Research Methods for Public Administrators

Y0-BRC-750

Research Methods for Public Administrators

SECOND EDITION

GAIL JOHNSON

M.E.Sharpe
Armonk, New York
London, England

Copyright © 2010 by M.E. Sharpe, Inc.

All rights reserved. No part of this book may be reproduced in any form
without written permission from the publisher, M.E. Sharpe, Inc.,
80 Business Park Drive, Armonk, New York 10504.

Library of Congress Cataloging-in-Publication Data

Johnson, Gail, 1947–
  Research methods for public administrators / by Gail Johnson.—2nd ed.
    p. cm.
  Includes bibliographical references and index.
  ISBN 978-0-7656-2312-6 (pbk. : alk. paper)
  1. Public administration—Research—Methodology. I. Title.

JF1338.A2J64 2010
351.072—dc22   2009018631

Printed in the United States of America

The paper used in this publication meets the minimum requirements of
American National Standard for Information Sciences
Permanence of Paper for Printed Library Materials,
ANSI Z 39.48-1984.

CW (p)   10   9   8   7   6   5   4   3

Contents

List of Illustrations

EXHIBITS

APPLICATIONS

Preface and Acknowledgments

This book reflects my belief that public administrators, policy-makers, elected officials, and nonprofit managers need to be able to determine whether those arguing for action are using convincing evidence based on credible research. Citizens also need to be armed with the ability to pierce through statistical arguments if they are to effectively participate in shaping public policy. My intention, therefore, is to reduce the mystery associated with research by making the concepts clear and accessible to nonresearchers.

This revised edition includes more examples to provide a realistic picture of the types of research and issues likely to be found in public administration. Some examples are based on my own research and some I invented. I also selected research that appeared in the media as well as from research organizations, such as the U.S. Government Accountability Office. I have added exercises at the end of each chapter to spark class discussions and provide opportunities to apply specific concepts.

I deliberately selected issues that were likely to challenge people to think about the evidence for their positions. However, public issues come and go; what was controversial in 2008 may not be on the radar screen in 2010, so current events will have to supplement the material in this book. Fortunately, research about public programs and policies appear almost daily in the media so feel free to use the concepts in this book to examine current controversial public policy issues.

Many students have contributed to the material presented in this book. To all the students who helped me learn how to teach research methods at Old Dominion University, Evergreen State College, and Troy University, I am forever in your debt. I am especially grateful for the encouragement and support of the students at Troy University who read the draft chapters before the copyeditor cleaned them up. Many students from Troy and Evergreen volunteered to critique various chapters and their critiques challenged me to work harder to make these concepts clear. Thank you for having the courage to tell me the truth about what worked and what did not.

I am also appreciative of the many colleagues who willingly took time from their overly full schedules to read chapters of the manuscript to provide me with very insightful feedback: Tom Barth, Pamela Dunning, Carole Edlund, Pamela Gibson, Amy Gould, and Stacey Plichta. Thank you!

I especially want to thank Harry Briggs, executive editor at M.E. Sharpe Inc., who saw the potential in a revised edition and encouraged me to complete this project. I am also very grateful for the assistance of Henrietta Toth and Laurie Lieb for their superb editing that dramatically improved this book. With all this help, it would be tempting to think that this book would be perfect. It is not and the mistakes are mine.

My son Jesse has consistently supported my work and provided some of the ideas in this book as well as some of the best lines. My longtime friend Lisa Weinberg was an excellent sounding board as I worked through my philosophy about research methods in public administration. I am very fortunate to have friends of the heart who are stalwart supporters. I deeply value their friendship.

Lastly, I dedicate this book to my friend Elizabeth Vogel, who loved research and especially enjoyed the intricacies of statistics. Her death is a tragic loss and I am one of many who miss her unbounded enthusiasm and joyous energy.

Research Methods for Public Administrators

1 Introduction

Research Methods for Public Administrators

With the tsunami of "facts" that wash over us daily—"nine out of ten dentists say . . . "—we have to be able to determine whether they are credible. Understanding the research process provides a way to pierce through the scientific veneer of facts and statistics. This knowledge helps us sort research results into the useful pile or the interesting but not useful pile. This ability to discern what is useful is as necessary in our public lives as it is in our personal lives when we must make decisions.

At the same time, experience as a researcher has taught me that the world stubbornly refuses to line up neatly to meet the requirements of social science research. Sometimes it is hard to figure out what to measure and how to measure it. Sometimes sources of data are illusive. Sometimes it is difficult to identify causal relationships or demonstrate program impacts.

Public administrators, therefore, face a dilemma. On the one hand, we look to science to help us make rational decisions, but on the other hand we often find social science research too weak to illuminate complex problems. It is not unusual to find opposing views supported by research: "More Guns, More Crime" screams one report while another screams just as loudly "More Guns, Less Crime" (Duggan 2001). We begin to understand what Benjamin Disraeli, the British prime minister in the 1860s, meant when he observed, "There are three kinds of lies: lies, damned lies, and statistics." Things have not changed much.

As a professor who often teaches the required public administration research methods course, I have struggled to find a way to help people understand this material. Few students are eager to be in the class. As one student put it, "I would rather bungee-jump over a lake filled with crocodiles with an extra long rope than take a research methods course." I suspect she speaks for many who have been traumatized by statistics courses, leaving a deep fear of all subjects with Greek symbols and square roots.

It is also true that most of the people in my classes—managers, elected officials, and frontline workers—are not going to do research. Yet there are practical uses for research in this age of measuring results. Still, I remember sitting in my required research methods and statistics courses when I was getting my Master of Public Administration (MPA) degree and wondering why I had to learn this material. As we calculated formulas by hand, I wondered why we did not have the computers do it—and in those days, the computers were big, slow, and unfriendly. Nor was it clear how this information could be applied. However, as I gained experience in conducting research in the workplace, I realized that research had practical applications and was a surprisingly creative process.

The challenge for those of us who teach research methods is to find a way to present this material so it reflects the needs of nonresearchers. I am not convinced MPA students need to know formulas or understand all those Greek symbols that fill the blackboards of traditional statistics courses—formulas dutifully transferred to class notes, memorized to pass an exam, and then quickly forgotten.

Therefore, this book presents research methods and applied statistics in a way that reflects my experiences as a teacher, researcher, and public administrator. It is faithful to the practice of research and is intended to be accessible to those who need to understand and use research results.

GOALS: RESEARCH AS A CRITICAL THINKING TOOL

The first goal of this book is to gently introduce research methods. This means making the concepts and approaches interesting, useful, and clear for a nontechnical audience. I have attempted to use a minimum of jargon (although it cannot be completely avoided) in presenting complex concepts. I use examples from my research, other people's research, current news, and fake data to illustrate basic concepts.

The second goal is to enhance critical thinking skills. Many examples in this book are taken from newspaper headlines and deal with controversial issues. Controversy is part of public life; plus, it makes this information more interesting. Of course, non-political research also shows up in the news, like the report that beautiful people earn about 5 percent more than their average-looking counterparts (CNNMoney 2005) and the finding that 81 percent of those aged eighteen to twenty-nine report playing video games (Lenhart et al. 2008). The examples provide opportunities to practice asking the tough questions needed to decide how much credibility to give the results. The toughest question is "Is it true?" Much that is presented as "fact" melts away like a snowman in July when subjected to scrutiny.

While most of us rapidly embrace research that agrees with what we already believe, we are often just as quick to dismiss research that does not. The challenge is to be aware of our beliefs and then be able to set them aside. This ability to be both aware of—and detached from—our bias is a component of critical thinking. Ideally, critical thinking enables us to see the world as it is. This enables us to ask questions and use information that challenges even our most cherished beliefs.

While I prefer to deal with facts and evidence in the public arena, I recognize there are many ways of knowing, such as intuition, vision, and reflective thought. These are valuable. For many of us, whether we admit it or not, our first filter is our own experience and perspectives. We can quickly assess whether some information is true or questionable based on our own experiences. However, while trusting his feelings might ground a Jedi knight like Luke Skywalker, most of us need to recognize that while our feelings can provide us with tremendous insight, they can also make it harder to recognize information that is different from what we want to believe.

Critical thinking requires that we ask ourselves how we know that the things we believe are true. This is followed by a second useful question: What would it take to convince us otherwise? It helps to keep in mind that most of us struggle with this detached yet open perspective; it took hundreds of years before people generally accepted the facts that the earth was not flat and that the sun did not revolve around the earth.

The final goal of this book is to meet the overarching objective of many MPA research courses, which is to encourage public administrators to use data to (1) think about the many wicked problems and understand complex relationships in the public arena, (2) develop policies and programs that will be effective, and (3) measure results to find out if what they are doing is working.

Public administration is not easy. Situations vary and sometimes defy simple prescriptions for action. What works well in one time and place does not necessarily work in another. We begin to see that "it depends" is not an excuse to avoid making fixed rules but a recognition that situations vary in ways that might affect why some things work and some do not. Ideally, the process of questioning what we believe opens us to new information and enables us to test new program and policy approaches. This courage to challenge our beliefs enhances our ability to serve the public.

RESEARCH IN THE PUBLIC SECTOR

Decision-makers and managers need to have the best information possible to guide decisions. Typically, they rely on researchers, either on their staff or from other agencies, consulting firms, or universities. But even the best facts are just one of a host of competing influences on public decisions. The political environment, with its competitive party system and continuous jockeying for power and position, is a reality that defies a totally rational approach. This is not a good or bad thing—it is just the way it is.

Values and beliefs play a large role in making public policy. It is important to recognize our beliefs, while also recognizing that we live in a pluralistic society where others hold different, and sometimes diametrically opposed, beliefs. As public administrators, we serve all the citizens and often find ourselves trying to find common ground among the divergent perspectives.

This diversity of views becomes apparent when we take a look at controversial policies. Does welfare help or hurt people? Should oil companies be prevented from earning too much profit? Is investment in primary prevention more effective in reducing crime than investment in law enforcement? Should we provide services to teenage mothers or do such services actually encourage more teenage parenthood? Is saving the spotted owl from extinction more valuable than the economic benefits of logging? Is the climate changing and, if so, are humans to blame?

In the public arena, a good story can be persuasive. Michael Moore's 2007 documentary *Sicko* presents a compelling argument for a nonprofit health care system by telling the stories of a few people who had medical insurance but were denied treatment. Denying treatment, Moore suggests, is cost-effective for the insurance companies, who are in the business of making profits. No doubt many people who saw the movie were left with a sense of injustice, convinced that no one should die from preventable illnesses. Moore goes further, noting that in Canada, England, and France everyone receives needed health care. For me, the most dramatic vignette is his account of several 9/11 rescue workers who were exposed to toxins while digging through the rubble of the World Trade Center. When their medical insurers refused to pay for the treatment and medications they needed, Moore took them to Cuba, where they received medical care for free.

A compelling story? You bet. Solid research? Not really. In the research world, this is called anecdotal evidence. Moore's film gives no idea of the scope of the problem. How frequently are insured people denied life-saving or potentially life-saving treatment? How many insured people go without needed treatment because their insurers do not cover it? Still, anecdotes can be persuasive—the stories of real people tug at policy-makers in a way that numbers sometimes do not.

Is there a more empirical approach to document whether there is a problem? Yes. In 2008, Will Dunham's article "France Best, U.S. Worst in Preventable Death Ranking" reported on the results of a study that has been tracking preventable deaths in nineteen industrial countries. If the United States performed as well as France, stated the researchers, there would be an estimated 101,000 fewer deaths in the United States per year. However, even with this scientific study, we would want to look more deeply before forming a firm conclusion

As an overall indicator of a country's health care system, this statistic suggests that Moore may have been correct in identifying that something is not working well in the U.S. health system. Indicators, however, do not provide information about the cause.

The story continues. In 2009, a whistleblower from one of the top health insurance corporations went public. Testifying before a U.S. Senate hearing in June, he stated, "My name is Wendell Potter, and for twenty years I worked as a senior executive at health insurance companies. And I saw how they confused their customers and dumped the sick, all so they can satisfy their Wall Street investors." Although Potter was part of the health insurance companies' public relations attack on Moore, he stated in an interview that he felt conflicted because "I knew it was an honest film" (Goodman 2009).

The Moore documentary is a great example of someone presenting information from a particular perspective. An allegation of bias might quickly come to mind and serve as the grounds for dismising the study. However, more than an allegation of bias is needed; to refute his documentary, one would need evidence that the information is incorrect. As more research is done, it may turn out that Moore accurately captured the health insurance situation. There are two key takeaway lessons. One is that anecdotal data may prove correct even though they lack the rigor of social science. The second is that it as challenging to support research conclusions as it is to refute them; mere proclamations of truth or bias are insufficient.

Simple statistics can spark hot political debates. For example, the *New York Times* reported that in 2007 the birth rate among teenagers aged 14 to 19 rose 3 percent, the first rise since 1991 (Harris 2007). It did not take long for the political spin machine to emerge. Senator Hillary Clinton said that the rates declined during the Clinton administration because it focused on family planning. Reproductive freedom activists used these data to claim that the Bush administration's abstinence-only program was not working. Those with a different political perspective dismissed these critiques as "stupid." But these statistics merely present a picture of what is happening; they do not tell why. To determine the reason, more research is needed.

The paradox that public administrators face is that however much we seek facts to help us make good decisions, we too often find that facts may not appear the same to others. The tale of the blind men trying to describe an elephant seems to capture our experience in seeking the truth about reality. Our perceptions are partial; if we feel the elephant's legs, we think we are dealing with a tree. If we feel the elephant's trunk, we think of a snake. Hitoshi Kume suggests that even our own experiences are not facts: "We must be aware that our knowledge and experiences are finite, and always imperfect" (1985, 208).

In a rational world, data should inform public decisions. However, the research needed to provide useful and credible results takes time and resources, with inevitable trade-offs between quality and costs. The consequence is less than perfect research. Besides, not everything in public administration lends itself to quantification. From a philosophical perspective, not everything is even knowable. Furthermore, the best data do not always win the day in policy-making, where power agendas often rule.

My premise is that all research is flawed, so it is essential for managers to be comfortable with some risk-taking based on their assessment of the credibility of the research. It also means accepting that better information may emerge next week or next year showing that the policy was doomed to fail. It is not a personal failing when new information reveals the flaws in the previous data. Good managers make decisions based on the best information available and demonstrate flexibility in making midcourse corrections when new information shows that they are on the wrong course.

In the mid-1980s, for example, an argument to do away with the death penalty was based on its disparate impact on African-Americans. In 1987, the Supreme Court ruled in a death penalty case that the statistical study did not present substantial evidence of a discriminatory effect (*McCleskey v. Kemp*, 481 U.S. 297). But research on complex public issues is difficult to do, so it is also possible that concluding that race is not a factor might have been a mistake. The results of continuing research consistently show that the death penalty is more likely to be imposed if the victim is white. The effect of the race of the defendant, however, remains in statistical dispute.

Research should lead to deeper understanding and insight to guide policy choices and program implementation, even if the answers are a work in progress. Public administrators need to make decisions within this reality, which is why it is wise to always remain open to new information that challenges old decisions.

WHAT IS RESEARCH?

Research is a systematic search for answers to questions using a clearly specified process for gathering and analyzing data. It is empirical, meaning that the information is derived from experiment, observation, or experience. In other words, research results should be based on something more than beliefs and opinions.

People do research all the time. Comparing prices and characteristics of cars, comparing the qualifications of the staff and the services offered at different day care centers, interviewing prospective employees, and gathering and reading the research of others are all forms of research.

The research methods and analytical tools presented in this book are based on social science and emphasize rigorous attention to detail. They provide a solid foundation for policy analysts and increase managers' understanding of the kinds of issues researchers face. Researchers make choices that might affect the conclusions that can be drawn. Using rules and guidelines from social science to minimize bias and errors, researchers in the public sector strive to accurately reflect reality. These rules and guidelines of the research process provide useful criteria for assessing the credibility of research results.

The research process consists of three interrelated phases: planning, doing, and reporting (see Exhibit 1.1). While the steps are presented in a linear fashion, the actual practice is not. This is an iterative process, which means researchers may move through a few steps only to have to return and go through them again because new information or problems emerge. Some steps may have to be done together, such as deciding on samples and data collection strategies. There are a lot of back-and-forth decisions.

First-time researchers are often surprised by how hard it is to plan a research project. They are often frustrated by discovering that their initial ideas are too broad to be researchable. But frustration is a normal part of the process that leads to eventual clarity.

Managers contracting for research may feel that the researchers are going around in circles. Actually the researchers are working their way through a funnel, moving from general concepts to a narrow, very detailed focus.

Typically, research begins with general concerns about a situation, a problem, or questions about a public program or issue. These tend to be broad and unfocused. The goal of the planning phase is to transform broad questions and unfocused issues into narrow questions with a specific strategy for collecting data to answer each one. It does not take many failures before researchers come to believe, "If you do not know where you are going, you can wind up anywhere."

As strategies for doing the research are considered and assumptions tested, obstacles typically emerge. Problem-solving is a big part of the planning process and it takes time to figure out solutions. However, it is worth taking time in this phase to get the solutions right. If mistakes are made in the planning process, no amount of statistical wizardry will save the research. Patience and perseverance are virtues during the early phases of the planning process.

Suppose researchers want to find out what people in a community think are major

Exhibit 1.1 **The Research Process**

Planning
- Determine the issues

  ° Build on the work of others
  ° Use models to clarify the issue within its context or environment
  ° Assess stakeholders' needs

- Determine the research questions
- Select measures
- Select an appropriate design
- Develop data collection strategy and instruments
- Develop a sampling approach
- Develop data analysis strategy
- Review and test the methodology
- Prepare a work plan with resource and time requirements

Doing
- Gather the data
- Analyze the data
- Verify the accuracy of the data and analysis
- Formulate the findings

Reporting
- Report major findings
- Suggest clear, specific proposals for action: who should do what by when
- Present evidence to support recommendations
- Use charts and tables to communicate the results: reports, briefings, executive summary
- Give oral presentations

public problems that need attention. They begin by developing a list of issues as they talk with various stakeholders (e.g., the people in the community, elected officials, and the various agencies who provide services). They also read about other community assessments and talk with other researchers to learn from their experiences in conducting this kind of research.

The researchers will probably wind up with too many issues and need to narrow the focus. This is a good time to engage the stakeholders in setting the priorities for the research. It helps to sort the "must know" from the "wouldn't it be nice to know" items. As the list of issues gets more precise and centered on answering the "must know" questions, the study will click into sharp focus.

Once the big research questions are clear, the researchers move into a deeper stage of defining the questions so they can be measured. A measurement strategy is developed so the researchers know very specifically what they will measure. The researchers will then choose the best research design. They then develop a data collection strategy, which means finding out where the best data reside so the researchers can effectively gather the data. This stage includes developing a sampling plan as well as data collection instruments, such as a questionnaire or interview guide. The data collection instruments are pretested and necessary changes are made before going live.

Once the plan is set, the researchers begin the doing phase. This consists of gathering and analyzing data. It is best to develop a data analysis plan so that the analysis stays focused on answering the initial questions. If the research plan has been done well, this phase should go smoothly. If not, problem-solving skills are required to overcome the hurdles. Quality control procedures should be in place to ensure accuracy and to keep bias from surfacing. Through appropriate analytical techniques, the answers to the research questions begin to emerge.

If the doing phase is an immersion in detail, the reporting phase requires a return to the research questions and the larger issue that prompted the study. It helps to think in terms of telling a story. The intention of reporting is to turn the data into information that can be used by the larger audience to guide decisions. This is a dangerous moment. They may be tempted to make bigger conclusions than can be supported by the research. Bias can also creep in as researchers make sense of the data, and. Surprisingly, even quantitative analysis can be ambiguous. It is possible for people to look at the same data and draw different conclusions. Many possible stories can be drawn from the same data so choices have to be made about which story gets told. Interpretation is part of the process and can be highly subjective.

Lastly, researchers face an ongoing struggle when reporting results. They need to find the balance between summarizing so tightly that readers feel they are not getting the whole story and providing so much detail that the readers are overwhelmed.

Very good studies typically raise more questions than they answer. The research might paint an accurate picture of the current situation, but not explain much about why the situation exits. Sometimes the research methods prove too flawed to give definitive answers. The mantra "More research is needed" is not a full-employment program for researchers; it is just another step in the research process. Albert Einstein observed, "To raise new questions, new possibilities, to regard old problems from a new angle, requires creative imagination and marks real advance in science" (1938, 95).

TYPES OF RESEARCH

The world of research can be divided into many categories. One way is to look at the primary purpose of research. From this view, I divide this world into scholarly and applied research to reflect the uneasy relationship that exists in the field between the people who teach public administration in universities and those who practice public administration in government agencies. Each group holds different overall views of the purpose and intended uses of research. However, both are needed in public administration. There is also crossover between scholars and practitioners; it is not unusual for scholars to weigh in on policies, including testifying before Congress, or for practitioners to publish in scholarly journals.

Scholarly research seeks to understand why the world works as it does by exploring and testing theories. The goal is to contribute to knowledge. If a theory is correct, it helps administrators understand, explain, or predict why things happen. For example, economists believe in the theory of supply and demand. If this theory is correct, then prices should decrease when supply exceeds demand; conversely, prices should increase when demand exceeds supply. Gas prices are a good example: if supply decreases or demand increases (thus demand exceeds supply), the cost per gallon should go up.

Scholarly researchers might want to look at motivation theory. Abraham Maslow (1987) offered his theory of the hierarchies of needs to explain what motivates people. He believed that people move through levels of motivation, beginning with physical needs. When these are met, people begin to look at security needs. When these are met, people seek to have ego needs met and then a sense of belonging. The highest need is self-actualization. But is Maslow's theory correct? Managers, believing that people are motivated primarily by money, may set up individual recognition and rewards systems, based on a competitive model. But what if belonging is the highest need? If that is true, then highly individualistic work environments and competitive reward systems may reduce morale and motivation rather than enhance it.

Public administrators tend to use applied research in developing public policies and public programs and assessing whether those programs and policies are making a difference. The desire is for information that can be of immediate use to managers, lawmakers, advocates, and citizens. Administrators want research results that can be used to test new programs, make adjustments to existing programs, or solve problems. Elected officials are often interested in determining whether public dollars spent on various programs make a positive and measurable difference. Advocates want information about various policy options to influence decision-making. Citizens want information to support their policy preferences as they lobby their elected officials. Theory and scholarly research inform applied research, but theory testing is rarely the sole focus of research in the public sector.

Another way to categorize research is whether it is quantitative or qualitative. Public administration research still carries the scars of the qualitative versus quantitative wars of the 1980s and 1990s. Simply defined, qualitative research focuses on stories and observations, seeking an in-depth understanding based on a firsthand experience of people and their environment. Qualitative approaches include case studies, observations, interviews, and focus groups but are often combined with quantitative research, which uses numbers, such as census data, available data, and surveys, to understand the world and to describe and measure a particular phenomenon. The study of preventable deaths mentioned above is an example of quantitative methods. Statistics and quantitative analytical tools used in public administration research reflect many of the methods used in the sciences; some are relatively simple while understanding others really does require a PhD.

For years, qualitative research was dismissed as mere storytelling. It was just too soft and too biased compared to hard numbers, leading some to passionately argue that only quantitative research counted as good research. Others argued just as passionately that qualitative approaches provide a broader perspective of the context and a deeper understanding of the situation than can be obtained by quantitative techniques. The results, they state, yield a more holistic picture. As Mary Lee Smith observed, "Many of us who were disillusioned with experiments and other hypothesis-testing, causation-seeking studies found greater satisfaction with qualitative approaches in which the researcher could be sensitive to local context, participant interpretations, historical and cultural stories interacting holistically, and social actions and processes. . . . For some of us, this was a fair trade in spite of accusations that we are numerical idiots or mere storytellers" (1994, 40).

It is important to remember both approaches are used in public administration research. My view is that neither approach is inherently better or worse than the other. Neither is inherently harder or easier; they are just harder and easier in different ways. All research approaches have strengths and limitations within the particular situation. They also share similarities. Both research methods require careful planning, logic, and attention to detail. Whether using qualitative or quantitative methods, researchers collect data systematically, strive for error-free analyses, and honestly report both their methods and results. Both approaches can be used to critically question an issue in the public arena and influence policy or to add to basic knowledge. Both can also be used in highly participatory teams.

The kind of research question and the data needed will determine whether to use a quantitative or a qualitative research approach. Clinging to a preferred type of research, despite the situation, is counterproductive. The saying "If the only tool you have is a hammer, then every problem becomes a nail" applies here. The results are not pretty. My point is simply this: good researchers know how to do both types well and sophisticated users of research results need to understand what constitutes quality in quantitative and qualitative research. Public managers should not be afraid to use data from either type of research in guiding their decisions.

ETHICS AND PRINCIPLES OF GOOD RESEARCH

Ethics are essential in all aspects of public administration research, just as in public administration practice. At the top of my list of ethical research is the dictum "Do no harm" (see Exhibit 1.2). Research should not harm participants in any way.

One of the most blatant abuses of ethics in public administration was the Tuskegee syphilis study by the federal government (Associated Press 2008). The experiment, which began in 1932, monitored the health of two groups of African-American males for forty years. One group had untreated syphilis and the other group did not have any symptoms of syphilis. There were no safe treatments for syphilis when the study began, but by the 1950s penicillin was an effective treatment. However, the participants in the study were denied treatment.

This research violated the Nuremberg Code. This code was a result of the Nazi war trials in 1949 and requires, among other things, that experiments should avoid all unnecessary physical and mental suffering and injury and all participants should give informed consent. Informed consent means that the participants have sufficient understanding of the experiment to make a decision that protects their own interests. Participants should be told the nature and purpose of the experiment, the methods to be used, the duration of the experiment, and any possible harm it could cause them. Informed consent precludes the use of force, fraud, and coercion. Participants should also have the freedom to bring an end to the experiment if continuation will bring harm (National Institutes of Health 1949).

The Milgram experiment is another example of how research can potentially harm

Exhibit 1.2 **Ethical Principles of Good Research**

Do no harm
- Protect participants from being harmed by the research
- Guard the confidentiality of the participants
- Do not coerce people to become participants
- Do not deny people benefits to which they are entitled
- Do not quickly conclude that a program does not work just because the research did not find an impact

Honesty
- Do not lie or distort
- Fully disclose methods, definitions, assumptions, biases, and limitations

Accuracy
- Build quality control procedures into data collection, analysis, interpretation, and written product
- Strive to be error-free

Technical correctness
- Use appropriate designs, data collection methods, analysis, statistics, and charts

Reliable and valid measures
- Measure what matters using systematic approaches with fixed measurement rules

Objectivity
- Be aware of personal biases
- Strive to see clearly
- Build in quality controls to minimize bias

participants. Dr. Stanley Milgram (1974) was trying to understand obedience and the extent to which ordinary people will agree to do things that cause pain to other people when asked by someone "in authority." The participants were asked to take part in a "scientific experiment" in which they would give increasingly painful electric shocks to people who gave the wrong answers on a test. The electric shocks, however, were not real and the test-takers, who were part of the experiment, merely acted as if they were in pain. The ethical question concerned the potential harm to the participants when they realized that they were capable of inflicting harm on another person just because an authority figure in a lab coat told them to do it. Universities now have Human Subjects Review Committees to ensure that researchers are conducting ethical research and that participants have given their informed consent.

There are other types of harm. People who participate in research experiments should not be placed in threatening situations. Researchers should never coerce people into participation and no one should lose benefits or be denied benefits to which they are entitled (such as social security or veteran's benefits) because of the research. If participants are promised confidentiality, then protecting their identities is essential; this is especially true when the research is exploring illegal behavior, such as use of cocaine or cheating on income tax. Data collection procedures and the handling of all identifying information must be done in ways that protect the participants' privacy.

An often unspoken harm can occur when researchers conclude that a program does not make a difference. It is possible that the program does work but the research was not strong enough to accurately capture the true impact. It is equally important to resist the temptation to form firm conclusions about a policy or program based on a single study. Given the potential harm in erroneously concluding that a program does not work, it is best to conduct more research to get a more accurate measure before making a final decision.

Right below the principle of "do no harm" are honesty and accuracy. Honesty is sometimes a slippery concept because it really is possible to interpret the same data in different ways. While differences are normal, researchers need to be wary of "spin," when the reported results are clearly being driven by a political agenda.

Objectivity is crucial even if it is not absolute. Even in the hard sciences, scientists' beliefs can influence the results. For example, consider what happens when measuring light. If the scientists test for a wave, light behaves as a wave. If they test light as a particle, it behaves as a particle. This creates the uncomfortable awareness that the scientists' beliefs influence the results.

For me, objectivity means approaching the research with the intention of seeing the world as clearly as possible and then truthfully reporting the results, even if they are opposite from what I wanted to find. The fact that it is not possible to be absolutely objective does not let researchers off the hook in pursuing that goal. Keeping their biases in check, to the extent possible, is a good thing. Quality control measures help. For example, researchers can have other people with different perspectives review the research plan, the data analysis, and the final report to identify bias. Another option is to use different teams to independently analyze the results and identify the key findings.

Every effort should be made to accurately gather the data, using specified, systematic measurement rules and technically correct statistical applications. Researchers should report the data as well as fully disclose all methods and their limitations. In the conclusion sections of reports the researchers may potentially venture far from their evidence, so it is necessary to check that the conclusions are actually supported by the data.

It is reasonable to expect in any research report a clear description of how the research was conducted, a statement about the limitations of the research, and cautions in interpreting the results. Be suspicious of studies that appear to be perfect. None are.

At the same time, it is important not to dismiss all research because of serious flaws. Even flawed research can provide useful insights. It may prompt important conversations about the issue and the challenges in exploring that issue or it may provide ideas for new research approaches. It is necessary to be able to assess whether research flaws are minor or fatal. Perfection is not a useful standard. While there are some rules, generally this is a gray area. Of all the take-away lessons of a research methods course, this ability to work in the gray areas is the most essential because research is imperfect.

OVERVIEW OF THIS BOOK

This book follows the research process. After describing the basic research concepts in Chapter 2, the book goes through the various steps in the planning process in Chapters 3 to 10. Research flaws are almost always a result of the choices made during the planning phase; no amount of sophisticated statistical analysis will correct poor choices. Chapter 11 presents information about analyzing qualitative data, while Chapters 12 to 15 present commonly used analytical techniques and statistics, including analyzing quantitative data, descriptive statistics, exploring relationships between variables, and inferential statistics. The emphasis is on understanding how these statistics get applied and interpreted. Chapter 16 focuses on reporting the data so that public administrators can use them to make informed decisions. The concluding chapter pulls together all the threads: revisiting the process, reminders about ethics, issues of research quality and credibility, the limitations of science, and the challenges of research at the intersection of politics and administration. Some advice, observations, and key take-away lessons are offered.

The appendixes contains additional material, including mathematical formulas in Appendix A, a handy guide to definitions of the many terms used in the book in Appendix B, and references and resources in Appendix C.

EXERCISES

1. In the news: Select an article from a newspaper or online news source that reports findings from a research study (a poll, interviews, economic data, or other scientific research) and summarize the main points of the article. Does it strike you as academic or applied research? Explain. Is it quantitative or qualitative research, or a combination? Does the choice make sense given the situation? Are the results believable? Why or why not?
2. Review these strategies for bringing about policy changes:
   a. Would advocates be more effective when meeting with the governor by saying they are concerned about the negative effects of toxic waste sites or by showing the governor a map detailing all the toxic waste sites in the state and the cancer rates within five miles of those sites? Which approach would be more convincing? What questions should the governor ask to determine the veracity of the data?
   b. Would the director of a prison be more likely to initiate an innovative education and counseling program if presented with data showing that such a program effectively reduced the recidivist rate in other jurisdictions or with statements that the program was more humane? What questions should the director ask to ensure that the data were credible?
   c. Would a union official be more effective in convincing the city manager that there is a management problem by saying there is a problem or by showing data from an employee survey that indicates a high degree of dissatisfaction with management practices? Should the city manager accept the survey results without any questions? If not, what question should the manager ask?
3. What does critical thinking mean to you? How is it the same as, or different from, skepticism? Is either or both important in deciding whether to apply research results to policy or program decisions?

2 Basic Research Concepts

OVERVIEW

Public administration research comes out of the tradition of social science. Using the scientific method of repeated systematic observation and experimentation that is deliberate, intentional, and organized, researchers test ideas in order to understand why the world works as it does.

When we think of a scientist, the image of a person in a white lab coat doing experiments with rats comes to mind. However, people dressed like the person in the cubicle next door do public administration research.

While research in the public sector can take many forms, evaluating programs and measuring results are very common. Evaluation is an assessment, as systematic and objective as possible, of a planned, ongoing, or completed policy or program intervention (Wholely et al. 2004). The intention is to provide useful, credible information to guide decision-making and enable continuous learning.

Policy analysis is also a staple of public administration research. It can be used in a variety of ways. It can evaluate a specific policy to determine its impact or examine a social problem to recommend possible solutions. It can also be used to assess the likely costs and impacts of various proposed policy options that might be implemented under different circumstances (Bardach 2005).

As researchers move from the big policy picture to the details that are needed to do the research, they use a set of interrelated concepts in order to specify exactly what will be observed and measured. This chapter presents these basic concepts and explains the secret language of science. Some terms, such as *theory, hypotheses,* and *variables*, might be familiar. Other concepts, such as independent and dependent variables, levels of measurement, and direction of relationships, may be less familiar. These concepts are important in both the research planning and data analysis phases. In addition, this chapter presents a tool—called the logical framework—that is helpful in the program-planning phase as well as in evaluating the program after it has been fully implemented.

THE SECRET LANGUAGE OF SOCIAL SCIENCE

THEORY

Typically, social science begins with a theory to guide the research. Theory can be defined as a coherent group of general propositions or as a verified explanation accounting for known facts or phenomena, such as the theory of relativity or the theory of gravity. Theories are used to explain reality or make predictions. Untested theories might be considered beliefs.

Theories can be developed from the ground up or from the top down. Researchers may look at an existing situation and then begin to theorize why the situation exists. They are looking for possible explanations. They observe first and then begin to create possible explanations about their observations. This ground-up process is called inductive logic.

Alternatively, deductive logic is used to conduct research that flows from a preexisting theory. Like Sherlock Holmes, researchers begin with a theory and then test it to see if it is true. Inductive and deductive logics can be connected. A theory generated from the ground up inductively might be tested deductively.

Theories, whether stated or not, are the foundation of public programs and policies. Public programs are based on a belief that if we do this (X), we can cause a desired result (Y). For example, micro-lending programs lend small amounts of money to women without access to employment or assets to start a business (Mallick 2002). The money can be used to buy seeds and tools for small-scale gardens; goats or chickens for small-scale production of milk, cheese, or eggs; or materials needed to produce handicrafts for sale. Micro-lending is based on the theory that entrepreneurship will result in economic self-sufficiency. By making it possible for women to obtain money to start their own businesses, the program enables women to increase their families' income and move out of poverty, thus reducing poverty in their community.

Ideally, there should be some evidence that the theory is connected to reality so that the program has some chance of actually achieving its intended outcomes. A perceived crisis can bypass that requirement. For example, what is the evidence to support the belief that empowering the secretary of the Treasury to bail out the sinking financial markets to the tune of $700 billion will save our economy from a recession?

HYPOTHESIS IN ITS MANY FORMS

Hypotheses are conjectures put forth to predict likely relationships that will be observed if a theory is true. Hypotheses serve as the basis for testing theories. I tend to think of hypotheses as the researchers' best guess about how the world works if the theory is true. Hypotheses, typically set up as "if-then" statements, are a way to look at the theory in a concrete way. Stating hypotheses is, therefore, the first step in setting up a research project.

For example, here are some testable hypotheses for the micro-lending program theory. If micro-lending works, then women who participate in this program will be more likely to start small businesses than women who do not. If micro-lending works, then women who participate in this program will be more likely to increase family income than those who do not. If micro-lending works, then, over time, communities with successful micro-lending programs will see a reduction in poverty compared to other communities without the program.

The researchers choose the testable hypothesis (or hypotheses) that is the most relevant to the situation. Measuring whether more women start businesses may be a good choice for an early evaluation of the program. Measuring whether community poverty has been reduced because of the program is best tested after the program has been operating for at least a few years. Assuming the program is run well, the best test of the theory is this: Does entrepreneurship among poor women reduce poverty?

Some research reports, however, do not specify a theory or even a hypothesis. Researchers might simply state a proposition; that is, a statement about what would exist if the theory were true—for example, micro-lending increases the earning capacity of women and reduces poverty in the community. An advocate is likely to make this affirmative proposition. However, without evidence to support it, it is merely a testable hypothesis in a different guise.

Researchers might also pose questions to focus their research. For example: Does micro-lending result in increased family income and reduce community poverty over the long term? I tend to use research questions in my work; they seem direct and likely to result in clear, specific answers. This book reflects my bias. But no matter whether researchers use hypotheses, testable propositions, or research questions, they all have to work through the phases in the research process.

Let us look at another example that is closer to home. Suppose a city manager is concerned about high turnover in one department. Why are people leaving? She may remember some theories about motivation from her MPA program, which may influence her thinking. She is also likely to base it on her own experiences and beliefs. Her unstated assumption is that satisfied employees are less likely to leave and that a number of factors will affect satisfaction. She develops a list of possible factors (see Exhibit 2.1) and shows it to the human resources director. The human resources director recognizes these as part of various theories but she is also aware of another theory: public service motivation (Naff and Crum 1999; Perry 2000). This theory states that public employees are motivated by the desire to serve, to make a positive difference to their community, and to place the public interest over self-interest. To the extent that this theory exists, city employees may be dissatisfied if the desire to make a positive difference is blocked by organizational dysfunction. The human resources director suggests adding public service motivation to the list of factors to be tested.

The takeaway here is that theories and hypotheses may guide the research either explicitly or implicitly. They are the starting point as the researchers and public administrators work through the research planning process, which will take them deeper into the detail needed to conduct the research.

VARIABLES

Variables are the observable characteristics of a concept. The factors that might affect employee satisfaction, such as salary, retirement benefits, treatment by a supervisor,

Exhibit 2.1   **Possible Factors Affecting Employee Satisfaction**

Factors	Outcomes
Salary	
Control over work	
Working conditions	
Flexible schedules	
Being treated with respect →	Employee satisfaction
Working with friendly people	
Health benefits	
Retirement benefits	
Job security	

Exhibit 2.2   **Variables and Possible Values**

Variable	Values
Gender	Male and female
Job satisfaction	Very dissatisfied (1—2—3—4—5) Very satisfied
Annual salary	Actual dollar amount

and doing work that makes a difference, are variables in the language of science. By measuring each variable, the researchers can determine the relative impact of each factor on employee satisfaction. Is salary more important, for example, than how people are treated? Is the opportunity to make a positive difference more important than salary?

Variables are measured individually. However, it is possible to sum up variables to create a composite measure. For example, responses to four questions about salary and benefits can be combined into a single variable called compensation. Composite measures are sometimes used in advanced research studies.

VALUES

The next level of detail is the values of the variables. Values are defined as the concrete categories or measures of the variables. For example, gender, job satisfaction, and annual salary have values by which they are measured (see Exhibit 2.2).

LEVELS OF MEASUREMENT

Values may be measured differently; social science categorizes them in terms of levels of measurement: nominal, ordinal, interval, and ratio.

Nominal data, which are also called categorical data, have values that are measured by name or category. They are descriptive, such as gender (male, female), religion (Christian, Jewish, Hindu, Muslim, other), or city (Tokyo, Seattle, London). There is no order to the values; one is not better than or more than the others.

Ordinal data have names or categories, but the values also have an order to them. The highest educational degree obtained is ordinal because high school, bachelor's, master's, and PhD degrees have an underlying order. The categories are moving from fewer years of education to more years of education.

Scales that go from less to more are another type of ordinal measure. For example, people are often asked to rate the importance of something on a scale from 1 (least important) to 10 (most important). Another common example is asking people to rate how strongly they agree or disagree with specific statements on scale from 1 (strongly agree) to 5 (strongly disagree). Ordinal scales have an order.

The thing to remember about ordinal data, however, is that the numbers are not real. The researchers could have set the scale from 1 to 100 or 1 to 1,000; the numbers have no meaning in a mathematical sense. In ordinal data, numbers merely anchor a concept along a measurement scale. The numbers are more like metaphors than mathematics.

Interval data have values that are real numbers of equal distance but do not contain a zero point. SAT, GRE, and IQ scores are examples of interval data. A SAT score of 800 is not twice as good as a score of 400 because there is no zero point.

Ratio data, on the other hand, do have a zero point. These are real numbers. Income, weight, or number of children can be averaged. Someone earning $100,000 earns twice as much as someone earning $50,000.

The key point to remember is that data analysis techniques vary depending on the level of measurement used. These will be discussed in the analysis chapters.

DETERMINING CAUSALITY

Determining the relationship between two or more variables is difficult outside of laboratories because the world is complex and too many things happen simultaneously. However, researchers are often asked to determine whether relationships exist between variables. Are there racial disparities in who is sentenced to death? What are the factors associated with unmarried teen parenthood? Is pay the most important reason explaining turnover in city hall? Does micro-lending reduce poverty? Will a federal bailout of the financial market prevent a depression? Are humans causing climate change? These are all questions about relationships.

Four conditions must be met in order to demonstrate that a causal relationship exists:

1. There has to be a logical theory connecting the variables.
2. There has to be appropriate time order: the causal variable has to come first.
3. There has to be covariation, meaning both variables have to change.
4. All other possible explanations for the observed changes are ruled out; this means eliminating rival explanations.

Much of this book deals with causal relationships because questions about causality are so prevalent and the hardest to answer. If researchers want to conclude that one variable causes change in another variable—for example, claiming a causal relationship—then all four conditions must be met.

INDEPENDENT AND DEPENDENT VARIABLES

Social scientists often are interested in examining the relationships between variables. Variables are labeled "independent" and "dependent" to identify which variable the researcher believes causes change in the other variable. The dependent variable is the effect or the variable being explained. The independent variable is the causal or explanatory variable. If I do X (the independent variable), then I predict I will get Y (the dependent variable) as a result.

I do not know why social scientists decided to use the terms *independent* and *dependent*, other than capturing some idea that the changes to the dependent variable depend on the causal variable. They could have used the *changer* for the independent variable and the *changed* for the dependent variable. But they did not, so it is best to use the social science jargon.

The determination of whether variables are independent or dependent is contextual. For example, in one study researchers may be testing the hypothesis that if people believe they are paid fairly, they are more likely to report being satisfied. If they feel they are not paid fairly, they will be more likely to report being dissatisfied. More technically, perceived compensation equity is believed to be the variable that affects employee satisfaction, so perception about compensation equity is the independent variable and employee satisfaction is the dependent variable. The relationship could be depicted as follows:

Perceived salary equity → employee satisfaction

However, employee satisfaction is not always the dependent variable. In a different research context, employee satisfaction could be the independent variable. For example, suppose the question is framed as: What is the relationship between employee satisfaction and turnover? The underlying hypothesis is that employees with high levels of satisfaction are not likely to leave; conversely, those with lower levels of satisfaction (i.e., more dissatisfied) are much more likely to leave. Employee satisfaction is the independent variable and the decision to stay or leave is the dependent variable. This relationship could be depicted as follows:

Employee satisfaction → turnover

CONTROL VARIABLES

Sometimes there are other factors that might influence the results. For example, employee satisfaction and turnover might vary based on gender. The hypothesis might be that women are less attached to a job than men and are therefore more likely to leave if they are dissatisfied. The research question is: Are dissatisfied women more likely than dissatisfied men to leave their jobs? The initial relationship is still between employee satisfaction and turnover. The researchers identify gender as a control variable and reanalyze the data. By controlling for gender, they will look at the relationship between satisfaction and turnover among men and compare it to the relationship between satisfaction and turnover among women. If their hypothesis that dissatisfied women are more likely to quit as compared to dissatisfied men is correct, they should see higher levels of turnover among dissatisfied women as compared to dissatisfied men. In this case, gender would be called a confounding variable. If no differences are found, then gender is not a factor in explaining why dissatisfied employees leave or stay. It is also true that sometimes relationships are not always as related as they initially appear. A classic example is the seeming relationship between ice cream sales and drowning. As ice cream sales increase, so do the number of drownings. But do ice cream sales cause drownings? Or are they both caused by something else—say, warmer temperatures? Temperatures is the control variable. A relationship that completely disappears when a control variable is used is called spurious. Controlling for other factors explores complexity between many variables and tests for possible rival explanations.

DIRECTION OF RELATIONSHIPS

Causal relationships must have covariation, meaning that as the independent variable changes, so does the dependent variable. These changes also have a direction: direct, inverse, and nonlinear.

A direct relationship occurs when both variables change in the same direction. Both variables can increase or both variables can decrease. As age increases, health problems increase; as the perceived equity of salary decreases, job satisfaction decreases.

An inverse relationship occurs when the two variables change in opposite directions: as one variable increases, the other decreases. As age increases, memory decreases; as the number of layers of supervision decreases, job satisfaction increases.

Both direct and inverse relationships are linear: as the independent variable increases at a steady rate, the dependent variable also changes at a steady rate. Sometimes, however, variables are not in a linear relationship. They might go up, then down, and then up again. For instance, household income and drug use among youth are related but their relationship is nonlinear. Researchers have found a high percentage of reported use among youth from low-income households, a lower percentage of reported use among middle-income households, and a higher percentage of reported use among youth from high-income households.

PROGRAM EVALUATION: RESEARCH IN THE PUBLIC SECTOR

Program evaluation is a major type of research in the public and nonprofit sectors. There are several different kinds of evaluation: feasibility, formative, and summative.

Feasibility evaluations begin before a program starts and are used to improve program design. These assess the feasibility of the program and identify potential supports and barriers to successful implementation.

Formative evaluations (also called program monitoring) are used during the implementation phase so they can provide feedback about operations and processes. Is the implementation going as planned? If not, can barriers can be identified and removed? Midpoint evaluations can begin to focus on lessons learned and the relevance, effectiveness, and efficiency of a program. These answer the question: Are we doing things right?

Summative evaluations (also called impact evaluations or ex-post evaluations) are used after a program has been running for a long enough time to actually see outcomes. Although these evaluations can be done after a program is over, they are usually done to assess ongoing mature programs. The central issue is whether the theory that the program is based on is correct. The question is: Are we doing the right thing? For example, if a community invests in a program to train beauticians, the question is whether that is the right focus. No matter how well the program is implemented, if the belief that beauticians are needed in the community is wrong, the program will fail because graduates will be unable to find jobs.

Summative evaluations not only attempt to measure impact, but also can be used to identify the key lessons learned from implementing and managing the program, lessons that can be used by others. These evaluations might also look at other issues, such as unintended outcomes, program sustainability, program efficiency, or the costs and benefits.

USING MODELS FOR A HOLISTIC VIEW OF RELATIONSHIPS

Models can be very useful in seeing a problem, program, or policy clearly within its complex environment. While models are important to researchers, they are also important to public administrators. By beginning with the end in mind—that is, what a program or policy should accomplish—public administrators can see the connections between their program and all the necessary pieces that have to be in place for the program to work in their community.

A good starting point in developing a model is to draw a picture. For example, if an administrator believes that training the chronically unemployed will increase their quality of life and ultimately reduce poverty, the model might look like Exhibit 2.3. But is training by itself sufficient to make this happen? Other factors are likely to make a difference in this situation. For one thing, there have to be sufficient jobs in the local economy and the training should be geared specifically for those available jobs. Training people to be beauticians when there is no demand for more beauticians will not be effective and the sequence of events will be stalled. If the ultimate goal is reducing poverty, then program success will depend on having jobs that pay a livable wage.

There also may be other factors associated with unemployment besides not having the right skills. Do people also need coaching in how to apply for jobs and develop effective interviewing skills? Should that be added to the program to increase the likelihood that graduates of the training program get hired? Are services like childcare and transportation needed to enable people to complete the training program and hold a job? Should the program manager work with providers in the community to make sure the trainees have access? Do larger issues related to disabilities or discrimination create barriers to employment? If so, should the program manager begin working with local employers to overcome these barriers?

A model helps make program elements clear, and a feasibility study might identify the key supports and barriers for an employment program in this community. While

Exhibit 2.3 **Model: Training Program for the Chronically Unemployed**

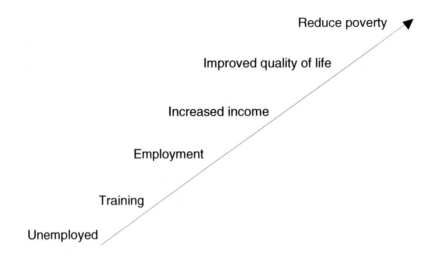

the program manager is not likely to have sufficient resources to minimize these barriers, seeing the program in context might help in identifying the major roadblocks to success. Models, therefore, can help in designing programs and shaping the research that will be used to measure the results.

When attempting to fix complex social issues, it really does help to see the picture in all its complexity. Let us look at unwed teenage mothers. Politicians, health officials, and educators have raised concerns about too early parenthood, offering a wide range of remedies. A model shows that teenagers face a web of decision points rather than a single one (see Exhibit 2.4). The model thus opens the policy-making to a range of interventions targeted at different decision points.

The teenager's first decision is whether or not to become sexually active (this model assumes consensual relationships). Programs to encourage teenagers to "just say no" might be implemented to prevent early sexual activity. However, if the teen decides to become sexually active, then she has to decide whether or not to use birth control. Factors such as knowledge of contraceptives and access to birth control might be an issue. If a teenager becomes pregnant, another set of factors might impact the decision whether to continue the pregnancy. If she decides to continue the pregnancy, she then faces another decision about whether to place the baby for adoption or not. While these decisions are presented here as a linear series, in reality they are interactive. For example, a teenager might make a different decision about pregnancy or sexual activity if she knows that marriage is or is not a likelihood.

From a policy perspective, program activities to prevent sexual activity will be different from programs designed to prevent unmarried parenthood after a pregnancy has occurred. Alternatively, policy-makers may decide that programs focused on ameliorating the problems encountered by teenage mothers might be a wise investment. Day care programs in high school, for example, can teach necessary parenting skills

Exhibit 2.4 **Teenaged Parenthood Model**

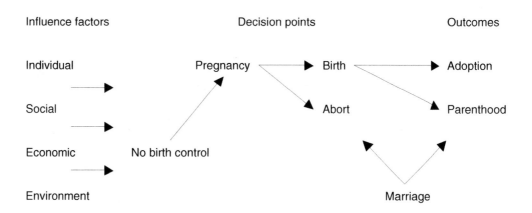

and encourage teens to finish school so they can get a good-paying job. Other policy-makers might oppose such programs, fearing that they might encourage other girls to become unmarried teenage mothers. We are back to the mantra that interventions in this policy area are controversial and the best data may not be the deciding factor.

From a research perspective, models help to explain the context and force some decisions about the research question. Do the researchers want to know what might work to prevent unwanted teenage pregnancies? Do they want to know why marriage is not the option of choice? Do they want to know what services are needed to help teenage mothers continue their education and be effective parents? Working with models keeps the policy-makers and the researchers aware of the complexity.

THE LOGIC MODEL

Without the kind of simple bottom line typical of the private sector, many state and local governments focus on other ways to determine whether programs are achieving the desired results. Measuring results is a variation of program evaluation. Although measuring results is harder to do than many people realize, the process can be very helpful in providing a deeper understanding of the program (Hatry 2007). While administrators may fear that it will be used solely to cut their programs, that should not be the intention. The problems that public administrators try to solve are often wicked and measuring results should be used to understand the situation, including identifying barriers to success.

However, if a community program trains people for employment but none of the trainees ever get a job, the question of whether to continue funding the program has to be asked. To answer this question, the program administrators need information. Does the program have enough resources? Is it recruiting the right people? How many clients complete the program? Is there a good connection between the jobs available and the training program? Why are local employers refusing to hire the graduates of this program? Is the economy on a downward slide?

Exhibit 2.5 **Components of the Logic Model**

Inputs	The resources put into a program: money, staff, facilities, equipment, and technical expertise.
Activities	What the program does.
Outputs	The services or products produced. Outputs are a quantifiable statement of the activities, such as the number of program participants or the amount of money spent per participant.
Outcomes	The short-term results of the activities and outputs. An outcome is the immediate thing that gets changed because of the program.
Impacts	The long-term consequences of the program, which could be divided along a time continuum or a chain of outcomes, with the more immediate outcomes leading to a more distant and typically larger impact. Typically, impacts refer to goal attainment.
Environment	The external factors that might affect each program component.

The key is to be able to break a program into distinct measurable parts, and a useful tool to accomplish this is the logic model (also called the program outcome model) (Fisher et al. 2006; Frechtling 2007; W.K. Kellogg Foundation 2004). The logic model considers a program's inputs, activities, outputs, and outcomes within the context of its dynamic environment. The environment plays a role and has to be considered.

The components of the program are identified and can be assessed separately. Exhibit 2.5 describes the components of the logic model. At its simplest, resources are invested in a program to carry out very specific activities. These activities result in the delivery of specific services, which are considered outputs. For example, a city invests $1 million in a training program for the chronically unemployed. By providing the training, the city expects that people will get jobs. That is the desired outcome. The long-term impact is that people will stay in those jobs and rise out of poverty. The components form a model that can be presented in a visual format.

Before looking at an application, there are a few caveats. First, it should be noted that these terms are not rigid. Sometimes it is hard to decide where an output ends and an outcome begins, or where an outcome ends and an impact begins. For instance, while I would categorize graduates of a training program as an output, other administrators may see them as an immediate outcome. However, regardless of the label, the researchers need to measure the number and percent of graduates, thus providing information that serves as program feedback to the public administrators.

Second, it is easier to measure inputs into a program and describe the activities than it is to measure the outcomes. It is also difficult to determine whether the program caused the outcomes; there may be rival explanations.

Third, while the intention is to measure the program outcome, managers might use this model to look at activities that are outside the program itself. For example, the manager, recognizing that the lack of childcare for the trainees' children is a huge barrier to the program's success, might decide to invest resources in working with local childcare providers to ensure sufficient spaces for the children; this might involve meeting with the childcare providers, writing grants, and lobbying the legislature for

Exhibit 2.6 **Logic Model: Job Training Program**

Inputs →	Activities →	Outputs →	Outcomes →	Immediate impacts →	Long-term impacts

Staff
Money
Class space
	Recruit participants
	Develop job training
	  classes
	Develop workshops
	  on résumé writing,
	  interviewing,
	  applying for a job
		Number of classes
		  and workshops
		  offered
		Number of
		  participants in
		  classes and
		  workshops
		Number of
		  graduates
			Number who get
			  jobs
			Average salary
			  earned
				Percent who
				  earn above the
				  poverty line
				Long-term
				  employment
					Reduction in
					  community
					  poverty

	Develop program
	  support activities
	Partner with childcare
	  center to develop
	  additional spaces
	  for trainees' children
	Write grants to obtain
	  money for a jitney
	  transport service for
	  trainees
		Number of slots
		  made available
		Grants applied for
			Number of slots
			  used by trainees
			Grants obtained:
			  number and
			  amount of funds
			Reduced trainee
			  absenteeism
			Absenteeism
				Contributes to
				graduation
				rate—
				necessary
				components
				to support the
				program but
				not the actual
				impact of the
				training program	

childcare funds. The manager would want to track whether these efforts are successful and whether they reduce trainee absenteeism.

Fourth, the environment is an important factor that should be considered. In a job training program, the unemployment rate and the state of the economy will be important environmental factors. While the program managers may not be able to do anything about the environment, it still provides important information about possible supports and barriers to program success.

APPLYING THE LOGIC MODEL

Let us continue working with the training program for the chronically unemployed that is intended to reduce poverty in the local community. The program is broken into components: inputs, activities, outputs, outcomes, and impacts (see Exhibit 2.6). The program managers, funders, and researchers need to determine the measures for each component. It is relatively easy to count the number of participants in the training program and the number of people who obtain jobs at the end of the training program. It is possible to have them report their income immediately after getting a job. However, it will be harder to track them over time to determine whether they remain employed, experience an increase in income, and move out of poverty. It will be harder still to determine whether or not it was the training program that caused the reduction in poverty. But seeing the components in the model helps in deciding what things to measure.

The environment is a factor. Does the program have enough resources? Government funding may vary; in a budget crises, the legislature might reduce funding to the point where the program can barely function. The economy may affect the number and types of jobs available; it may also affect wages and therefore poverty levels. A foundation may or may not be funding job-training programs. Childcare may or may not be available.

The manager cannot control some things but might be able to affect other things. This is where strategy becomes important. She can work closely with local businesses to ensure that she is training people for jobs that exist and building partnerships with people likely to hire graduates of the training program. She can work closely with local governments and foundations to increase the chances of receiving necessary funding. She can work with community groups to increase the availability of childcare. Some of these actions take time, so these factors might still negatively impact the early results of the program. It is important to take these environmental constraints into consideration when assessing program results.

A logic model format used by the City of Olympia, Washington, is another way to set up a logic model (see Appendix D on page 262). Managers and researchers can develop their own format as long as it includes the basic components. This approach is useful for both planning the project and thinking about needed evaluations at the beginning, at the midpoint, and after full implementation. This approach is also useful to identify information about the context or environment as well as any assumptions that may help explain what is observed in the program and possibly why things did not go as planned.

By staying focused on the outcomes and impacts, program managers can design research that will tell them how well the program or policy is reaching its desired goals and objectives. It is also possible to establish some benchmarks: the number of training classes, the expected number of participants, and target number of graduates each year.

In sum, the logic model attempts to break an intervention or program into component pieces so that both the components and the overall results can be measured. The researchers, collaborating with the public administrators, decide which components to focus on and develop concrete measures. The choice will depend on whether the program is just starting, has completed a full cycle of service delivery, or has been operational for years. Every evaluation is guided by the particular situation.

CONCLUSION

Public administrators have turned to social science methods as an empirical way to provide nonpartisan data to guide policy-making and program implementation. Program evaluation, policy analysis, and performance measures are used extensively in both public and nonprofit administration. While policy decisions are often based on things other than research results, factual information can be useful in bringing a sane voice to the political process, balancing the mischief of factions who will say anything to win the argument.

The basic research concepts apply to scholarly and applied research, including policy analysis and program evaluation. Theories provide the big picture, and hypotheses provide a concrete way to test the theories. These are especially important when examining cause-and-effect relationships and program impacts. Depending on the characteristics of the variables and values, different analytical techniques will be needed; the choices can make a big difference during the analysis phase. Relationships between two variables can be direct, inverse, or nonlinear. To demonstrate a relationship is causal; there needs to be a logical theory to explain why the variables ought to be connected, appropriate time order, covariation between the variables, and elimination of rival explanations. Sometimes researchers look at the relationship between two variables, but, more often, they add other variables. This is called adding a control variable or controlling for other factors. A relationship may appear or disappear when controls are applied.

Models provide a way to identify and explore a complex set of possible relationships in a visual format. They also provide a handy framework that helps managers and researchers to plan research. Since most public administration research focuses specifically on results, the logic model or the logical framework helps researchers and managers identify what outcomes and impacts to measure while keeping the larger context in view.

Studying public administration is a bit like learning a foreign language. This chapter presented many new terms, which will often recur before the end of the book. Definitions of many of these terms are provided in Appendix B on page 248.

EXERCISES

1. In the news. Pick an article from the news that reports research results and look closely at how the researchers applied the basic concepts described in this chapter. Did they use a theory, hypothesis, or research question? What variables did they use? Did the concept of independent and dependent variables make sense in this study? Did the researchers use a model—or imply the use of a model—to make the connection between the variables and the results? Should they have used one? Why or why not?

2. Translate these research questions into testable hypotheses:
   a. Is there pay inequity in the organization based on gender?
   b. Is there a correlation between prenatal care and infant mortality?
   c. Do training programs help people move off welfare into jobs?

3. For each of the following relationships, identify the independent and dependent variables, the likely values of each variable, the type of data (nominal, ordinal, or ratio/interval), and the direction of the relationship.
   a. Researchers believe that people with higher education earn higher salary.
   Independent variable: _____ Values: _____ Type: _____
   Dependent variable: _____ Values: _____ Type: _____
   Direction of the relationship: _____

   b. Pollsters predict that younger voters and older voters are more likely than middle-aged voters to support redistributive economic policies.
   Independent variable: _____ Values: _____ Type: _____
   Dependent variable: _____ Values: _____ Type: _____
   Direction of the relationship: _____

     c. Death rates in automobile accidents are higher in less densely populated areas.

        Independent variable: _____   Values: _____   Type: _____

        Dependent variable: _____   Values: _____   Type: _____

        Direction of the relationship: _____

4. The mayor would like to evaluate a micro-lending program that began one year ago and has asked you to make suggestions. What type of evaluation would you suggest and why?

5. Look at the model of teenage parenthood in Exhibit 2.4. What are some likely individual, social, and economic variables that might be associated with the different decision points? Explain.

6. The army is interested in increasing retention of its soldiers and has asked you to develop a model that identifies the possible factors that influence the decision to reenlist.

    a. What would you do to help build a model?

    b. Sketch a possible model that captures at least a few of the factors that you think might affect the decision to reenlist.

    c. Some human development experts believe that the desire to serve, to make a positive difference, and to place the public interest over self-interest is strong among those entering the public and nonprofit sectors. They call this desire public service motivation. Do you think public service motivation exists and should be added to this model? Why or not?

7. Applying the logic model: Below is a list of inputs, activities, outputs, outcomes and impacts in random order. Please check the column that best describes each statement.

Statement	Input	Activity	Output	Outcome	Impact
Poverty rates decline in areas that are empowerment zones.					
Built new training facilities.					
More than 500 unemployed adults attended classes last year.					
Almost 80 percent of graduates are hired at above-poverty wages.					
The training program hired ten new teachers to deliver the program in remote locations.					
The federal government and local businesses provided $3 million in loans and grants to run the training program.					
Implemented a curriculum to teach practical skills for the marketplace.					
After the new teachers were hired, test scores improved by 20 percent.					
More than 1,000 students graduated in the past three years.					
Employers are satisfied with the skills of the graduates.					
Provided 300 students with classes in job search strategies last year.					

3 | What Is the Question?

OVERVIEW

The first step in the research planning process is figuring out the question (or questions) to be answered. This is surprisingly difficult. Sometimes what researchers think they want to find out, at least initially, is so general that it is impossible to define it. Other times, they might feel overwhelmed by many possible questions and ways to ask them.

Because the research questions are the starting point for all the subsequent choices that have to be made in planning the research project, it is worth spending a substantial amount of time getting them right. In public administration, this means asking questions that will provide accurate, relevant information that can be used by administrators and policy-makers to make decisions.

The focus of this chapter is on the big, overarching research questions. The chapter covers the issues related to determining the research question, the different types of questions, and the special requirements involved in answering cause-and-effect questions.

DETERMINING THE RESEARCH QUESTION

The research planning process begins with defining the question. Slightly different questions may require different research approaches, different data, and different methods of collecting the data. For example, suppose the state legislature spends a fair amount on the state park system each year and wants to know what the taxpayers are getting for their money. Here are some research possibilities:

1. What research approaches might be needed if the question is "What is the health of the public parks?" To answer this, the state might bring in ecosystem experts to look at the health of the trees, plants, and water. A slightly different question about the quality of the built environment would require engineers to assess the buildings, walkways, parking lots, and boat ramps.

2. Researchers may want to measure the overall use at the individual parks if the question is "How frequently are the parks used?" An unstated but important subquestion might be whether some parks are used more frequently than others, which may then lead to a question about why there are differences in use. Another possible question along this concept of "use" is "What amenities are used most in the various parks?" The researchers would have to gather more information than just a count of how many people used the parks.

3. Asking park users how satisfied they are with the parks makes sense; a short customer feedback questionnaire would work fine. However, if the researchers ask a slightly different question about why people do or do not use the parks, then asking the general population would be necessary.

The research question typically evolves, starting as a single general question and getting refined as the most important concerns become clear. Sometimes several questions are embedded in the initial question and have to be teased out. However, whether the researchers ask one research question or several, each question goes through the planning process.

Every situation is different and various factors should be considered when determining the research question. Some factors will be more important than others in specific situations, so the researchers need to ask the right question(s). Here are some useful questions to ask in determining the research question:

- Who is requesting this research and why?
- Are there any mandates for data by policy-makers or funders?
- Who are the likely users and/or stakeholders of the research and what are their specific issues and concerns? What is the relative importance of each of the possible issues and concerns?
- If the concern is about a program or policy, does it make sense to focus on its goals and objectives? Are they measurable and concrete?
- What is already known about this issue?
- How have others conducted this research in the past?
- What are the resource requirements, data availability, and relative ease of answering the possible questions?
- What is not being considered that might be important?

For example, the downtown business community is concerned that too few people come to shop. Storeowners meet with the mayor to ask for help, pointing out that downtown development is in the city's interest too. "The neighboring city collects more sales tax revenue from its downtown than we do," they state. "We need to be more competitive. Will you help?"

The mayor agrees to look into this issue and meets with the city manager and agency heads the following week. As the conversation meanders, someone suggests that maybe the other city's downtown is thriving because it has a parking garage. "Would people come to our town if we had a parking garage?" the mayor asks. Someone then suggests surveying citizens to find out if they would shop downtown if there were a parking garage. In a short time the city officials have chosen their research question and a broad plan about how to conduct the research. It seems pretty simple.

But is parking really the problem? It makes sense to step back at this point in the process and look at a range of factors that might explain why the neighboring city's downtown attracts shoppers. Maybe the stores in the neighboring city are more interesting or have more convenient hours of operation. Maybe the neighboring city provides free shuttles that make it easy to get around town, or maybe people feel safer walking around the other city's downtown area. Maybe the other city has a wealthier population and has upscale stores that are attractive. Maybe the neighboring city gives a sense of vibrancy. There are lots of maybes.

By failing to work through the process, the city jumped on the first question that popped up without asking whether it was the right one. The city officials run the risk of spending time and money on research that will not tell them why citizens do not shop downtown.

LEARNING FROM OTHERS

Most researchers do several things almost immediately to help determine the research question. One action is to gather information. What has been published on this issue? Governmental agencies, nonprofits, think tanks, lobbying groups, advocacy groups, and universities may have done prior research on this topic. An early action step is to gather all the studies that seem most relevant.

Researchers use several methods in tracking down existing studies. If they are working for an agency or know people in the local agencies concerned about this topic, they might ask for prior studies; some studies are formally published but others may be insider documents.

To find information in the public domain, Google is not a bad start. However, libraries have much better searchable online databases available that are likely to identify academic studies as well as government reports that have some degree of rigor. Once a few books, articles, and reports are identified, their bibliographies or cited works provide additional studies that might not have turned up in the initial library search.

Researchers are on the lookout for the handful of studies that everyone cites. Not only are they likely to provide useful information, but also their inclusion is a signal to others who know the issue that the researchers have done their homework. These studies become the backbone of the researchers' literature review.

Prior studies provide research results and background information, setting up the context for this new study. They also specify the research questions used and provide examples of different research approaches, including measurement strategies, specifics about data collection, clues about data that might be readily available, and analysis options. Good studies will often highlight problems they encountered and offer suggestions for the next study. Knowing what worked and what did not in earlier studies is an important piece of information. Researchers build on the work of others and if someone has already figured out how to do the research, there is no point in reinventing the wheel. Replication can be very useful because it can speed up the design process and provide a comparison point.

It is important to keep in mind that even the best study may need to be adapted to fit a particular situation. If there is too much adaptation, however, the results lose their comparability. This may or may not be a good trade-off. The researchers need to find the balance point between unreachable perfection and being good enough to withstand scrutiny.

Lastly, the literature review should reveal the experts on the topic. The researchers can contact them informally to get advice and assistance. Alternatively, the experts might be asked to play a formal role in advising the research team or briefing the elected officials and agency heads about what is already known. Depending on the situation, convening an expert panel may be enough to answer the research questions.

ENGAGING THE STAKEHOLDERS

Simultaneously with the literature review, researchers work closely with the requester of the research (see Application 3.1). The requester—the primary stakeholder—could be an immediate supervisor, agency head, legislator, committee, funder, or some combination. Researchers need to understand the requester's concerns, including what motivates the research and the intended use of the results.

The researchers also need to think about other possible stakeholders and consider ways to engage them. Having key stakeholders involved in some way will add to the quality of the research planning as well as increase buy-in of the results. Researchers who desire to engage stakeholders need to decide how participatory the project should be and how wide the circle should be drawn.

The wider circle of stakeholders might include customers or clients of the specific services, citizens, representatives of other public or nonprofit agencies, elected officials, business people, and interest groups. Although this circle can become large and unwieldy, sometimes the situation requires casting a wide net. For example, if both the research process and the research results are intended to bring people into the policy-making process, then inclusiveness is essential. Engaging others in the research process is sometimes called participatory research, action research, or empowerment evaluation

Two different issues come into play when thinking about including stakeholders. One is diversity. Are different interests and viewpoints represented? When considering whom to invite, the researchers need to decide what perspectives should be included and whether they are diverse enough to preclude bias. What diversity looks like will depend on the particular research topic and the community.

The second issue concerns the number of stakeholders to be included. Does everyone need to be involved or will a handful of people who represent the diverse perspectives be sufficient? There is a trade-off here. Not everyone has to be involved in order for diverse perspectives to be at the table. However, will those not invited feel left out, thus creating some hard feelings that may surface later? Those planning the research need to consider the politics of the situation.

While ensuring diversity at the table is essential, not all tables are even; some person (or persons) with a particular agenda may try to dominate and control the process. If this happens, the research may wind up seriously flawed. The challenge for the researchers and managers is to ensure that all views are heard and that the integrity of the research is protected.

As with any group endeavor, strong group facilitation and negotiation skills will be required to manage the inevitable conflicts that will arise. Conflict is useful and should be allowed to bubble up. In my experience, if there is no conflict, it is time to get worried about "group-think," when there is false agreement about what is really going on: everyone says you are going in the right direction as you walk backward off a cliff.

WORKING TOGETHER

The working relationship between the researchers, managers, and other stakeholders is important. It begins in this first step of determining the research question. There needs to be mutual respect between the researchers, managers, and stakeholders. The researchers need to be able to explain in clear terms research approaches and concepts, especially those that are necessary to ensure the quality of the research.

The researchers might be working with specific subcultures with different values, norms, and terminology. There may be some history that is essential to understand before moving forward. For example, prior researchers may have behaved unethically, leaving a legacy of suspicion that new researchers will have to overcome.

At the same time, the researchers need to be aware that the people sitting at the table have information and insights about the situation and the specific issues that are essential to successfully plan the research project. The takeaway lesson here is that the researchers do not know all they need to know and are dependent on the other people at the table. Humility is an important characteristic of the researchers if they are to be successful.

Conversely, the managers working with a research team need to recognize that the researchers bring important knowledge and skills. While it is easy to dismiss the researchers' concerns as "academic," it is worth the time to understand the researchers' concerns. However, the needs of a researcher are not necessarily the same as a manager, so managers need to make sure the research meets their requirements. The takeaway for managers is to recognize that planning a research project is a process that requires both time and good communication.

TYPES OF QUESTIONS

The research question is the starting point in the research process; depending on the type of question, different designs and/or data collection strategies are needed. One way to divide the universe of questions is into descriptive, normative, and relationship questions (see Exhibit 3.1).

DESCRIPTIVE QUESTIONS

Descriptive questions seek to capture a snapshot of the current situation, process, or program. They might elicit a description of a neighborhood, clients, or program

Application 3.1
United Way of Thurston County
Facing Our Future

In 2002, United Way of Thurston County in Washington convened a group of stakeholders to plan a collaborative community assessment. The Community Partnership consisted of representatives from more than thirty agencies and organizations, including business, public social service, schools, hospitals, nonprofit agencies, and elected officials. The partnership was charged with overseeing the research planning process and disseminating the results.

The intention of this effort was to identify community strengths as well as needs that would guide community interventions. According to Pam Toal, the executive director of the United Way of Thurston County, the assessment would "help improve the quality of life in our community and get a snap shot of the services in our community." These results would be used by nonprofits to obtain funding and to guide future allocation of United Way dollars (Olympian 2002).

The research questions were:

1. What do people view as the strengths, challenges, and issues facing our community?
2. Do citizens, community leaders, and service providers share a similar sense of community strengths and challenges?

The Community Partnership located people with needed expertise, including someone to do the data entry and a graphics designer to produce the report to the community. The local MPA program offered a community assessment course whose students did much of the data collection as part of the hands-on learning experience.

A subcommittee worked with the MPA faculty to design the survey. The subcommittee worked to find the right balance so the survey would be both comprehensive enough to cover the many community issues and short enough to hold people's attention. The survey team looked at what other communities had done, including other United Way agencies, to get ideas. Planning the assessment took more time than originally allotted, but, in the end, the Community Partnership was satisfied that the assessment was focused on issues that mattered.

Students and faculty from the MPA program analyzed the results. The final report was developed by a few members of the Community Partnership and approved by the large group. The Community Partnership held a press conference when the report was released and made presentations to local groups. Six month later, the partnership convened the Facing Our Future Forum to discuss the key findings and develop action teams. Over 300 community members attended to discuss the results and plan action steps.

Creating the Community Partnership brought to the table key players who participated in the overall research design and approach. They had substantive knowledge of specific community issues and helped to make sure the right questions were asked. Their engagement also sent the signal to the community that this was something that mattered. The local paper provided coverage of the study and published the report.

Exhibit 3.1 **Three Types of Research Questions**

Descriptive questions describe, "What is."
- How many teenagers dropped out of high school last year?
- How many people were served last year?
- What are the steps in the process?
- How satisfied are the participants with the program?

Normative questions compare "what is" to "what should be."
- Is the dropout rate in area high schools higher or lower than the dropout rates in comparable cities?
- Did we achieve our goal of serving 1,000 people?
- Do the benefits outweigh the costs?
- Are we providing enough computer training classes to meet the need?

Relationship questions examine relationships (cause-and-effect, impact, or associations).
- What factors are associated with drug use among youth?
- Are public service employees more likely to evidence public service motivation than those in the private sector?
- Did the mentoring program result in increased job satisfaction?
- What was the impact of the welfare-to-work training program?

---

employees. Think of a journalist's questions—who, what, when, where, how, and how much—when asking descriptive questions. This information might be used to target services, understand the clientele, identify bottlenecks in a process, or identify attitudes.

Sometimes all that people want to know is a description of the situation without making any judgment as to whether it is good or bad. Descriptive questions might seek to show changes over time, but they do not explain why there are changes; for example, Portland, Oregon, estimates the number of daily bike trips on selected bridges and roadways (i.e., the number of bikes that cross those bridges and roadways) and the number of miles of bike paths. Exhibit 3.2 gives a picture of changes over time. However, there is no judgment or explanation about why things changed; just the facts.

Descriptive questions are very common. While not necessarily easy to answer, descriptive questions can help set the context of the program or issue. I almost always include a descriptive question as part of the set-up in my research projects.

Small modifications to the wording can change the type of question. Asking *how*

Exhibit 3.2 **Portland, Oregon: Bicycle Trips and Miles of Bikeways, 1997 and 2006**

	1997	1998	1999	2000	2001	2002	2003	2004	2005	2006
Total estimated number of daily bike trips	5,225	5,690	5,910	6,020	7,624	8,250	8,562	8,875	10,192	12,046
Miles of bike ways		166.3	182.6	213.2	221.7	235.0	251.9	254.4	260.0	262.1	266.1

Source: Portland Auditor's Office, Service Efforts and Accomplishment Report, 2006–2007.

Note: Bicycle trips over Broadway, Steel, Burnside and Hawthorne Bridges (total per day based on one-week count).

a program works—that is, the processes it uses—is descriptive. Asking *how well* a program works implies a measure against some kind of criterion and changes it into a normative question.

NORMATIVE QUESTIONS

Normative questions compare the current situation (what is) to what someone thinks it should be in terms of a quantifiable target, standard, benchmark, or criterion. Once a normative question is posed, the criteria for comparison are essential. In fact, a normative question cannot be answered without a comparison to something.

The word *normative* connotes judgment, a determination that something is good or bad based on a set of values. As used here, however, the word means only that a judgment is made based on whether the measure meets a specified, quantifiable standard.

There are different ways we can ask how our program stacks up. How many service units do we provide as compared to other organizations? How much does it cost to provide a unit of service this year as compared to last year? These questions may sound descriptive, but the criteria are implied: are we doing better or worse in comparison to other agencies or to our past performance? Another example of a normative question can be found in cost-benefit questions, which assume that costs should not exceed the benefits.

Let us walk through an example to highlight some complexity. Suppose Congress passes a bill requiring the Environmental Protection Agency (EPA) to clean up 200 toxic waste sites per year and provides a budget of $5 billion. At the end of the first year, Congress, as part of its oversight function, wants to know whether EPA cleaned up the 200 toxic waste sites during that year. This is a normative question. The researchers can collect data to count how many sites were cleaned up in the past year and compare that figure to the criterion of 200 toxic waste sites.

If EPA cleaned up 200 sites, then the researchers would report that EPA was in compliance with congressional mandates. If EPA only cleaned up 100 sites, the report would find EPA not in compliance. However, additional questions might be posed. The researchers might want to determine what barriers the EPA encountered and whether those barriers can be removed.

When there is a simple, single criterion—did the agency meet a concrete and measurable goal?—it is easy to draw a conclusion. Sometimes, however, whether or not the agency met the criterion might not the only factor to be considered. What if EPA cleaned up only 100 toxic waste sites, but they were the 100 worst in the country? Judgments about compliance need to be made within the context of the legislative intent and the situation.

Who makes the judgment? Sometimes the researcher decides, but often program managers, policy-makers, interest groups, and citizens get to weigh in with a judgment also.

If there is no agreed-upon benchmark, the researchers, in collaboration with the stakeholders, have to establish one. Researchers may look at what other investigators have used in the past and consider adopting their standard. Or they may opt to

Exhibit 3.3 **Profits of the Five Largest Oil Companies, 2003–2007** (in $ millions)

Company	2007	2006	2005	2004	2003
Exxon Mobil	40,610	36,130	25,330	25,330	21,654
Royal Dutch Shell	27,564	25,310	18,183	18,636	12,606
BP	17,287	22,341	15,371	16,208	10,437
Chevron	18,688	14,099	13,328	13,328	7,506
Conoco-Phillips	11,891	13,529	8,129	8,129	4,585
Total	116,040	113,415	82,346	84,635	56,788

Sources: U.S. Congressional Research Service, 2007, 2006, 2005. Fortune Global 500, MoneyCNN. com, 2002–2008.

convene a group of experts and ask them to set a standard. If this strategy is used, it is essential that these be generally recognized experts in the profession and represent a range of perspectives.

Here is a real-life example: oil companies' profits. If the question is descriptive—for example, how much profit have the big oil companies made in the last five years?—it might take a bit of digging but we can find that data. Exhibit 3.3 shows the profits of the five largest integrated oil companies over the past five years. Exxon Mobile was the clear winner, earning a record $40.6 billion in 2007. However, if the question is framed in terms of whether these oil companies are making too much profit, it shifts into a normative question. Now we have to define "too much profit." The definition offered by the oil companies is likely to be different from the definition offered by a consumer advocacy group or angry citizens who believe price gouging caused gas prices to soar (Jacobe 2008). From a research perspective, we need to ask whether an entity has a particular interest in how that criterion is defined.

The takeaway lesson here is that criteria are the key issue in answering normative questions. Whenever criteria are used to answer a normative question, a good researcher states the criteria along with the rationale for selection. Sophisticated users will consider whether the criteria are fair, objective, and generally accepted as reasonable. If the criteria are not provided, the sophisticated user will have to dig to find them. The tough question is simply this: are the criteria biased in such a way to lead to a predetermined desired result?

RELATIONSHIP QUESTIONS

Relationship questions are called by many names: causal, cause-and-effect, impact, correlation, and association. They are intended to determine the extent to which two or more variables are related. Cause-and-effect questions reflect public administrators' desire to understand the root causes of public problems and to determine the impacts of policies and programs. Did the program cause the intended result?

While I lump the various names of cause and effect questions together for ease of presentation, sometimes researchers are investigating only if variables are associated; this means that two variables occur together but are not causally related. For example, when researchers identify "risk factors" associated with drug use among youth, they are not claiming a causal relationship. Although one of the risk factors for drug use is the use of tobacco and alcohol before the age of fifteen, the researchers are not saying that early smoking and drinking cause the later use of drugs. The early use is like a canary in a mineshaft; it is a signal that early intervention is needed to prevent the movement to more harmful drug use. The key point to remember is that association does not mean causation.

A variation of cause-and-effect questions looks into the future and is often used when policy analysts need to predict what will happen if the government does or does not take certain action; to compare the likely costs and outcomes of various policies under consideration; or to forecast future revenues, expenditures, and service demands. Answering "likely future" questions is a common activity among economists, policy analysts, and budget officers. The U.S. Congressional Budget Office, for example, routinely determines cost estimates for all proposed legislation. Since these estimates (or projections) are made on assumptions, it is essential that all assumptions be carefully stated. Debates typically focus on the assumptions.

Answers to questions about the future are always tentative. Life has a way of messing with the assumptions on which the predictions are based. For example, states that have a substantial tax on gas discovered that as the price of gas went over $4 per gallon in 2008, people drove less. As a result, the forecasted revenues vanished, leaving many states with budget shortfalls.

Cause-and-effect questions are the hardest to answer because isolating the independent effect of one variable on another is difficult. As discussed in Chapter 2, four conditions need to be in place in order to demonstrate causality: a logical theory, time order, covariation, and elimination of rival explanations. Researchers need to use very specific designs to answer cause-and-effect questions; these will be presented in Chapter 5.

The reason I go through this drill on types of questions is so that is clear when researchers or requesters are asking cause-and-effect question. It is easier to answer a question about whether program participants are satisfied with the program than to measure the impacts of that program. Of course, if the requester really wants to know the program's impact, then providing an answer about participant satisfaction will not do.

CONCLUSION

The question is one of the drivers of the research project so it makes sense to invest time in getting it right. Engaging stakeholders, reviewing prior studies, and talking with knowledgeable people can be very helpful. Building models or reframing relationship questions as hypotheses can also make the issues clearer.

The research design depends on the kind of question asked. There are other ways of categorizing types of questions than the descriptive, normative, and relationship typology used here. It is also possible that questions fall into more than one of these categories, depending on how people understand the words used. What is important, however, is to recognize the different types of questions when designing a research study or when reviewing other research. Normative questions have to state the criteria and cause-and-effect questions have to eliminate rival explanations.

It is also not unusual for researchers to develop different research designs to answer the different types of questions in their study. For example, a single research project about a job-training program may describe trainees and program components (descriptive questions), check whether the program met its enrollment targets (normative question), and determine what percent of the trainees got jobs as a result of the program (impact question).

Researchers and managers need to resist the temptation to lock in on the first question that comes to mind; it is unlikely to be the question that gets at the heart of the issue. Instead, they need to consider many questions during the early phases of planning the research project, without regard to how hard or easy it will be to gather data and without any preference of data collection methods. This step in the research process will help the key players articulate what they really want to know. What matters most is that the right research questions are chosen for the situation.

EXERCISES

1. In the news: Look at a research article and identify the likely stakeholders and/or audiences for this study. What research questions were asked? Using the descriptive, normative, and cause-effect categories, what types of research questions were asked?
2. For each of the following, identify the type of question being asked. Develop at least three possible subquestions that you would want to answer as part of the study.
   a. How does the post office purchase land?
   b. Has the bailout of the financial corporations been subject to adequate financial oversight and audit?
   c. What is the adequacy of prenatal care obtained by women who are enrolled in Medicaid or who are uninsured?
3. Identify the type of question: descriptive, normative, impact? If the type is not clear, rewrite the question.
   a. Was the crackdown on speeders successful?
   b. Since its inception, how many individuals have been served by the state's job training program?
   c. What teaching methods are most effective for adult students?
   d. How effective are the current recycling efforts in our community compared to the nearby cities?
   e. Have there been fewer complaints of sexual harassment after all managers went through a training course that emphasized prevention?
   f. How many books were borrowed from the library last year?
   g. Was there a change in reading levels after the "It's fun to read" program was implemented?
   h. Did the program reach its goal of enrolling 100 children in "It's fun to read" in the first month?

4. In order to demonstrate a causal relationship, the researchers must have a logical theory, appropriate time order and covariation between the variables, and must have eliminated rival explanations. What is missing, if anything, in these cause-and-effect assertions?
   a. A study looks at the promotion time for women and concludes that women face barriers to promotions.
   b. A recent report states that the arctic ice caps are melting faster than expected because of overpopulation and the dramatic increase in carbon emissions by humans over the past fifty years.
   c. Proponents of free college education for all argue that teenage pregnancies and crime would be lower if everyone had the opportunity to go to college.
   d. An e-mail circulated stating that a study found that a majority of women who had breast cancer had used deodorant containing a specific chemical and that it should be banned.
5. Some people have argued that the oil companies have made too much profit over the past five years. Is it possible to make too much profit? Why or why not? Assuming you are required as a congressional committee staff member to determine whether the oil companies have made too much profit, how would you go about determining the criteria to decide what is "too much"?

4 Identifying Measures and Measurement Strategy

OVERVIEW

Once the research questions are posed in general terms, the next step is to determine what specific information is needed to answer each research question. Counts, percentages, rates, and averages, which are commonly used statistics in measurement (see Exhibit 4.1), will be discussed in greater detail in Chapter 12. However, the measurement strategy is something more than statistics. The measurement strategy defines exactly what will be counted.

This chapter covers basic issues about measures and the steps necessary to develop a measurement strategy. In order to assess the credibility of research results, it is essential to understand the measures used in any research study.

DEFINING KEY TERMS

The first step is to define key terms in the research questions. Although concepts may be difficult to define in English, every term in the research question must be defined. This is necessary in both quantitative and qualitative research. For quantitative research, there is a second step: to develop operational definitions that attach numbers to the conceptual definitions. In social science language, this is called "operationalizing the terms."

CONCEPTUAL DEFINITIONS

Let us go through the process to get a clear sense of the level of detail that is ultimately necessary in developing a measurement strategy. Suppose a legislator poses a descriptive question: "What is the extent of drug use among youth?" To answer this question, the researchers must determine what is meant by each key term.

- *Extent*: Should extent of use be defined in terms of numbers, percentages, or rates? What amount of drug use is a problem? Is any use at all a problem? Is

Exhibit 4.1 **Frequently Used Measures**

- Frequencies (numbers, a count of how many)
  Fifty students graduated from the training program last year.

- Percent (proportion) distributions
  The majority (51 percent) of the students were women.

- Mean (average)
  The average age of the students was 36.

- Median (midpoint)
  The ages ranged from 22 to 60, with the midpoint being 29.

- Mode (the most frequent value)
  The most frequent reported age was 32.

- Money (costs, revenues, expenditures)
  The yearly tuition cost is $18,000 for a full-time student in 2008.

- Percent change between two points in time (sometimes called rate of change)
  Between last year and this, enrollment increased by 40 percent.

- Ratio (the number of one thing compared to another)
  The student to faculty ratio is 15 to 1.

- Rate (number expressed per something)
  The teen birth rate in the city was 165.4 per 1,000 girls aged 15 to 19 in 1996.

- Comparisons (could be numbers, percentages, means)
  The average salary for graduates of the MPA program was $52,000. In contrast, graduates of
  the MBA program earned an average of $75,000.

10 percent of youth using drugs a problem? 30 percent? Does it depend on the type of drug or age of the person using it?

- *Drugs*: Does this include all drugs or specific illegal ones, such as marijuana, cocaine, and heroin? What about alcohol and tobacco? Since it is illegal for youth to use alcohol and tobacco, should they be included?
- *Use*: Does this include use at any previous time or only recent use? If recent, then the word *recent* needs to be defined: in the past week, month, or year? Alternatively, *use* might be defined in terms of frequency of use: once, several times, or many times? Does problem use vary by type of drug? For example, is there a difference between having an occasional beer and binge drinking? Is there a difference between use of illegal substances and abuse? If so, how would each be defined?
- *Youth*: Does this refer to children age 14 and under, or only those between 14 and 18, or everyone under 21?

Defining these terms depend on a number of factors. First, have experts already developed definitions? If they have, will their definitions meet the needs of the legislator? It is acceptable to differ with the experts but the rationale for using different definitions should be explained. The rationale must also be able to stand close scrutiny—especially if someone with a particular political agenda believes that using different definitions creates a bias.

Resource constraints become a factor as the researchers wrestle with what to measure. What can be done in the time and with the resources available? The more inclusive the measurement, the larger the study will need to be. For instance, a much longer data collection instrument will be needed if all illegal drugs are included than if the study is limited to alcohol and marijuana.

Researchers should look at the results of previous studies to see if there is a way to justify a narrow focus. If studies over the last ten years indicate that alcohol is the illegal substance of choice among youth, followed by marijuana, this information could be used to justify focusing the study on these two substances. Ultimately, a balance has to be struck between inclusiveness and resources available to conduct the study.

Sometimes researchers discover that data have already been collected that they might be able to use. The researchers will need to assess the measurement strategy used for that study: there really is no getting around this step in the planning process. The definitions used in the earlier study may not be perfect, so the researchers have to decide whether those measures are close enough to use for the current study. There is a trade-off here: it is cheaper to use available data than to embark on original data collection. However, if the measures are not close enough to what is needed, then this is not a good trade-off.

OPERATIONAL DEFINITIONS

The next step in the measurement strategy is to develop operational definitions that specify exactly what will be counted to answer the research question. It means attaching numbers to concepts (see Application 4.1).

In the youth drug study, suppose that the researchers decide to measure the proportion of youth aged 14 to 18 who used marijuana, cocaine, or alcohol in the past week and the past month, as well as the proportion who ever used these substances. The researchers decide not to ask about how frequently people have used drugs over the past year because people may have difficulty accurately recalling their behavior over a long period of time (known as "memory decay"). Instead, the researchers opt to ask a yes-or-no question about whether the respondents have ever used drugs. For the alcohol portion of the study, researchers define problem drinking in terms of binge drinking, which is operationalized as five or more drinks at one time.

Having operationalized these terms, the researchers are in a position to write survey questions to measure exactly what they want to measure. Sometimes it helps to create a matrix of the subquestions and measures so the details are easier to identify (see Exhibit 4.2); this matrix is based on my work on the U.S. Government Accountability Office's study of drug use among youth in 1993. The takeaway lesson is to realize how detailed and specific this measurement step has to be.

Once the researchers develop their basic measurement strategy, they would meet with the legislator to make sure there are no problems. It is not unusual, however, for another question to be posed at this point. The legislator is seeking to create a preven-

Exhibit 4.2   **Drug Use Among Youth: Measurement Strategy**

Question	Subquestions	Measurement	Comments
What is the extent of drug use among youth aged 14 to 18?	What percent have ever used marijuana? How frequently have they used marijuana in the past week and month?	Percent ever used (yes/no) Frequency: 1 time, 2–3 times, 4–5 times, 6 or more	Asking number of times ever used might elicit inaccurate answers due to memory decay. It is better to ask about the past week or month.
	What percent have ever used cocaine?	Percent ever used (yes/no)	Cocaine in any form (including crack)
	How frequently have they used cocaine in the past week and month?	Frequency: 1 time, 2–3 times, 4–5 times, 6 or more	
	What percent have ever used alcohol?	Percent ever used (yes/no)	
	How many days in the past week have they had a drink?	Frequency in past week	
	How frequently have they binged in the past week? Past month?	Frequency: 1 time, 2–3 times, 4–5 times, 6 or more	Binge drinking: five or more drinks in one sitting

tion program and wants to ensure that it is targeted to youth most at risk. She suggests a new question: what are the risk factors associated with drug and alcohol use?

Faced with a new research question, the researchers run through the same planning steps. The researchers begin by looking at what is already known about risk factors. They gather existing research and talk to experts in the field about a variety of possible social, psychological, and economic risk factors. Finally they select and operationalize the factors that seem most applicable. Some factors, like family structure, are surprisingly complex. Children may reside in families with both parents, with only one parent, or with a stepparent. Children might be living with grandparents or other family members. Some may be in foster care. If data were gathered through a questionnaire, then it would have to accommodate a variety of possible family arrangements.

As sophisticated users of research results or managers contracting-out for research are aware, the number of tiny decisions that shape any research project is substantial. The devil is in the detail, as the saying goes, and it is important to understand how every term is defined. Researchers cannot assume that "drugs" or "abuse" mean the same thing to everyone. The key point is that the research question must be carefully and concretely defined so there is no ambiguity.

SETTING BOUNDARIES

Part of the defining process means setting the boundaries or scope of the study. This is the statement about what is included and what is not. Boundaries establish things like the specific topics, the number and characteristics of participants, geographic

---

Application 4.1
Measuring a Training Program

A researcher is asked to measure the impact of a training program provided in public housing projects. The goal of this program is to help the chronically unemployed find steady work so they can move out of poverty. The research question is: Is the program successful in training the chronically unemployed so they can obtain steady jobs? Next, the researcher identifies the five terms that need to be defined in order to answer this question: program, successful, chronically unemployed, steady, and jobs. It may seem odd to include program here. However, if a program is delivered in different locations, the experiences might also differ. It is something a researcher would want to pay attention to, and the readers of the report should expect some statement about any differences in the program locations that might affect the results.

What does success look like? One measure would be the percent of people who get jobs after completing the training program. The researchers might also set a criterion for success: 30 percent of the trainees? 50 percent? 75 percent? Again, prior studies and experts in the field might help identify an accepted benchmark of success.

Alternatively, success might be defined through the research design by using a comparison group. In this case, success would be defined in terms of whether a higher percentage of participants in the program got jobs as compared to the comparison group.

What is meant by the term chronically unemployed? Does the program define this? It could refer to people unemployed at the start of the program who may or may not have been unemployed for very long. Alternatively, it could only consider people who have been unemployed for more than half of the past three years as chronically unemployed. It is important to know how the researcher defines this term.

Steady is also tricky. Does it mean forty hours per week or does it include part-time work? Does it mean that the trainees kept the job for more than two months? Six months? One year? What is meant by job? Is it only paid employment or does volunteer work count?

As the researcher and stakeholders work through this process of developing a measurement strategy, the research question could change. For example, if the research question is stated slightly differently, it could change from asking whether people got jobs to asking whether the participants moved out of poverty. In that case, the measures would also change and the researcher would have to once again work through the measurement step.

---

locations, and time periods that will be included in the research. For example, when researchers decide to look at only two drugs, marijuana and cocaine, rather than all illegal drugs, they are setting a boundary. They might describe this as "the scope of the study." They may decide to look at cocaine as a single drug rather than separating out crack cocaine. That further defines the scope of the study. Similarly, the researchers set boundaries by deciding to look at illegal use of these drugs reported by high school seniors rather than all youth.

From a practical point of view, setting boundaries is necessary. Time and resources are limited, so choices have to be made. It is often better to do a small, well-focused study that can be completed than one that is so large and broad that it is impossible to finish within the time available.

The unit of analysis is another way to think about boundaries. The unit of analysis defines the target of the research. Suppose a city council member is concerned about the availability of food to residents in the poorest neighborhoods. He asks for an investigation and the city manager hires a researcher to design the study. The researcher finds a study done by Curtis and McClellan (1995) and uses that as the starting point in developing two possible research questions.

One question asks whether the prices for comparable food items in supermarkets are higher or lower in the poor communities as compared to those in the middle-income communities. In this case, the unit of analysis is food prices. The researcher can design a study that will systematically collect and compare prices for a very specific "basket" of food in supermarkets in low-income and middle-income communities: a gallon of milk, a pound of margarine, price per pound of in-season fresh fruits and vegetables, and the price per pound of specific types of meat.

The second possible research question is whether people feel they have access to affordable food. The unit of analysis will be people's perceptions about access. If this question is selected, then the researcher will design a study to systematically collect and compare people's perceptions about access to affordable food in low- and middle-income communities.

The measures and the questions should align: the measures should make sense in terms of the unit of analysis. Sophisticated users of research results would want to know the boundaries of the research and why those boundaries were selected. Do the boundaries make sense given the situation? The tough question: Would these results be likely to be notably different if the boundaries were different?

VALID AND RELIABLE MEASURES

Measures should be valid, relevant, and reliable. Unfortunately, sometimes measurement strategies suggest the person looking for his lost keys under a lamppost. When asked if he lost them on this street, he says, "No, but this is where the light is." In measurement, the measure should be what is needed to answer the question, not just what is easiest to collect.

For example, if the question is about people's behavior, then behavior must be measured; behavior is the unit of analysis. Asking people how many hours they spend working productively on the job is likely to elicit very different results from what might be observed. However, asking people to estimate the number of their productive hours on the job is much easier than trying to do observations. This is one of those trade-offs: ease of collection is balanced against the accuracy of self-reported data. If the researchers decide they do not have the resources to do observations, they need to restate their research question to reflect the change from behavior to perceptions. Their research question is now about people's perceptions of their productivity on their job. This shift reconnects the measurement to the research question. And as long as

Exhibit 4.3 **U.S. Poverty Thresholds, 2008**

Persons in family or household	48 contiguous states and Washington, DC	Alaska	Hawaii
1	$10,400	$13,000	$11,960
2	14,000	17,500	16,100
3	17,600	22,000	20,240
4	21,200	26,500	24,380
5	24,800	31,000	28,520
6	28,400	35,500	32,660
7	32,000	40,000	36,800
8	35,600	44,500	40,940
For each additional person, add	3,600	4,500	4,140

Source: Federal Register 73, no. 15 (January 23, 2008): 3971–3972.

the conclusions reflect that the researchers measured perceptions about productivity rather than actual productivity, there is no problem.

VALIDITY

Valid measures are precise; they measure what the researcher thinks they measure. In social science, this is called construct validity. For instance, are the numbers of jobs advertised in the classified section of the newspaper a valid measure of job availability? No. The classified ads merely show how many jobs are advertised in that particular medium.

Sometimes a commonly used measure is not really as good as it seems initially. The poverty line (threshold) is a routine measure. How is poverty defined and measured? Poverty is measured by the amount of cash a family receives. If it is less than a specific amount, the family is counted as "below the poverty line." That is simple enough. However, how was the poverty line initially operationalized? The story of the poverty measure goes back to 1963, when Mollie Orshansky, an employee in the Social Security Administration, developed a measure of poverty based on the cost of food that took into account family size. This measure was adopted in 1965 by the federal government as the poverty line.

Orshansky calculated the cost of purchasing the cheapest of four food plans developed by the Department of Agriculture, a food plan designed for emergency situations. Using other research, she learned that families of three or more persons spent about one-third of their after-tax income on food. So she multiplied the cost of the cheapest food plan by three to arrive at the minimal yearly income a family would need. Using 1963 as the base year, she calculated that a family of four (two adults and two children) would spend $1,033 for food per year. Multiplying that by 3, she set $3,100 a year as the poverty threshold for a family of four in 1963. That operational definition has stuck, with only annual inflation adjustments. The 2008 poverty thresholds are listed below (see Exhibit 4.3).

This operational measure of poverty has been criticized (National Academy of Science 1995). Some critics argue that it fails to include the in-kind cash benefits from programs like food stamps, the Women, Infant and Children feeding program, free school lunches, housing subsidies, and taxes saved by taking the Earned Income Tax Credit. The measure also does not consider the monetary value of food that people grow themselves. If these were included, the number of people falling below these poverty thresholds would probably be fewer.

Other critics point out that family size is not all that useful in estimating minimum living requirements. A family with a growing teenager will need more money for food than a family with a small child. A family of four with two adults might have different food requirements than a family with one parent and three small children. Using a more realistic operational definition of living requirements would probably increase the number of people falling below the poverty line.

Still others argue that the living costs are unrealistic and should not be applied according to a one-size-fits-all formula. Even within the same state, housing costs vary; the cost of housing in New York City is not the same as in Buffalo. In addition, the costs of childcare, transportation, and health insurance are not reflected in Orshansky's calculations.

Changing the measure, however, is problematic. First of all, there is no agreement about what should be counted as income. Second, there is no agreement about what expenses should be included in a new measure of poverty. Third, adjusting the measure to account for variations in family composition and housing costs in different geographic areas would add almost impossible complexity to the calculation. So the operational definition of poverty remains as it was in 1963, even though its validity is in question.

However, the debate continues. In July 2008, Mayor Michael Bloomberg of New York City announced a more realistic measure based on the work of the National Academy of Sciences. "No formula would be perfect, but Mr. Bloomberg's employs common sense," opined the *New York Times* in an editorial (2008a); "It is absurd, for example, that the poverty threshold in New York City, one of the most expensive, has been the same as the least expensive: $20,444 for a family of four. The mayor raised New York's poverty ceiling to a more believable $26,138." The result? New York City's poverty rate rose from 19 percent under the Orshansky formula to 23 percent under Bloomberg's. Among the elderly, it rose from 18 percent to 32.

Another frequently used measure is racial identity. Race is a very common demographic question asked on surveys and in polls. How would a person with an African-American parent and a white parent be classified? What about a person whose grandparents were Hispanic, Asian, and African-American? Such questions suggest the term "race" might not be as valid as we tend to treat it.

The U.S. Census asks many questions about race and ethnicity; that is a clue that the distinction between race and ethnicity is unclear. It is also important to keep in mind that there is only one race and that is the human race. *Race: The Power of Illusion*, reports scientific evidence showing very little genetic difference between people who believe they are of different races (California Newsreel 2003). This lack of scientific evidence has led some to argue that the U.S. census should no longer ask about race.

If there is no scientific evidence for racial differences, why does the census ask?

Race is a social construct in American culture; that is, social meaning has been attributed to this concept called race. Based on this social construct, people have been treated differently. American history has far too many stories of harm done to people who were seen as a different race, and the concern is that racism is still very much alive. Although we saw history being made in 2009 as the first African-American was sworn in as president of the United States, it is necessary to continue to measure race in order to determine whether progress is being made in eliminating racial discrimination in American society. And yes, people will answer surveys in terms of how they identify themselves, including using the newly added biracial or multiracial categories in the U.S. Census. That is about as accurate as this measure is going to get.

RELIABILITY

The last component of a good measure is its reliability. Reliable measures have uniform definitions that are concrete and unambiguous. Reliable data are collected using the same decision rules every time. The metaphor is one of a fixed rather than an elastic measuring tape.

Some measures seem straightforward but quickly become complex once examined. Take income, which is a common demographic question asked on surveys. How should income be defined? Should income be counted in terms of the individual or the household? Should only wages be counted or should investment income be included? What about stock options and other benefits? What about income transfers such as food stamps and housing subsidies? Should child support be counted as income? Lastly, what time frame should be used—income for the past week, month, or year? A researcher would have to specify exactly how income is defined so that people completing a survey answer the same question. If one person reports only earnings and another person reports earnings and investment dividends, the data are not reliable.

The poverty measure discussed above has the advantage of being very reliable despite its limitations in terms of validity. This reliability enables poverty to be tracked over time; we know if poverty in America is increasing or decreasing. If the measure is changed, it loses its comparability.

Reliability is also an issue in survey research. Statisticians have developed a way to measure the overall reliability of survey responses by testing for internal consistency. This is checked once all the data have been collected and entered into the computer. The computer can then look at the internal consistency of the answers. The test is called a reliability coefficient or Chronbach's alpha. The values vary from 0 to 1. If there is little internal consistency, the reliability coefficient will be close to 0. If there is a great deal of internal consistency, it will be closer to 1. There is no firm cutoff point, but generally, it probably should not be lower than 0.7. Some survey researchers will report this test. However, it does not indicate whether the data are accurate or meaningful.

Reliability is a challenge when working with qualitative data. For example, suppose researchers want to determine whether women candidates for governor are portrayed differently than men candidates in newspaper stories. The researchers might decide to measure the extent to which physical descriptions of the candidates appear in the major newspapers and whether the descriptions have a positive or negative tone. However, each member of the team is likely to see positive or negative tone differently. For these measures to be reliable, the people doing the measuring have to share the exact same understanding of what positive and negative tone means.

Quality control procedures need to be used in this situation to ensure reliability. The method is called inter-rater reliability. The researchers should have all their raters code a small sample of the same newspaper articles and then compare the results. If there are differences in how the stories are coded, it is a signal that the coders are using "elastic rulers." The definitions need to be tightened up and then tested again until the raters code the same data in the same way.

WHY MEASUREMENT MATTERS

It is easy to skip over the measurement step of the research process and assume that the researchers would have used valid and reliable measures. And many times that would be a good assumption. However, at this step in the process it is not unusual for researchers to discover that the concepts are too vague or hard to quantify. Measurement is not always easy.

Sometimes even things that seem routine prove not to be. Take high school dropout rates, for example. For one thing, it is not always clear whether students stopped attending school or just moved away. For another, graduation rates might not be measured the same way in every school district. Some school districts count students who complete a General Education Development (GED) exam as part of their graduation rate while others do not. Dropout rates may not be reliable across different school districts.

Operational definitions can even become the focus of political debates, especially if the issue is controversial. If there are no agreed-upon definitions, the process of operationalizing research terms gets harder once the issue gets into the political spin cycle. For example, the report of the U.S. Government Accountability Office (GAO) on Iraq's progress in meeting specific benchmarks briefly became controversial when Congress considered whether to sustain the increased number of soldiers in Iraq (2007a). How did the GAO measure "progress," "success," and "failure"?

One key measure was the reduction of sectarian violence. Military data showed a reduction in the level of sectarian violence in Iraq between June and August 2007. However, that measure was not as solid as one might assume. The Department of Defense acknowledged that the numbers were underreported because not all violence was known. According to a *Washington Post* story, GAO's comptroller general, General David Walker, told Congress, "Let's just say that there are several different sources within the administration on violence, and those sources do not agree." Among the many challenges, one was the way sectarian violence was operationalized. "If a bullet went through the back of the head, it's sectarian," stated an intelligence official in Washington. "If it went through the front, it's criminal" (DeYoung 2007). This is a dramatic example of why it is necessary to know exactly how variables are measured.

CONCLUSION

How measures are defined and operationalized will impact the data collection strategies and affect the results. The scope of the study also frames the research boundaries, which might affect the conclusions that can be drawn. The key point is that the measures should be valid and reliable. A sophisticated user of research results should be skeptical of any study that does not fully explain the scope, the conceptual definitions, and the specifics about exactly what was counted; the operational definitions are crucial to any study using quantitative measures.

Given how difficult it is to develop measures, warning sirens should go off when someone claims to measure something that is essentially unknowable. Many examples can be seen in the news. The number of times people use handguns to protect themselves, the number of illegal drug sales, the amount of discrimination and the number of illegal immigrants are not actually known.

At the same time, a study should not be dismissed simply because the measures are less than perfect. This is not inherently a fatal flaw. If the researchers have clearly defined their measures and if they are the best that can be achieved given the situation, they deserve attention.

The three tough questions to ask are:

1. Do these measures actually measure the concepts that are at the heart of the research (i.e., are the measures valid)?
2. Are these measures reliable?
3. Are these measures biased in some way to get a particular desired outcome?

EXERCISES

1. Critique this study about political ideology and brainwaves that appeared in the *Los Angeles Times* (Gellene 2007): In a simple experiment, scientists attempted to discover whether political orientation is related to differences in how the brain processes information. Participants were college students whose politics ranged from "very liberal" to "very conservative." They were instructed to tap a keyboard when an M appeared on a computer monitor and to refrain from tapping when they saw a W. M appeared four times more frequently than W, conditioning participants to press a key in knee-jerk fashion whenever they saw a letter.

   Each participant was wired to an electroencephalograph that recorded activity in the part of the brain that detects conflicts between a habitual tendency (pressing a key) and a more appropriate response (not pressing the key). Liberals had more brain activity and made fewer mistakes than conservatives when they saw a W, researchers said. They concluded that liberals were more comfortable with ambiguity than conservatives.

   a. What are the key elements of this research and what terms need to be defined and operationalized?

   b. What problems might you see in terms of measurement strategy? Does the measurement strategy make sense to you? Why or why not?
2. In the following questions, identify the terms that need to be defined and some possible measures, including both English and operational definitions.
   a. What is the adequacy of prenatal care obtained by poor women?
   b. How satisfied or dissatisfied are students in the MPA program?
   c. How likely is age a factor in whether someone supports redistributive economic policies?
3. Questions asked using different words can change the unit of analysis. This means that different measures are needed. What measures would you use for each question below?
   a. What factors explain differences in infant mortality rates in various countries?
   b. What factors explain the death of children before their first birthday in your state?
4. The local MPA program has a goal of graduating students who make a positive difference in their communities. The accrediting agency has asked the program to demonstrate that it is achieving its goal. If you were asked to advise the director, how might you define and operationalize the phrase *make a positive difference*?
5. The measure used to construct poverty rates in America was adopted in 1965. It was based on the cost of a "basket of food" for various family sizes. Since that time, this measure has been adjusted to keep up with inflation. Some critics have argued that the current measure is not valid; others say that the measure is reliable.
   a. Explain what people mean by the terms *valid* and *reliable* when describing measures. How is it possible for a measure to be reliable but not valid?
   b. If you had the power to change the poverty measure, would you? Why or why not? If you would, what would you change and why?
6. Consultants have been hired to measure the extent to which the employees in your organization feel empowered. The consultants define empowerment as the extent to which employees feel they have (1) authority to make independent decisions without checking with their supervisors in routine matters, and (2) opportunity to have input on any major decisions that affect the way they do their work. The consultants have operationalized empowerment by measuring the percentage of employees who agree or strongly agree that they can make independent decisions and feel they have input into larger decisions. Do you agree with these conceptual and operational definitions? Why or why not?

5 Designs for Research
The Xs and Os Framework

OVERVIEW

In some ways, designing a research study is like architecture. The architects want to build a house in a particular setting to meet specific requirements using principles of good design. However, since life is less than perfect, the builders have to deal with challenges inherent in the site location and constraints in terms of time and money. Architects try to anticipate the likely consequences of the various options but, despite their best efforts, unexpected problems tend to emerge; problem solving becomes an important skill as they seek ways to maintain quality while dealing with the less than ideal situation.

It is much the same when researchers design a study. They deal with a particular situation and have only so much staff, time, and money. Ethical standards and accepted best practices for research provide the boundaries for their work. They also deal with the desires of stakeholders, which may or may not be clear or realistic. In many ways research becomes the art of the possible because the world stubbornly refuses to align itself in a way that makes research easy.

One thing that sometimes gets in the way of understanding research is its vocabulary, especially when the same words are used to mean different things. Take the word *design*. The word sometimes is used to talk about the broad plan to systematically gather and analyze data. The broad plan includes all the steps in the research process discussed in Chapter 1. This chapter, however, focuses on a narrow definition of design, which is comprised of three design elements: when measures are taken, whether comparison groups are used, and whether there is random assignment. These design elements are important when answering cause-and-effect questions (also known as impact questions), especially in eliminating rival explanations. The combinations of these elements result in three large categories: experimental, quasi-experimental, and nonexperimental designs. Each has strengths and limitations.

DESIGNING AN EXPERIMENT

Let us walk through this process of designing an experiment. Suppose researchers want to determine whether a relatively inexpensive organic fertilizer is effective in increasing the crop yield of corn. Researchers can create two separate growing areas in a greenhouse and randomly assign the corn seeds to the test area with the organic fertilizer and to another area without it. Both areas receive the same soil, temperature, sunlight, and water. The scientists thus control for all the key variables so that the only difference between the two areas is the organic fertilizer. The yields are measured when the corn is harvested. If the test area with the organic fertilizer has a higher yield of corn than the comparison area without the fertilizer, then the scientists will conclude that the organic fertilizer made the difference.

But what happens if the research is conducted in the field instead of the controlled environment of the greenhouse? If the two areas are close together, the fertilizer might run off into the comparison area, thus giving an imperfect measure of the impact of the fertilizer. The researchers might move the comparison area to a different part of the field to avoid run-off, but then the soil, light, temperature, and/or rain may be slightly different. Even if the corn yield with the organic fertilizer is higher than the corn yield without it, whether the fertilizer alone caused the differences in the yield is not absolutely clear.

Clearly, working in the field does not give researchers as much control as they have in the lab, making it more challenging to conclude that a cause-and-effect relationship exists. Similarly, because public administration research often takes place "in the field" rather than a laboratory, it is difficult to control everything.

APPLYING THE DESIGN ELEMENTS: THE Xs AND Os FRAMEWORK

Researchers design their studies using various combinations of the design elements. While they may prefer to use specific elements, the situation constrains their choices. Sometime the researchers can use before-and-after measures, sometimes they can use many measures before and after, and sometimes they can only use a single measure gathered after the program is implemented. Similarly, sometimes they have a comparison group and sometimes they do not. I call this very narrow concept of research design the Xs and Os framework because of the particular notation used as shorthand for describing the design elements:

> X is the causal factor, program or treatment (you might think of this as the independent variable).
> O is the observation or the measure of the effect (you might think of this as the measure of the dependent variable).

To understand the different ways these design elements can be applied and their limitations, let us walk through the design options available to determine the impact of a stress reduction program in an organization. I will present them using the non-experimental, quasi-experimental, and experimental categories.

NONEXPERIMENTAL DESIGN

The human resources director asks for volunteers to participate in a stress reduction program and accepts the first fifty employees who raise their hand. At the end of three months, they are given a stress test to measure whether the program was successful in reducing stress. This *one-shot design* is the simplest and the notation looks like this:

X O
(the stress reduction program)   (observation or measurement: the stress test)

If the researchers find that the majority (75 percent) of the participants have low stress tests after the program, can the human resources director claim that the program is a success? Although she may make the claim, it lacks credibility because too many other factors might actually explain the observed results. Maybe the fifty participants were longtime meditation gurus so their stress levels were already low. Without a baseline—a measure taken before the program began—it is hard to say whether the program actually changed the participants' stress levels.

Alternatively, the researchers might opt to use a before-and-after design. They administer a stress test to the participants before starting the program (O_1): this is the pretest or the baseline measure. At the end of three months in the program, they readminister the stress test (O_2)—this is the posttest. The notation would look like this:

O_1 X O_2
(stress test)   (the program)   (stress test)

Have the stress levels changed? Suppose the researchers find that stress levels in the posttest are lower than they were before the program started. Does that mean the program was successful? Maybe. However, rival explanations might exist to explain the observed drop in the stress tests. Perhaps the agency's stress-provoking director left the organization during the first month of the program and that really explains the lower stress levels observed in the posttest.

Alternatively, the researchers could have chosen to use a comparison group of employees who do not participate in the program but who take the same stress test as the participants three months after the program begins. This is called a static group design and the notation would look like this:

Program participants X O
Comparison group O

Perhaps the researchers find little difference between the groups. Did the program fail? Maybe. But it is also possible that the comparison group learned about the stress reduction techniques from people in the program and began using the techniques on their own. Alternatively, they may have already been using various stress reduction techniques. While the temptation would be to conclude that the program did not work, the reality is that the researchers do not know.

These three designs, which are called nonexperimental designs, share a weakness in being unable to control very much. Nonexperimental designs are perfectly fine to answer descriptive and normative questions. Sometimes researchers just want to take a snapshot of a situation at one point in time. For example, what do citizens say are the most pressing problems facing the city right now? This is just a snapshot at one point in time. The researchers may compare responses of people based on income or educational level, using statistical controls, but this too is often just descriptive information. Other times, however, researchers will use statistical controls to demonstrate causal relationships. Therefore, sophisticated users of research results will look very carefully at the intention of the research to determine whether the researchers want to simply describe a situation or demonstrate a cause-and-effect relationship.

Nonexperimental designs, however, are the weakest for answering cause-and-effect questions because they cannot do much to eliminate rival explanations. That said, sometimes researchers find that no other design option is available given the particular situation. As a general rule, sophisticated users of research results should be very cautious in making firm conclusions or policy decisions when a nonexperimental design is used to answer a cause-and-effect question.

QUASI-EXPERIMENTAL DESIGN

Using more of the design elements will increase the strength of the design by giving the researchers more control over rival explanations. As a group, these methods are categorized as quasi-experimental because they have some but not all the features of a true experiment.

One type of quasi-experimental design is to expand the before-and-after design by taking several periodic measures instead of just a single postmeasure; generically, this is called a *longitudinal* design. For example, the researchers could extend the program for nine months and take stress measures every three months. While there might be an initial drop after the director leaves, what happens over time? This design is likely to moderate the effect of the departure of the stress-provoking director. The notation would look like this:

$$O_{before} \qquad X \qquad O_{3\ months} \qquad O_{6\ months} \qquad O_{9\ months}$$

However, this design does not eliminate all other possible explanations. A major problem is that these volunteers might be unique. Perhaps they are highly motivated to reduce stress and do other stress reduction activities outside of work. Would this program work for those not so motivated? That is unknown based on this design.

If the researchers combine a comparison group with a before-and-after design, they will have a nonequivalent comparison design. This is noted:

Program group	O_1	X	O_2
Comparison group	O_1		O_2

In this design, both the participants and the comparison group (also called a control group) take a stress test before the program begins. The participants then engage in the program while the comparison group does not. At the end of three months, both groups take another stress test. The changes between the before-and-after measures of the program participants are compared to the changes in the comparison group.

This design controls for events such as the departure of the agency's stress-provoking director. If the stress level declines are still greater among program participants than in the comparison group, we would be more willing to give the program credit for at least some of the reduction.

These groups, however, are not exactly the same (hence the name nonequivalent), so it is still possible that something about the groups themselves affects the results rather than the program. For example, suppose both groups are interested in stress reduction and actively meditate outside of the program. The research might not, therefore, show much change no matter how good the program is because both these groups were already at the lowest point in terms of the stress test. In this scenario, the program would appear not to work.

What else can the researchers do to design a stronger study?

CLASSIC EXPERIMENTAL DESIGN

The researchers can choose the third design element: random assignment. By adding it to the nonequivalent design, the researchers now have a *classic experimental* design, which randomly assigns people to the stress program and the control group. This is noted:

Random assignment	Program group	O_1	X	O_2
Random assignment	Control group	O_1		O_2

Random assignment makes the groups comparable by distributing a range of differences to both groups. The health nuts, meditation gurus, workaholics, and couch potatoes are randomly assigned to the program or comparison group. Neither group is dominated by one type of person. Given the relative equality of the groups, the researcher can feel confident in concluding that the program had an impact if the program participants show a substantial reduction in stress as compared to the control group. If, however, there was no difference between the groups, the researchers can feel confident in concluding that the program had no impact.

It should be noted that I am presenting a simple version of the classic experimental design here. Depending on the exact nature of the research, experimental designs can be very elaborate. For example, they can be designed so that the participants do not know if they are in the treatment or the control group (called a blind study), and sometimes the researchers do not know either (called a double-blind study).

In studies testing medications, for example, the people in the control group might be given sugar pills to control for the "placebo effect." Researchers have found that the belief that taking a pill will make them better causes some people to get better. So everyone receives pills and no one knows whether it is the real medication or a sugar pill. If a substantially greater percent of the people in the treatment group get better as compared to the control group, the placebo effect has been eliminated as a rival explanation.

While the classic experimental design is the strongest in ruling out other rival explanations, random assignment in public administration research may not be possible due to ethical, legal, equity, practical, or political constraints within a particular situation. Clinical trials to test the efficacy of various drugs, for example, might raise ethical issues. Is it ethical to assign some people into an experimental group that gets treatment that may increase life expectancy and assign others into a control group that gets a sugar pill? In this situation, researchers might test various dosages of the potential life-saving drug rather than use sugar pills.

There may be legal constraints that prevent random assignment. It is not legal for an employer to force people to participate in an experiment, even one like the stress reduction program. It is also illegal to deny people public programs or benefits to which they are entitled by law, such as food stamps, training program for disabled veterans, or unemployment benefits; this means that people cannot be forced to participate in a nutrition experiment, for example, under the threat of losing their food stamps. Equity may also be a constraint. Are the choices about who gets to participate fair, especially if participation provides a benefit?

Sometimes random assignment is simply impractical. It is unlikely, for example, that Congress would randomly assign some states to a program and others to a comparison group that does not get the program. When laws are implemented in every county or every state at the same time, there is no way to form comparison groups (see Application 5.1).

Random assignment might also pose a challenge to political deal making. For example, it is difficult to randomly assign cities to receive a program that will bring in millions of dollars from the federal government. Elected officials from other cities are likely to negotiate to have their cities included in the experiment. As a result, the cities are no longer randomly assigned (because political influence has gotten them included), and the pot of money might be divided up to the point where it is insufficient to be effective in any city.

There may be situations, however, when an experimental design can be used. For example, when a program is not large enough to accommodate all those who apply, random assignment is possible. Since relatively few can participate, random assignment not only provides a strong design, it is also more equitable because it rules out bias and favoritism in selection. In the mid-1980s, for example, a public-private partnership funded a huge evaluation of welfare training programs (Gueron 1988). Eight states were selected and over 35,000 people who volunteered to participate in the training program were randomly assigned to one of three groups: the full training program, a program with limited job search services, or the no-service control group. In states with a typical unemployment rate, the programs worked; those who participated in the full training program earned more than those who did not, although the differences were generally small. This is a good example of how an experimental design can be used in the public sector.

DESIGN VARIATIONS

Every situation is different and therefore constrains the ability to use one or more of the design elements. In some situations, random assignment is possible but there is no way to get a preprogram measure. For example, suppose researchers are testing a training program for people on welfare. The researchers go through the welfare rolls in their town and randomly assign clients to the training program or not. The outcome measure is whether they get jobs and keep them for six months. Since they are on welfare when the program begins, there is no premeasure. Some people may have had prior work experience, but random assignment equalizes the groups since people with and without prior work experience are in both groups. My point, however, is that there will be no premeasure in this experimental design.

The notation would look like this:

| Random assignment | Training program | X | O |
| Random assignment | Comparison group | | O |

Sometimes researchers stumble on a situation that is naturally a quasi-experimental design. For example, until Indiana's state legislature decided to put the entire state on daylight saving time in 2006, only fifteen of its ninety-two counties turned their clocks forward in the spring and back in the fall (Lahart 2008). This created a natural experiment by which the energy use in the counties could be compared. Using data from monthly meter readings for three years, researchers were able to compare energy use before and after daylight saving went into effect as well as compare the usage of residents living in counties that were using daylight saving before 2006 with those who were not. The result? The researchers concluded that daylight saving time does not save energy or money: residential energy usage increased between 1 percent and 4 percent, amounting to an additional $8.6 million a year that consumers paid.

Another quasi-experimental variation is to find a group that is matched on key characteristics. Researchers might, for example, select two schools that share very similar demographic characteristics to compare a specific program offered in one school but not the other. The assumption is that if the demographics are the same, the schools are relatively comparable so any observed difference is likely to be due to the program.

USING STATISTICAL CONTROLS TO CREATE COMPARISON GROUPS

Creating comparison groups by using statistical controls is another very common quasi-experimental design. In the jargon, this type of design is typically called correlational with statistical controls, but variations are called an ex post facto or causal comparative design. Basically, they use statistical techniques to make comparisons.

Suppose researchers want to determine whether the Head Start program has a lasting impact on the reading abilities of the children who participate in the program. Assuming the data is available in school records, the researchers design a study to gather information on all the eighth graders in an inner-city school district. This data includes whether or not they attended Head Start, various test scores, grades, and demographic information.

Using statistical software, the researchers separate the students into two groups:

those who attended Head Start and those who did not. The software then performs various statistics procedures to determine whether there is a noticeable difference in reading scores between the former Head Start and the non–Head Start students. Specifically how this is done will be presented in the analysis chapters.

What else might affect a child's reading scores? Maybe the educational level of the mother, family income, or having attended nursery school makes a difference. These become rival explanations, and the researchers use statistical controls to examine reading scores associated with these factors, assuming they are in the permanent record. Using statistical controls is a strong quasi-experimental design to use in the field.

We often see statistical controls used in analyzing polling data. For example, a national exit poll conducted by NBC was used to analyze how young people voted in the 2008 presidential election (Keeter et al. 2008). Defining young voters as eighteen to twenty-nine years old and old voters as aged thirty and over, the polltakers found that 66 percent of all young voters reported they had voted for Barack Obama. In contrast, 50 percent of the older voters reported voting for Obama.

Statistical controls allow the researchers to make even finer slices. How did race affect the votes of the young and the not so young? Race is now the control variable. The NBC poll found that 54 percent of young white voters said they voted for Obama. In contrast, 41 percent of older white voters said they voted for Obama.

LONGITUDINAL STUDIES

Longitudinal studies are another type of quasi-experimental design that can be used to measure change after a program or event. These have more measurement points than a simple before-and-after design. There are two approaches for gathering the data for longitudinal studies. The cross-sectional approach takes a different "slice" of the population of interest at each point in time; the result is that different people are used each time the data is gathered. A good example of a cross-sectional longitudinal study is the National Institute of Drug Abuse's annual survey of high school seniors. A different random sample of high school seniors is selected every year. This longitudinal design allows researchers to track the self-reported use of illegal drugs over time, creating a trend line.

The second approach is a panel design that gathers data from the same group of people over time. For example, the Department of Labor's Bureau of Labor Statistics conducts the National Longitudinal Survey of Youth (NLSY). It began in 1979 with a random sample of 11,406 people between fourteen and twenty-one years of age. Follow-up interviews were conducted annually with this same group of people though 1994. After that, biennial interviews were conducted. In addition to a standard set of questions about employment, other questions were included from time to time. For example, drug use questions were asked a few times, making it possible to identify factors associated with drug use for this particular group of people.

Longitudinal studies can also use statistical controls as part of their analysis if demographic data or other variables that control for rival explanations are gathered. For example, are there differences in drug use based on urban or rural settings, gender, or family income? These statistical controls are used to create comparisons that might explain why some people use drugs and others do not.

Time series analysis is another longitudinal design option. Its key feature is that it uses many points in time to describe a trend over time. In the notation, this analysis is just a series of observations:

$$O_1 \; O_2 \; O_3 \; O_4 \; O_5 \; O_6 \; O_7 \; O_8 \; O_9 \; O_{10} \; O_{11} \; O_{12}$$

Note that there is no *X*—just a series of periodic snapshots (observations) that can be used to describe trends over time, such as crime rates, poverty rates, budget deficits, electricity usage, teen birth rates, stock prices, or average temperatures over time. This is a good design for descriptive questions, but time series analysis does not explain why trends rise or drop.

Predictions are also possible based on trend lines, but there are some limitations in driving forward by looking through the rearview window. Changes in the larger environment can dramatically alter forecasts.

An interrupted time series design is a good option for program evaluation when there are multiple data points before and after a program or policy is implemented. Researchers would be looking for a change in the trend line after a program was implemented. In the notation, it looks like this:

$$O_1 \; O_2 \; O_3 \; O_4 \; O_5 \; O_6 \; O_7 \; O_8 \; O_9 \; O_{10} \qquad X \qquad O_{11} \; O_{12} \; O_{13} \; O_{14} \; O_{15} \; O_{16}$$

Sometimes it is possible to use an interrupted times series design with a comparison group. This is called a multiple time series analysis. This is a useful design when a program is implemented in one place and not another. For example, this design could be used to look at the fatality rates before and after some states rescinded the laws requiring that motorcyclists use helmets compared to the others that did not. The notation would look like this:

$$O_1 \; O_2 \; O_3 \; O_4 \; O_5 \; O_6 \; O_7 \; O_8 \; O_9 \; O_{10} \qquad X \qquad O_{11} \; O_{12} \; O_{13} \; O_{14} \; O_{15} \; O_{16}$$

$$O_1 \; O_2 \; O_3 \; O_4 \; O_5 \; O_6 \; O_7 \; O_8 \; O_9 \; O_{10} \qquad\qquad O_{11} \; O_{12} \; O_{13} \; O_{14} \; O_{15} \; O_{16}$$

Whether to use a longitudinal design (covering just a few years) or a time-series analysis (covering many years) will depend on the situation. Clearly, if researchers need quick results, they will not choose a time series analysis unless the data are already available.

The key point with any data collected over time is whether the data are measured in exactly the same way every time. Any change creates apples-to-oranges comparisons; more technically, the data are no longer reliable.

While these are strong designs, it is important to keep in mind that they are limited in answering a cause-and-effect or impact question unless they are able to rule out those pesky rival explanations. Trend lines, in particular, are not useful in explaining changes.

Application 5.1
True Confessions of a Researcher

The Immigration and Reform Control Act (IRCA) of 1986 prohibited employers from knowingly hiring unauthorized workers. The intention was to stem the tide of illegal workers by penalizing employers who knowingly hired them. Employers were required to have all employees complete I-9 forms, which required that new hires show two pieces of identification verifying their status as legal workers.

Before the law was passed, some congressional legislators feared that employers might begin a practice of not hiring legal workers because they looked or sounded foreign. As a compromise to get the bill passed, a provision was added requiring the U.S. Government Accountability Office (GAO) to determine whether there was a widespread pattern of discrimination against eligible workers applying for jobs solely because of employers' fear of sanctions. If GAO found discrimination, Congress could invoke an expedited repeal provision written into the law.

Clearly, this is a cause-and-effect question: did the law cause discrimination? The best type of design is experimental: random assignment to the program group or a comparison group, with both before-and-after measures. However, there was no way GAO could randomly assign states so that some would implement this new law and others would not. Random assignment was out.

Working down the list of options, the next best design would be a quasi-experimental design, with a comparison group and before-and-after measures. However, there also was no way to allow some states to implement the law while others did not—so comparison groups were out. The best possible design now was a before-and-after design. However, the law was implemented quickly without any chance to develop a baseline measure of discrimination based on whether people looked or sounded foreign. A before-and-after design was out. The only research design left was a one-shot design: implement the policy and measure the results. As a researcher on this study, I knew this was the weakest design of all to answer a cause-and-effect question. However, I had to accept the constraints of the situation: there was no getting around the fact that the program was implemented nationwide and GAO had to determine whether or not there was discrimination.

One of the data collection methods used was a cross-sectional survey of businesses across the United States. Among the questions, the survey asked if these employers discriminated against people who looked and sounded foreign because of IRCA; 19 percent said yes. If you were a member of Congress, would you consider this evidence strong enough to repeal the law?

INTERNAL VALIDITY

Researchers talk about internal validity when operating within the Xs and Os framework. Internal validity is the shorthand reminder for considering whether other factors may have influenced the results. Social scientists have identified some common threats to internal validity, including history, maturation, testing, instrumentation, regression to the mean, selection, and attrition.

History is a potential threat if a particular event took place while the study was being conducted that might impact the results. For example, the departure of the stress-provoking manager after the stress reduction program started is an example of a history effect. Using a comparison group reduces this threat. If it is not possible to have a comparison group, it is important to find out what was happening at that time that may have affected the results.

Maturation is a potential threat when it is possible for skills or abilities to increase because the participants got older. For example, improved study skills among children might be a result of maturation rather than their participation in a study skills program. Using a comparison group reduces this threat.

Testing can be a potential threat in research when a test is used to measure change before and after a program. Why? It is possible that people might have learned how to take the test. Using a comparison group reduces this threat because both groups would have learned how to take the test. If the program made a difference, participants in the program should still have higher scores.

Instrumentation refers to any changes in what gets counted or how it gets counted. This is a threat in any design that uses before-and-after measures because it creates an apples-to-oranges comparison. For example, a school implements a zero-tolerance-for-weapons program that includes posting "no weapon" signs, educational events and conflict resolution training for all students. The school uses the number of children who brought a weapon to school before the program began as the baseline (pre-measure). The program runs for three years and then measures the number of children who brought a weapon to school during the last year of the program. If the school changed the definition of *weapon* during those three years to include more items, such as Swiss army knives and metal nail files, the results would not be a good measure of whether the program worked. The threat would be reduced if there were a similar comparison school that did not have the program but confiscated weapons during that same time period and made the same definitional changes about what was considered a weapon.

Regression to the mean is only a threat if a program or policy is implemented because of an unusually high or low measurement. Regression to the mean is based on the idea that things vary over time and tend to balance out. It is kind of a statistical version of "what goes up must come down." For example, when a crackdown on speeders is implemented because of an unusually high number of highway fatalities one year, it is possible the number of highway fatalities would have gone down the next year without the program.

One way to avoid this threat is not to intervene solely on the basis of a single extreme high or low score. However, sometimes there is public or political pressure to do something about a perceived crisis so public administrators implement a program or regulation. To minimize the regression to the mean threat, researchers would want to look at data over time and/or use comparison data from neighboring jurisdictions to get a clearer picture of the impact of the crackdown in the context of the natural variation in traffic fatalities.

Selection of sites or people can be a threat. The criteria for any selection have to be made clear along with potential impacts on the results. For example, if different sites are selected, are there some differences between them that affect the results?

Are the volunteers in the stress reduction program different from other employees in some particular way that affects the results? Similarly, when only a small proportion of people asked to participate in a survey actually do, are they different from those who do not in some way that affects the results?

Selection is also a possible threat when a program manager chooses some people to participate in the program but not others. What are the criteria for selection? Are those participants different from a typical client? More skeptically, did the program officials select the people most likely to succeed in order to make the program look successful?

In fairness to program managers, however, this is a tough situation. From a management perspective, selecting people who are most likely to benefit from the program may be the best use of taxpayers' dollars. However, from a research perspective, selecting the best—the cream of the crop—will not give a good measure of program impact because the best people might have done just as well without the program. For example, selecting welfare recipients with at least a high school education and some work experience to participate in a training program makes it hard to tell whether the training program actually made a difference. It is possible that a high percentage of these recipients would have gotten jobs without the training program.

Attrition is a potential threat in any design that tracks the same people over time. It is possible that the people who dropped out of the study were different in some important way. For instance, researchers want to determine the efficacy of a drug treatment program, so they track the participants over time. The researchers state that 75 percent of the participants who answered a survey a year after completing the program were drug-free. Success? Maybe. If a hundred people started the program and only fifty completed it, attrition is a threat to validity. What happened to the other fifty who did not complete the program? A 75 percent program success rate looks like the program had a positive impact but it is based on only half the initial group; the program might not be as successful as it initially appears.

WHY VALIDITY MATTERS

On March 16, 1964, President Lyndon B. Johnson delivered a speech announcing his proposal for a nationwide war on poverty (Grier and Jonsson 2004). He told Congress and the nation: "Because it is right, because it is wise, and because, for the first time in our history, it is possible to conquer poverty, I submit, for the consideration of the Congress and the country, the Economic Opportunity Act of 1964." The antipoverty program includes a wide range of programs, including Head Start, VISTA, food stamps, Job Corps, legal aid, and community action agencies.

Exhibit 5.1 shows the poverty data for the United States. The trend data over time (think time series) shows a continued drop in the percentage of people below the poverty line after 1960. In 1964, the poverty rate was 19.0 percent. In 1973 the poverty rate hit its lowest level, with just 11.1 percent living in poverty. It rose and bumped along at 13 to 14 percent through the 1980s and 1990s. In 2007, an estimated 12.5 percent of Americans lived below the poverty line, totaling over 37 million people.

Do these figures mean that President Johnson's poverty program failed? Maybe yes, maybe no.

Exhibit 5.1   **Percentage of People Living in Poverty, United States, 1960–2007**

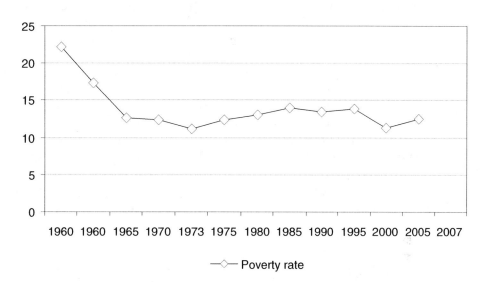

Source: U.S. Census Bureau, 2008, www.census.gov.

The libertarian Cato Institute and the conservative Heritage Foundation agree: it is a failure. According to the Cato Institute, the government has spent trillions of dollars yet poverty remains "perilously close" to what it was in 1964 and the availability of welfare has made things worse by trapping people into a state of dependency (Tanner 2006). The Heritage Foundation challenges the statistics, saying poverty is overstated and government rewards dependency (Rector and Johnson 2004).

On the other hand, the liberal Center on Budget and Policy Priorities argues that these programs, sometimes called the safety net, have accomplished a great deal (Parrott et al. 2005). The percentage of people living in poverty is less than it was in 1960 and severe hunger is rare in America today because of the food stamp program and other nutrition programs such as the Special Supplemental Nutrition Program for Women, Infant and Children (WIC) and school meals.

Other antipoverty advocates, however, also point to the failure of the antipoverty program. "What is discouraging is that poverty rates have remained stagnant . . . suggesting that policies aimed at the low-income populations have failed to substantially reduce income inadequacies," stated Legal Services of New Jersey in 2008 (Livio 2008). The organization advocates expanding assistance to low-income New Jersey-ites, including raising the minimum wage, developing a paid family leave program, and providing more food supports.

From a research perspective, however, measuring the impact of the antipoverty program on reducing poverty has some internal validity problems. Certainly, there was no random assignment to the poverty program or not. Without a comparison group, we do not know whether poverty would have been worse if the antipoverty program had not been in place when the recessions hit in 1970, 1974, 1980, 1981–1982, 1990, and 2001. It is possible that the percentage of citizens in poverty might have been higher without those programs. On the other hand, it may be that the antipoverty program failed.

My point is that while there are different opinions about whether the anti-poverty program failed, any research would be inconclusive because it was not possible to use an experimental or quasi-experimental design. In addition to the challenges of defining precisely what constitutes the "antipoverty program," there are too many uncontrollable factors at play to get a precise measure of program impact. The truth is that no one really knows the answer based on social science research. However, it is perhaps inevitable that when people are invested in being "right" on a policy issue, they will ignore internal validity issues. Appearing tentative—"the research suggests" or "while not precise, it appears that"—is just too weak to win the political argument. The takeaway lesson is that what people believe to be true is not the same as knowing what is true.

EXTERNAL VALIDITY

While internal validity refers to the internal structure of the design, external validity refers to the likelihood that the results will hold true in the larger world. Many experimental designs are strong on internal validity but weak in terms of external validity if they are relatively small and based on nonrandom samples.

It is easy for program managers to become enthusiastic about an innovative program or policy. "Let's implement it in our agency," they say. However, the tough question is whether that program or policy will work in their particular situation. Technically this is called an issue of external validity. More commonly, public administrators have long known about the limits of "cookie cutter" or one-size-fits-all approaches. Communities are different and what works in one might not work in another. Sophisticated users of research results who are concerned about external validity will ask, "Does what happens in this study reflect what occurs in other places where the program is also being conducted?"

When critiquing study results, it is reasonable to expect the researchers to identify potential threats. When possible, they should take steps to mitigate these threats. If things are beyond their ability to control, it is reasonable to expect the researchers to identify possible limitations and provide cautions about drawing conclusion from the results.

CONCLUSION

The situation and type of research question determine which design elements are used. No design is perfect nor can a single design be applied to every research question because every situation is unique. Exhibit 5.2 summarizes the common research designs in the *X*s and *O*s framework. If the researcher is asking a descriptive question or a normative question, then a nonexperimental design is sufficient. However, to demonstrate that a program had an impact or that a cause-and-effect relationship exists, the design has to be rigorous enough so that other possible explanations are ruled out.

Exhibit 5.2 **Common Research Designs Using the *X*s and *O*s Framework**

Experimental

Always uses random assignment to treatment and control groups. The classic experimental designs also collect data before and after treatment. However, variations may not collect before measures. It is the strongest design for controlling threats to internal validity but weak in external validity. While hard to do in the public sector, it is not impossible.

Quasi-experimental

No random assignment. Selection is a potential threat. May be reasonably strong to answer impact and cause-and-effect questions; generally strong in controlling for history and regression to the mean. May be weak on external validity.

- *Nonequivalent groups:* Comparison of group with program to group without the program. Controls for history and maturation if comparison group is a close match; selection and attrition may be threats.
- *Natural experiments:* Situations in which there are naturally occurring comparison groups and before-and-after measures.
- *Matched groups:* Matches program and comparison groups on key variables to control for selection threat.
- *Correlational design with statistical controls (sometimes called causal-comparative or Ex post fact):* Collects data from all or a sample of people, cases, units, etc., and uses statistical techniques to create comparison groups in order to compare outcomes and control for rival explanations.
- *Longitudinal*

  □ *Data collected over time:* The key is that the measures are defined and data collected the same way; attrition, testing, and instrumentation are possible threats.
  □ *Cross-sectional:* Collects the same data at a few points in time from different people.
  □ *Panel:* Collects same data from the same people at various points in time.

- *Time series:* Collects the same data at many points in time. Useful for describing trends but does not explain why things change.
- *Interrupted time series:* Data before and after the program from different people or the same people. May face selection and instrumentation threats.
- *Multiple time series:* Comparison of data over time

Nonexperimental

While useful in answering descriptive and normative questions, it is weak for answering impact or cause-and-effect questions.

- *Before and after:* Collects data on key measures before and after program; controls for history and maturation if comparison group is a close match; selection, regression to the mean, and attrition may be threats.
- *Static group comparison:* Collects key day after the program and compares with control group. Selection, history, and regression to the mean may be threats.
- *One-shot:* Provides a snapshot after a program or policy is implemented or a picture of one point in time. There are no before measures and no comparison. History and selection may be threats.

The strongest design for cause-and-effect questions is an experimental design. Random assignment is its unique feature and this controls for all kinds of factors that might affect the observed results. However, quasi-experimental designs are more commonly used in public administration research because it is often not possible to randomly assign people to programs or policies.

One takeaway lesson for sophisticated consumers of research results is to look beneath the surface whenever anyone claims to have found a program impact or a program failure. If it is difficult to discern a strong research design in terms of the Xs and Os framework, then caution is warranted in accepting claims of causality as truth. Three tough questions to ask are:

1. Is there something else other than the program that could explain these results?
2. Has something been left out of the study that might alter the results or reflect a bias?
3. Is the research design strong enough to support the conclusions?

The final takeaway lesson is to remember that given all the challenges in designing strong impact studies and eliminating all the threats to internal and external validity, we often know a lot less than we think we know about cause-and-effect relationships and program impacts.

EXERCISES

1. In the news: A recent study looked at the relationship between happiness and the amount of time people spend watching TV (Rabin 2008). The researchers found that happy people watched less TV than unhappy people. Does watching TV cause people to be unhappy or does being unhappy cause people to watch more TV? Explain your reasoning?
2. County officials administered a drug use survey to all junior high students in September. The officials then selected the junior high school with the highest drug usage based on this test to receive a drug education program; the other junior high schools were to be used as comparisons. The officials administered the same survey to all junior high students in June. First, draw the design, using Xs and Os. Second, identify the likely threats to validity of this study.
3. Your boss has just read a newspaper article declaring that naps in the afternoon increase productivity. Since you have completed a research methods course that your organization paid for, your boss asks you to design a study to find out whether allowing employees in your organization to take afternoon naps will boost productivity. Using the Xs and Os framework, which design would work best in this scenario? What are the possible limitations of your choice? Why do you believe this is the best option given the situation?
4. The state has implemented a program intended to reduce recidivism among juvenile offenders. Juvenile offenders will be randomly assigned to the treatment program or jail at the time of sentencing by the county judges hearing the cases.
   a. What is the likely outcome measure?
   b. Using Xs and Os, depict the best research design that can be used in this situation. Explain.

5. Using the *X*s and *O*s framework, identify the type of research design in these scenarios:
   a. A series of documentary films has followed a group of British children since they were seven years old. The subjects have been interviewed every seven years and the latest film captures them at age forty-nine.
   b. The National Institute of Drug Abuse does an annual survey of high school seniors to measure the extent of their drug and alcohol use.
   c. Researchers want to look at the impact of helmet laws across all fifty states by comparing the ten years since the laws took effect and the ten years before they were passed.
   d. The state implemented a program to encourage "green" construction of affordable homes and evaluated it a year later. The program was implemented statewide and there were no reliable measures of the number of green affordable homes prior to implementation.
   e. Researchers evaluated an early childhood learning program targeted to children whose families are at or below 200 percent of the poverty level. Since the program had the capacity to serve only 25 percent of all eligible children, the researchers randomly assigned the children who were signed up to either the program or a control group. The researchers tested all the children in both groups before beginning the program, at the end of the program, and six months later.

6 | Other Research Approaches

OVERVIEW

It is not surprising to come across case studies or cost-benefit analyses in public administration research. Yet they were not presented in the previous chapter, because, as if things are not complex enough, some research approaches do not easily fit within the *X*s and *O*s framework. In fact, some research approaches more accurately describe its dominant data collection method or analysis strategy. Still, they are often referred to as research designs.

Some commonly used research approaches are secondary data analysis, evaluation synthesis, content analysis, survey research, case studies, and cost-benefit analysis. There is also a mix-and-match quality to research designs and approaches. A one-shot design, for example, might use a survey. The analysis of that survey might use statistical controls to create comparison groups. A before-and-after study might use a cost-benefit analysis. A case study might use surveys and quantitative analysis. Research methods can be multifaceted.

The purposes of this chapter are to provide an overview on these different research approaches, identify the situations in which they might be used, and highlight some key issues specific to these approaches.

SECONDARY ANALYSIS OF DATA

While researchers look to prior studies to understand a particular situation, sometimes the whole focus of the research is on data collected by someone else for some other purpose. This is called secondary analysis of data. For example, researchers could go out into the world and gather data about drug use directly from drug users. However, they can also choose to use data that has already been collected by some other respected entity. The National Longitudinal Survey of Youth, mentioned in the previous chapter, was intended to measure employment and economic experiences as youth transitioned into adulthood. However, the GAO used it as the basis for its "Drug Use among Youth" study published in 1993. Another example is the use of the famous Framingham study on heart disease, which tracked 5,000 people from 1983 to 2003, to look at why people are happy (Fowler and Cristakis 2008). The researchers conclude that happiness is contagious.

The primary advantage of conducting secondary data analysis is that it is quicker and cheaper than doing original data collection. In the planning phase, therefore, researchers might want to consider whether the data they need have already been collected. If yes, a more careful review is needed to determine whether the earlier study contains the exact data that the researchers need for their new study. For example, if the researchers want to establish the extent of drug use among fourteen-year-olds, then data gathered from college students will not be of use.

If the database meets their research requirements, the researchers will have to obtain access. This may be relatively easy if the government owns the database. It may be more challenging if individuals or private organizations own the data. The researchers may be charged a fee for using the data. In addition to the database, they will need the data dictionary, which defines every variable in the database and how it was coded.

From a research perspective, the researchers must assess the quality of the methods used to collect the data. Did the original researchers follow the steps outlined in the research planning process? Did the researchers carefully document what they did? For example, exactly how did they select the people for their research? How many participated? What percentage of all those invited to participate actually did?

Lastly, the current researchers need to determine the accuracy of the database. This means that there should be very little difference between the source of the data and the database. What is the error rate? If it is high, then it is a problem and the researchers would have to reconsider their design options.

If the quality is high and the data are appropriate for answering the research questions, then secondary analysis of data is the appropriate choice.

EVALUATION SYNTHESIS (META-ANALYSIS)

In some ways, evaluation synthesis (sometimes called a meta-analysis) is an expanded version of secondary analysis. It is used when many studies on exactly the same issue have been conducted. Using this approach, these studies can be systematically summarized to provide descriptive information about common themes as well as to assess the effectiveness of a program or draw a general conclusion about the issue.

In addition to being cheaper to do than original data collection, meta-analysis has the advantage of creating a much larger data base that is potentially very powerful in drawing conclusions. Each individual study might be small and have unique limitations, but, when combined, they provide a larger picture with many more cases. If the results are fairly similar across the different studies, the researchers can be more confident in making general statements about program impact.

The first step is to identify all the relevant studies. Titles can be deceiving so it is important to review the actual studies to make sure each one is relevant. Next, the researchers must establish criteria to rate the quality of the studies. Each study is carefully rated based on the criteria, and only those meeting those criteria are included in the analysis. The researchers typically summarize the key findings and impact measures. They are looking for consistency in the findings. Conclusions will be drawn if the findings from the high-quality studies are consistent. If not, the researchers will report that no conclusion can be made and perhaps suggest what other research might be needed.

A variation of this approach is to obtain the actual data from the studies and construct a meta-database, which can then be analyzed. For example, data from many small studies (e.g., case studies of prison sentencing in particular jurisdictions) can be combined into a database that would be sufficiently large to permit high-powered statistical analyses.

Of course, there are some downsides. One is obtaining the data and all the necessary documentation. The more difficult problem, however, is that the studies might have measured different concepts or measured the same concepts differently. This is the apples-and-oranges problem, which makes it difficult to summarize the data. However, in situations when meta-analysis might be appropriate, it should be considered as a research approach.

CONTENT ANALYSIS

Although content analysis also does not fit into the *X*s and *O*s framework, it is a very useful research approach when the intention is to systematically measure the number and/or the message of communications (see Applications 6.1 and 6.2). It can be used to analyze content in a wide range of settings: speeches, books, newspapers, e-mails, greeting cards, magazines, memos, movies, songs, or television shows. Sometimes content analysis is used when working with narratives such as personal diaries and journals. In the strictest sense, content analysis converts qualitative data into quantitative analysis. However, it is often used qualitatively to identify common themes.

Measurement and coding of data are the Achilles' heel of this approach. For example, perhaps researchers want to investigate media images of women governors—specifically, whether they are portrayed as strong or weak. Each quality—strength and weakness—must then be defined (operationalized) so the research team will know it when they see it.

Reliability is the key issue in coding. Everyone on the team must understand the conceptual and operational definitions so they can code the same material in exactly the same way. Clear and very detailed decision rules are required. We are talking about serious detail here and those who are doing the coding must be well trained. The coders and the coding rules must be tested to make sure everything is working before they go live with the research.

For example, researchers at the Pew Forum on Religion and Public Life conducted a content analysis to determine the extent to which faith issues were reported during the 2008 presidential primary and which topics received the most media attention (2008a). They analyzed all the news reports about the primary and discovered that well over 80 percent focused on the "horse race," defined as stories about who was ahead in the polls and who was raising the most money. From a public administration perspective, it was disheartening to note that only 8 percent of all the media coverage during a long primary season focused on policy positions.

Application 6.1
Death Penalty Sentencing

The U.S. Government Accountability Office (GAO) issued a congressionally mandated report about racial disparities in death penalty sentencing (1990b). The agency had been asked to determine whether the race of the victim or the defendant was associated with the death penalty. Many studies on this topic had been done, so the GAO research team chose to do an evaluation synthesis.

The researchers began by conducting extensive computer and bibliographic searches to identify and gather all potentially relevant studies done at the national, state, and local levels. They also contacted twenty-one criminal justice researchers and experts to identify additional research. They screened more than 200 citations and excluded those that were based before 1972 and studies that did not examine race as a factor. That left fifty-three studies. The researchers then reviewed each study to determine both appropriateness and overall quality. Twenty-eight studies made it through that screening.

The team then rated the twenty-eight studies according to its criteria for research quality. Two social science analysts independently rated each study in five dimensions: study design, sampling, measurement, data collection, and analysis techniques. A third analyst reviewed the raters' assessment to assess the consistency between the scores. A statistician reviewed the analytical techniques used to determine whether they were appropriate and supported the conclusions.

The next phase focused on determining whether race was a factor in death penalty sentencing. This information was extracted from each study and then compared to determine similarities or differences in findings. The researchers found that the race of the victim was a factor; the death penalty was more often sought if the victim was white. However, the influence of the race of the defendant was unclear.

The issue, however, still remains in dispute. In 2008 Scott Phillips reported his research results in the *Houston Law Review*: race is a factor in death sentencing. "Death was more likely to be imposed against black defendants than white defendants, and death was more likely to be imposed on behalf of white victims than black victims," he concluded (812). Arguments now rage about the quality of this new study.

This research was not for the faint of heart. The data came from over 13,000 stories written from January 2007 to April 2008 for forty-eight different print, online, network TV, cable, and radio sources. The data were collected by the Project for Excellence in Journalism and published in its News Coverage Index (NCI). All the news stories were coded and the amount of detail is stunning.

How did the researchers decide that a news story was about "the horse race"? How was that defined? How were "faith issues" defined? To determine the nitty-gritty details, sophisticated readers would have to dig deep. But these details, along with their coding procedures, are essential in determining the quality of the research results. Suspended judgment is necessary until it can be determined whether the essential research procedures to control for bias were in place.

Application 6.2
Analyzing Citizen Feedback

In the summer of 2001, the Washington Department of Transportation (DOT) closed a major road and bridge in order to do repairs. Although DOT worked with local officials to publicize the closure, the severity of the impact of closing was not anticipated. The closure resulted in major gridlock, with three- to four-hour traffic delays.

The citizen reaction was intense. Angry drivers sent e-mails to the department and posted to a chat room created by the local newspaper. These responses provided a record of communication that could be analyzed, and the secretary of transportation requested that a study be done.

The e-mails were analyzed by two researchers independently to identify the common themes and provide a sense of the range of issues and concerns. While many e-mails calmly offered suggestions to resolve the problems that the drivers had encountered, the researchers observed a high level of disaffection and anger in other e-mail messages. The researchers agreed on several common themes based on their separate analysis of the e-mails:

- A sense that DOT was abusing power. "The DOT operates exactly like the rest of the state and local governments. Without thought, on impulse, and above all, power over the people."
- A belief that DOT did not understand the citizens and was disconnected. One citizen asked, "Do you people sitting in your ivory towers at the DOT have any idea at all what it's like to drive in the area?"
- A sense that government simply does not care about its citizens. As one e-mail claimed, "You really do not care about the people you are supposed to be helping."
- A clear taxpayer/government relationship (my job as citizen is to fund your work; therefore you work for me) instead of a citizen/government relationship (we are in this together). Many of the e-mail responses reflected the attitude that citizens will take their money away from government if government will not "wake up." For example, one citizen wrote, "I for one will not support additional gas taxes until you can more efficiently use the money you are taxing me for."
- A sense of insult and injury when drivers suffered the effects of the delays. One said, "You have made my life . . . a living hell."

SURVEY RESEARCH

While survey research is sometimes called a design or approach, I see it as a data collection strategy to gather data from people. As such, I talk about surveys in Chapter 9. Interviews and focus groups are other approaches to gather data from people and are discussed more fully in Chapter 8.

Briefly, surveys can be used in a variety of ways. A common application is in public opinion polls, using a cross-sectional random sample. However, surveys can also be administered to everyone in an agency or classroom. A very short customer feedback survey on the back of a postcard given out to everyone who comes into the post office is another example of survey research.

Surveys typically ask very specific questions and provide the respondents with a limited set of possible answers, more like multiple-choice questions rather than fill-in-the-blank. They may be administered in person, through the mail, by phone, by e-mail, or over the Internet. The real strength of using a survey approach is that it is possible to gather data from a very large group of people in a cost-effective way. Standardized responses also make it relatively easy to summarize the results.

Surveys do have some limitations. A survey must be short and easy for people to complete; it is therefore limited in its ability to explore complex issues, situations in which there are many possible answers, or issues that cannot be reduced to a meaningful check-a-box format. Surveys might be described as an approach that goes a mile wide rather than a mile deep.

There are also limitations to each of the distribution approaches. Briefly, a mail survey requires that people have the literacy skills to complete it; if they do not, then interviews would be the better approach. Phone surveys are another way to contact a large number of people and work well since most people have phones; many public opinion polls now include cell-phone users. E-mail and Internet surveys require that people have that technology; since not everyone does, using those methods to conduct a survey of the public will systematically exclude segments of the population. While phone surveys use random digit dialing, e-mail surveys require actual e-mail addresses, making e-mail surveys useful only when e-mail addresses are known. Researchers can also contact a particular group of people with known e-mail addresses and ask them to go to a website to complete a survey.

It is also possible to provide a survey on an organization's website. The specifics of designing questionnaires and the pros and cons of the various survey methods are presented in Chapter 9.

CASE STUDIES

Case studies are used to answer descriptive and normative questions that focus on one or more people, groups, organizations, communities, programs, processes, geographic areas, cities, or countries. It might help to think of case studies as the researchers' way of saying "for example." If researchers do not have the resources to do a national study of the Head Start program, they might opt to do a case study using a few sites across the country or maybe a few sites in their state.

Some research questions are nearly impossible to answer without using a case study approach. When researchers want to gain an in-depth understanding of a situation or how a complex process works, case studies make sense. When researchers want to learn about people's experiences that cannot be captured in a check-a-box survey, case studies also make sense. Case studies allow researchers to go a mile deep rather than a mile wide.

For example, researchers may want to do case studies when trying to learn about an innovative program. How did it get started, what supports did the program's managers have, and what barriers did they encounter? A case study could provide insight into the process of innovation, the role of leadership in innovation, and lessons learned that others could use to implement that program in their organizations.

Sometimes case studies can be used to put a human face on a particular situation. For example, a program designed to help students stay in school and go on to higher education might provide a few cases to balance out the quantitative data. These few stories can demonstrate the real impact of the program on the lives of young people.

One issue is how many cases should be used. There is no handy rule. More than one makes sense in order to make comparisons or to maximize diversity. Beyond that, the researchers will have to make choices based on their resources and what makes sense in the situation.

A second issue is how the case or cases are selected. That choice will also depend on the situation—including the research questions and the resources available. The researchers can select cases based on these factors:

- Convenience: the cases are easy for the researchers to access
- Particular aspects: best cases, typical cases, worst cases, or a mix
- Diversity: mix of locations, people, types of organizations, or perspectives
- Random selection: removing bias from the selection

No matter how they select the cases, the researchers need to state their rationale.

How might researchers select cases for the study? If researchers are looking at organizational innovation, they might select the best case in their community. If they have the resources, they may select several very different organizations to get a better sense of the factors that might vary in bringing about change in local government, nonprofit, and for-profit organizations.

If the researchers are trying to understand why different schools in their community perform so differently, they might opt to select the school with the highest achievement scores, one with average achievement scores, and the one with the worst achievement scores.

If the researchers are trying to find out what college seniors think about a public service career, the researchers might opt to go to schools in different parts of the country, to a few public and private colleges, or to schools with demographically different student populations.

When reviewing results from a case study, sophisticated readers will want to look carefully at the criteria for selecting the cases. They will also look carefully at the rationale and for any possible limitations stated by the researchers. The choices should have face validity, meaning that, given the situation, they should make sense to a reasonable person and do not appear to be biased.

Some people criticize case studies because the scope is so small that the results cannot be generalized to a larger population. This is a valid criticism. Case studies, like experimental designs, are weak in terms of generalizing back to the larger population; technically, they are weak in terms of external validity. They are also criticized because they lack rigor, meaning that they are qualitative. That allegation may or may not be true. It is not unusual for quantitative and qualitative data collection methods to be part of a case study; for example, case studies might include analysis of existing data, surveys, observation, and interviews.

This use of multiple methods to collect data is called triangulation. When traveling on the high seas, it is possible to determine a ship's position by taking measures from different angles. It is the same for researchers. By looking at the same situation from different angles—meaning using different measurement and data collection strategies—it is possible to describe the situation more accurately than by using only one method.

When done well, case studies are practical and provide useful information that can inform decision-making (Yin 2002). Careful and thoughtful decisions about identifying the research question, developing appropriate measures, using data collection techniques that minimize errors, choosing appropriate analysis tools, and writing conclusions that stay within the boundaries of the research will result in a high-quality case study.

COST-BENEFIT ANALYSIS

Developed by economists, cost-benefit analysis is another research approach used in public administration research (Adler and Posner 2006). At its most basic, cost-benefit analysis answers normative questions about whether the benefits justify the costs.

For example, is the Women, Infants, and Children (WIC) supplemental nutrition program cost-beneficial? To answer this question, researchers might gather data about the costs to run the program from budget documents. The challenge, however, is to calculate how much money is saved in health costs because mothers, infants, and children have improved nutrition. Estimating health cost savings takes some statistical wizardry, but the results can be expressed concretely. For example, a GAO study in 1992 reported that for every dollar spent on WIC, there is a $2.89 savings in the first year and a $3.50 savings in future health care costs.

The challenge of this research approach is in being able to define and measure costs and benefits. One key assumption is that everything can be measured in monetary terms. This, however, is not always the case. It is not necessarily easy to get the dollar measures. First, the researchers have to figure out the actual program costs. This seems straightforward except that some costs may be hidden in other programs, paid by someone else, or unknown until many years later. The full costs of caring for soldiers injured in Iraq, for example, will not be known until years from now.

Another type of cost is defined in terms of opportunity costs, meaning that the money could have yielded greater benefits if it had been used differently. One opportunity cost, for example, is the loss of interest that the money could have earned if it had been invested instead of spent. For example, the daylight saving study discussed earlier (Lahart 2008) found that residential electricity use increased under daylight saving, costing consumers an additional $8.6 million per year. This cost also represents an opportunity lost: what would be the benefit to the consumers if they had invested that money? It might have been worth more than the $8.6 million.

Or consider whether getting a college degree is cost-beneficial. A story in *U.S. News and World Report* noted in October 2008 that the estimated value of a college

degree is $300,000 in today's dollars (Clark 2008). On the benefit side, the research-
ers claim that college graduates earn an average of about $20,000 more than those
with high school degrees. Over a work life of forty years, that comes to $800,000.
However, there also are costs. The researchers report that the average cost per year
is $30,000 at a private university. So an investment of $120,000 for four years of
college yields $800,000.

Other adjustments also need to be factored in. One is the opportunity cost—that
is, the wages lost by going to college rather than getting a job. Then there is inflation.
When these costs are factored in, the $800,000 is reduced to a net value in today's
dollars of $300,000. Although it may not yield as much as people would like, a col-
lege education is still worth the investment.

Furthermore, some jobs are open only to people with a college degree. If people
want to do particular kinds of work, then a college degree is a necessity. In addition, a
college degree is required to pursue advanced degrees that might have high monetary
returns. Money, however, is not the only factor to be considered. For many students,
college is a life-changing experience, exposing them to new ideas and people. Many
Americans believe that an educated populace is essential to sustain a vibrant democracy. It is hard to reduce these intangible factors to a simple monetary figure.

Opportunity costs also look a little different in the public sector than in the private
sector. The private sector has the option of investing money that is not spent. That is
generally not the case in the public sector. Therefore, policy analysts are more likely
to try to estimate the benefits of several different program options rather than just
comparing the benefits from a program versus the benefits from investing that money.
For example, is it more cost-effective to create drug treatment programs for addicts or
to send addicts to jail? Is it more cost-beneficial to tax business firms and redistribute
the money to citizens so the can stimulate the economy by increased spending or to
cut business taxes so firms can expand and therefore create new jobs? These scenarios
assume cause-and-effect relationships, which may or may not be true. For example,
is there research that actually demonstrates a cause-and-effect relationship between
tax cuts and economic growth? These types of policy questions also reflect political
value differences that are likely to generate public debate.

The larger costs to society as a whole are called social costs. In the daylight saving
study, the researchers measured the social cost of increased emissions from additional
energy use; they estimated it to be between $1.6 million and $5.3 million. The tough
question is: How did they come up with this estimate?

Social costs might also be called external costs, externalities, or spillover costs. Basically, this means that those producing or using the goods and services do not pay the full
costs. The classic example is a mill in a town that provides jobs and tax revenues, but the
pollution that it produces has to be cleaned up by the delta town downriver. The people
in the delta town pay the costs for pollution they did not create. The producers of the
pollution have externalized that cost, meaning they do not pay for it. This is similar to
how the Environmental Protection Agency's Superfund works; when some corporations
pollute, the government comes in to clean up or mitigate the toxic waste site.

Measuring benefits is also challenging. There are different kinds of benefits: direct,
indirect, and intangible benefits. There also can be positive externalities or spillovers

such as the increased property values in neighborhoods with well-maintained gardens or with a small public park. A direct benefit resulting from a drug prevention program, for example, is the avoidance of future costs associated with addiction. Indirect benefits include the savings from avoiding the loss of productivity as well as the cost-savings in other programs, such as welfare or prisons. Intangible benefits are those that accrue by avoiding future pain, grief, or death. As researchers move from calculating direct benefits to intangible benefits, it gets harder to attach a concrete dollar value.

While there is an implied balance between costs and benefits, the reality is that who pays and who gains are not necessarily the same. Sometimes there is also a disconnect in terms of time; the costs occur now while the benefits will not be measurable until years later or the benefits can occur first while the costs show up later. For example, the current generation may enjoy the benefits of deficit spending but future generations will pay the costs later. When cost-benefit analysis is used to justify a political position, it is important to notice if there is any disconnect between who pays and who gains.

Although cost-benefit analysis has the appearance of concrete science, it is often based on estimates and assumptions that may or may not be valid. How did the researchers arrive at their estimates and what assumptions did they make? The tough question is: Do these estimates and assumptions affect the results in a particular way?

While cost-benefit analysis is not as simple as it might initially appear, it provides a useful framework for considering policy options. Ideally, it will provoke a deeper understanding of the many connections between policy options, their potential costs and benefits, externalities, and other equity considerations.

CONCLUSION

Researchers have many ways to approach a research situation. The choice of which approach to use is guided by the situation. If data are already available that will work, then secondary analysis is a good choice. Evaluation synthesis makes sense when there are already many studies on the topic. Content analysis is a good choice when the research question is about making sense of communication. Survey research makes sense when researchers want to gather people's opinions. Doing a case study makes sense when the researchers want to gain depth and richness of understanding; this is especially true for answering questions about how something works. It also makes sense when an in-depth description is needed or when a handful of concrete stories will illustrate the situation. Cost-benefit analysis makes sense when the costs and benefits are known and can be expressed in terms of dollars.

Whether researchers choose a design in the Xs and Os framework or one of the approaches discussed in this chapter, the sophisticated users of research results will want to look closely at the design choices. The design selected should be appropriate given the research question and the situation. When trying to answer a cause-and-effect question, the design choices are crucial and the Xs and Os framework should be used. Other approaches can be used, but the sophisticated user will want to carefully consider whether rival explanations have been eliminated.

All designs require a well-developed plan, including clearly defined measures, appropriate data collection strategy, and analysis procedures. The planning process can take considerable time to complete because there is typically a lot of back-and-forth decision-making until all the pieces are in synch.

The takeaway lesson is that no design is error-free and that every design has limitations that need to be taken into account in both the planning and the reporting phase. Sophisticated users of research results need to be mindful whenever estimates are used and look carefully for unstated assumptions that can allow bias to creep in.

The tough question about design is simply this: Is the research design strong enough to support the researcher's conclusions? If the researchers have asked a cause-and-effect question and used a one-shot design, then a sophisticated user will be wary of any definitive conclusions about causality. The design is just too weak.

EXERCISES

1. Indicate which research design or approach is the best choice in each scenario below. Explain your choice and note any concerns you might have before making a final decision.
   a. The WIC program provides nutritional supplements for low-income pregnant women and children under the age of five. You have been asked to determine the program's impact in reducing infant mortality. As you begin the exploratory research, you discover that more than 100 studies have been conducted measuring the program's impact.
   b. You have been asked to study an innovative program that has dramatically reduced the amount of time needed to do routine airplane maintenance at one U.S. Air Force base. Specifically, you want to understand the processes used, the training provided, and the views of the senior leadership about the key lessons learned that would be useful to military personnel wanting to implement this program on other Air Force bases.
   c. Citizens have organized to protect land on the waterfront from development. They claim that building a city park would be the most cost-effective use of the land. The park would attract people to the downtown and boost revenues for local businesses. They need to gather evidence of this result to convince the city council.
   d. Parents of children in the local high school believe that there is a conservative bias in the reading material and videos used in the history and social studies program.
   e. The oversight committee hires researchers to determine how the Department of Defense contracts for services to be provided in war zones. The committee members want to know the details of the process, from start to finish. They want to determine how long it takes and what creates delays. More than 500 contracts are signed every year.

f. The oversight committee hires researchers to determine whether there are differences in contracting in terms of the amount of time it takes, the number of contracts that are behind schedule for delivery, and the amount spent based on the branch of service. The Department of Defense maintains a contracts information system.

g. The local school board wants to find out citizens' views about education, especially whether the high school graduates are prepared for college. As the researchers are deciding how to design this study, one reads an article noting that the state published a study of all the school districts that shows SAT scores, graduation rates, and the percentage of graduates going on to college.

7 Data Collection I

Available Data and Observation

OVERVIEW

The choice of a data collection approach should logically flow from the prior decisions about the research questions and measurement choices. Basically, the data collection decision depends on three factors. The first factor centers on what the researchers want to know. For example, do they want to know what people think or what they do? If learning what people think is the goal, the researchers would choose a data collection approach that asks them. If the researchers want to know what people do, the approach to choose would be observation.

The second factor is where the data reside. Perhaps other researchers have already collected the needed data. If so, then the task is to obtain those studies, reports, and/ or databases. Alternatively, if the data are in files stored in a basement, then the tasks are to access those files and gather the needed information systematically. If the data are in the physical or built environment, the researchers will need to get out of the office and observe. If people have the desired information, then the researchers will need to decide whether to use interviews, surveys, or focus groups.

The third factor is the amount of resources available to collect the data. If sufficient money, staff, and time were available, then it would be possible, for example, to conduct face-to-face interviews with a large number of the people who have the desired information. If there is very little money, staff, or time, then interviewing just a few people or conducting three focus groups might have to do.

There are trade-offs in collecting data that ultimately affect the conclusions that can be drawn. However, regardless of what data collection approach is selected, researchers need to develop very clear, specific guidelines to ensure that data is accurate, reliable, and unbiased. The data collection methods should be described in the final report, along with any problems encountered and any limitations that might affect the conclusions.

This phase of the research process requires attention to detail and every detail has to be nailed down. The decision about the best data collection approach is interwoven with the measurement strategy and sampling approach. It takes time to make sure all the pieces align and requires flexibility because the initial plan may not work if the situation proves to have unexpected barriers. The next three chapters provide a toolkit for the most commonly used methods of data collection. This chapter discusses the large issues of structured and semi-structured data collection and then turns to several commonly used data collection methods: using available data, collecting data from records and files, and observation. The purpose is provide some "how to" basics so that it is easier to identify the strengths and limitations of each approach when reading research results.

DATA COLLECTION: THE DEGREE OF STRUCTURE

Researchers decide whether to conduct quantitative and qualitative research. Quantitative research is defined by its highly structured approach to data collection, while qualitative research is defined by its minimalist structure.

The difference between structured and semistructured data collection is like the difference between multiple-choice and fill-in-the-blanks exam questions. Multiple-choice questions have a limited number of specific possible responses and the students must select one; the responses are easy for the teacher to grade but might not match how the students understand the questions. Fill-in-the-blanks are open-ended, allowing the students to choose how to express their responses. However, these answers are harder to grade and might take more time to understand because handwriting might be scrawled or the meaning of the words is not clear.

The following examples illustrate the difference between closed-ended and open-ended questions:

1. Closed-ended question:
   What is the *highest degree* you have obtained (please check only one):
   a. ___ Less than high school
   b. ___ High school degree
   c. ___ Associate degree
   d. ___ Undergraduate degree (BA or BS)
   f. ___ Graduate degree or advanced professional degree (MA, LLD, PhD, etc.)
2. Open-ended question:
   What is the highest degree you have obtained? _____

Structured data collection approaches are used to collect quantitative data when there is a need to report numbers, when precision is essential, when many cases or people need to be considered, or when the measures are well defined and can be expressed numerically. Structured data collection means that data will be collected in exactly the same way every time. Think of a researcher with a clipboard who can reduce all observations to a "check-a-box" format.

Semistructured data collection approaches follow a general plan but are more fluid than a structured approach, allowing for changes and adjustments as more information is obtained. These open-ended approaches are the best option when the researcher wants to gain in-depth understanding of complex issues, experiences, processes, or interpretations. When researchers are uncertain about what specifically to measure, then exploring the situation using a semistructured approach also makes sense.

Semistructured approaches are used to collect qualitative data when:

- there is a need to tell anecdotes or stories
- it is important to understand the general issues and context of a situation
- when it is essential to understand how a process works
- the experiences of people are essential to understanding the situation
- the researchers want to gain insight into complex processes
- the measures are not clear or cannot be reduced to numbers

When collecting qualitative data, the researcher wants to capture as much information as possible. Good notes are essential. This means paying close attention to what people say and how they say it. Words may have special meanings. To the extent possible, responses should be captured verbatim. Any observations, including setting, body language, mood changes, and events that occur during the process of collecting data (for example, multiple interruptions during an interview), should be captured in the researcher's notes with as much detail as possible. Since humor or sarcasm might not translate as such when written verbatim, the researchers need to indicate the context of such statements.

Typically, researchers capture their immediate thoughts, reactions, and interpretations as they engage in qualitative data collection. These should be kept in a separate section of the notes so they are not confused with the actual data being collected. It is important that researchers do not confuse their interpretations and observations with those of the research participants. However, researchers should remain mindful of their own reactions because new ideas and hunches might emerge that open up new questions or ways of observing the situation.

Within this general framework of structured and semistructured data collection, there are many approaches. The choice of whether to use a structured or semistructured approach is always driven by the situation rather than the researcher's preference. A summary of the uses, characteristics, strengths, and limitations of some of the commonly used data collection approaches is presented in Exhibit 7.1.

Structured approaches are harder to develop but are easier to analyze than semistructured approaches. As a result, structured approaches require more time in the planning phase but less time in the analyzing phase. When working with semistructured approaches, researchers will find it relatively easy to begin collecting data but challenging and time-consuming to analyze it. Structured approaches are unforgiving of mistakes; if a question is poorly written, there is no way to change it once it is sent to 1,000 people. Semistructured approaches are very forgiving of mistakes; if a question does not work, it is easy to change it before the next interview; if new questions emerge, they can be easily incorporated into the next focus group.

While the choice to use quantitative or qualitative data collection methods might appear to be an either/or choice, it is not unusual for primarily quantitative research projects to include some of both. For example, researchers might collect available

Exhibit 7.1 **Data Collection Options**

Option	When to use	Characteristics	Strengths	Limitations
Available data	When data already exist to answer the research questions Secondary data analysis	Other studies and reports Computer files Electronic databases	Fast Easy Inexpensive	Access Quality of data May not be exactly what is needed
Document data collection instruments	Data are in files, budgets, records, books, computer files, newspapers, video Audits	Structured format to pull needed data from sources to create database	Consistent data collection Makes data available for analysis	Requires trained coders Need to ensure reliable coding Limited to material available Unforgiving of errors
Observation	Determine actual conditions or behaviors Few cases	Can be structured or unstructured Can be obtrusive or unobtrusive	Actual behavior—not self-reports Can provide a qualitative sense of a situation	May be hard to quantify May be hard to get consistency Time-consuming and costly in a large study Bias might be an issue
Structured surveys and interviews	Opinions and attitudes	Check-a-box Closed-ended questions	Large number of cases Consistent data collection Relatively inexpensive Easy to analyze	Hard to develop Researcher needs to know exactly what is wanted Precise data Cold and impersonal
Unstructured interviews and focus groups	People's perceptions and stories Exploratory: Not sure what to ask	A semistructured interview guide In-depth Open-ended questions	Personal Rich data Long interviews Complex topics Easy to develop	Not good for sensitive questions Time-consuming to conduct and analyze Requires skilled interviewers Potential for bias No counts Hard to analyze

data from records, observe activities, interview officials, and survey citizens. Sometimes researchers will use a qualitative method to help develop a quantitative method. For example, researchers might use preliminary interviews or focus groups to help develop a structured survey. However, sometimes a single data collection method is used; public opinion polls, for example, typically use only telephone surveys.

AVAILABLE DATA

If the researchers get lucky, the data they need have already been collected so they do secondary analysis (see Chapter 6). Public agencies routinely gather data, such as vital statistics, crime rates, census data, governmental budgets, and educational testing scores, and make it available to other researchers. Many governmental agencies and think tanks conduct studies on many different public issues; that information may also be available. For example, a national, longitudinal study on heart disease can be used to explore other issues, such as the relationship between depression and the amount of TV watched.

The researchers will need to do a number of checks before deciding to use data gathered by someone else. First they need to verify that the data are actually what they need. They then need to consider whether the data are current enough. If not, the data may serve as a comparison point but new data will have to be gathered as well. If the information is current, the researchers need to consider its credibility. Who collected it? Did those investigators have a bias? How good are the data? The researchers need to find out exactly how the data were collected and what quality assurance procedures were used in entering the data. Lastly, the researchers need to assess the reliability of the data entry. The data in the computer should match the source documents. If there were too many errors, the researchers might obtain the source documents and reenter the data. Alternatively, they might choose to collect original data.

The researchers must make sure the data dictionary comes with any electronic database; these are set-up in a way similar to a spreadsheet. The data dictionary describes what is in every row and column and identifies the names and codes for each value of each variable. For example, in Chapter 2, the values of the variable "gender" was presented as male and female; these are likely to be coded as 1 for male and 2 for female. The researchers need to know exactly how the data are coded so the analysis can be done correctly.

DATA COLLECTION INSTRUMENTS

When the data are not already gathered into a handy database, researchers must go through files, documents, and records to extract the needed information and create their own database. For example, if researchers could not access a database containing corporate income tax information from the Internal Revenue Service, they would have to go to the corporations' income tax returns to gather the key information in order to create their own database. This situation is not unusual. Data are often in nonelectronic formats, such as prior reports, budget documents, or file folders packed in boxes in a dusty storage facility. The researchers will have to collect the data systematically in order to create a database that they can analyze. Of course, the researchers will need permission to access this information if it is protected by privacy regulations.

A data collection instrument (DCI) is a systematic approach to gather loose data (see

Application 7.1). The DCI is basically a form that lists all the data that the researchers want to collect from the various documents. The more check-a-box items rather than fill-in-the-blank questions it contains, the easier and faster it is to complete. It also makes it easier to enter the data into a computer and analyze it. However, it might be necessary to have some fill-in-the-blanks as well if the data cannot be reduced to simple measures.

The researchers first review a small sample of the files or documents to determine whether the needed data are there. If so, they draft a DCI. Next, they test it to make sure it works—that is, that their check-a-box forms capture most of the data, leaving only a small amount of information that has to be written. Ideally, the DCI is as comprehensive as needed and easy to complete.

Once the researchers have a final draft, the big issue is reliability. The researchers will want to run some tests to make sure the team understands and codes the data in the same way. Using a small sample of the same records, each member of the team codes the data. The coding should be the same; this is called inter-rater reliability. If not, the problems should be identified and fixed. Then, the researchers should try another test.

For example, if the MPA program director wants to determine the average number of years between students' graduating from a four-year college and starting the MPA program, it will be necessary to look through the student records kept in file cabinets because the data have never been transferred into an electronic database. It makes sense to develop a simple form that several different people can use to gather the data from ten years' worth of files.

Before developing the DCI, the researchers might want to find out whether the program director has any other questions so all the data can collected at the same time. When asked, the program director might realize she also wants to know the demographics of the students, the undergraduate grade point average (GPA), the graduate GPA, and how long it took the graduates to complete the program.

The researchers would then develop the data collection instrument, which might look something like Exhibit 7.2. The identifier (File ID No.) provides the link to the actual file. This will be used so that information can be verified. To verify the data, the researchers select a random sample of student files and compare the data in the computer with what is in the files. If the error rate is low, the database is ready for analysis. If the error rate is high, then the data need to be fixed; sometimes it is necessary to reenter all the data. The DCI also contains a space for the researcher to add comments, perhaps a notation about missing information in the file or why a student left school without a degree. Providing a way for the researchers to identify issues, concerns, or their observations might be helpful.

Creating data sets from documents takes time and requires attention to detail. However, it is often cheaper than other methods and might be more likely to be accurate. For example, the MPA director could have sent a questionnaire to former MPA students asking about their GPA and how long they took to complete the program. However, they might not recall that information accurately. The MPA program might not have current addresses for many of them, making it difficult to contact them. Lastly, there is a good chance that only a small percentage of those who receive the survey would actually complete and return it. Going through the files, therefore, although labor-

Exhibit 7.2 **MPA Data Collection Instrument**

File ID No.	Date:
Researcher's name:	

1. Graduated from the program?

    Yes   If Yes, list your graduation year: ☐.☐☐

    No   If No, list last year of attendance: ☐☐☐

2. Area of concentration:

3. Year degree (BA/BS) was completed: ☐☐☐

4. Year entered the MPA program: ☐☐☐

5. Undergraduate GPA:

6. Cumulative GPA at either (a) graduation or (b) at time left the program:

7. Sex: Male   Female

8. Race/Ethnicity:

    Not stated   Other (specify):

    White   _____

    African/American

    Asian American   Foreign student (specify country):

    Native American   _____

    Hispanic

    Mixed

9. Date of birth: Month ☐☐ / Day ☐☐ / Year ☐☐☐☐

10. Research comments:

intensive and boring, will yield the best data in this situation; and sometimes there really are no other options. If the data reside in a file cabinet, then that is where the researchers have to look.

It is important to note, however, that access to agency files and documents might not be possible. The MPA director clearly has access but an outsider is likely to be refused access due to privacy issues. Outside researchers need to leave time to negotiate access.

Audits typically review documents to see if an agency has complied with applicable laws and procedures. This is another situation in which it is likely that researchers will be working with data in files. The process is the same: data is systemically collected in a structured way. Decision rules are in place to determine whether an activity is in compliance.

Gathering data from documents can also be used in a descriptive way that combines numbers with narrative. For example, researchers doing an organizational assessment may gather information from a wide range of documents: enabling legislation or charter, internal and external reports, budgets, memos, and news clippings (Harrison 2004). When was the agency started? What were the initial goals and objectives? Have they changed over time? If so, how and why? What is the organization's structure and has it changed over time? If so, how and why? What were some of the issues that emerged over time and what happened? Who are the heroes and enemies? My personal favorite is to look at clippings and cartoons on the walls and cubicles: does the humor say something about the culture of the organization?

While a check-a-box form is not likely to work, the researchers still need to be systematic in their data collection and keep a good record about what data they gathered from which documents. In this type of situation, interviews with key officials can be very helpful to verify the researchers' interpretation of the written information, explore issues that did not find their way into written form, and provide context. For example, the official organizational chart might not accurately capture the informal sources of power; interviews might shed more insight on the informal power structure in the agency.

OBSERVATION

Researchers can observe traffic, children in a playground, interaction between students and teacher in a classroom, the amount of time between bus arrivals, the friendliness of waiting rooms in public agencies, land use patterns in a county, the layout of city and rural environments, the quality of housing, or the condition of roads. Observation can also be used to assess the management skills of those who went through a special managerial training program or the availability of downtown parking during peak hours.

Observations can be made in a structured or semistructured way. In structured observations, a very specific checklist—a DCI with check boxes—can be used to count things precisely; counts may be taken according to a specific schedule or a stopwatch used to time activities. For example, if researchers are measuring the communication of men and women at meetings, they might time how long each man or

---

Application 7.1
Race and Death Penalty Sentencing Revisited

Is there a relationship between race and death penalties in federal cases? The Rand Corporation released a report in 2006 that concluded that the decision to seek the death penalty is explained by "the heinousness of crimes rather than race" (Klein et al. 2006). How did the researchers come to this conclusion?

The researchers began by looking at prior studies but decided to do original data collection rather than an evaluation synthesis. They reviewed a sample of federal murder case files to determine the information they contained. Based on a list of data that would be feasible and desirable, they constructed what they called a "case abstraction form," which is just a different term for a DCI.

They developed coding rules for recording data on victims, defendants, and case characteristics from the paper files. Five specially trained coders gathered the data. In addition, the victim and defendant data were gathered from electronic files. This effort yielded 312 cases for which the races of the defendant and victim were available.

To minimize bias in data analysis, Rand gave three independent research teams a copy of the database. Each team was free to determine its own analysis plan. The findings of the three teams were compared only after they had analyzed the data and written up their results. Despite the different analytical approaches, the three teams came to the same basic conclusion: the heinousness of the crime, rather than race, appeared to be associated with the decision to seek the death penalty.

Despite the efforts to provide reliable, technically appropriate data collection and to reduce bias by having three independent teams conduct the analysis, the researchers agreed that the research does not provide a definitive answer. "Analyses of observational data can support a thesis and might be useful for that purpose," they stated, "but such analyses can seldom prove or disprove causation." Among the potential limitations was that information that might have affected the outcomes of the murder cases—that is, whether the death penalty was imposed—might not have been included in the case files. The researchers therefore urged caution in interpreting their results.

---

woman speaks, count the number of interruptions, and keep track of who interrupts and who is interrupted.

In semistructured observation, researchers will make notes of whatever strikes them as interesting, typical, unusual, or important; they might note nonverbal communication, such as eye-rolling, leaning forward, turning away from the speaker, or who was speaking when people engaged in side conversations.

Observation does not have to be elaborate, but it does need to be clearly defined in measurable terms. For example, downtown business owners complain that people do not shop at their stores because there are not enough parking spaces. They decide to bring in MPA students to study parking downtown. First the students would have to clarify exactly what streets define "downtown." They then have to decide what options to use: they could count the number of parking spaces available within the defined boundaries of the shopping area or they could map the location of public parking areas in addition to just counting the number. Are the parking spaces close to the stores? Do shoppers have to cross a busy street? If so, how hard or easy is it to do?

Observation can answer a descriptive question about how many parking spaces are available; the number of spaces within the downtown area (however defined) can be counted. But if the question is changed to "Are there enough parking spaces?" it becomes a normative question. What is "enough"? Observation provides the necessary data about the number of spaces but criteria have to be asserted in order to decide whether this number is enough. Perhaps the students will define "enough" in terms of availability during prime shopping times. If so, the students will need to measure parking availability during prime shopping times as well as at random times.

The students might try to capture the subjective experience of parking downtown and approach parking like a prospective customer at random times. This is called participant observation. The researcher would note how hard or easy it is to obtain a parking spot at different times during the week. Are parking locations clearly marked if they are not on the main street?

The takeaway lesson is that researchers often have many choices. Those choices will reflect slight variations in the way questions are asked. The downtown business owners will need to ask: Why did the researchers make these particular choices?

OBTRUSIVE AND UNOBTRUSIVE DATA COLLECTION

When considering observation as a data collection strategy, researchers have two choices: obtrusive or unobtrusive approaches. Obtrusive observation means that people know they are being observed. For example, if a researcher comes into a workplace with a clipboard and is introduced as an observer, then all the employees know they are being observed. This knowledge might influence their behavior.

Unobtrusive observation is data collection in which people do not know they are being observed (see Application 7.2). In order to have the least influence on participants' behavior, unobtrusive observation is best. For example, if a researcher observes a class from behind a two-way mirror, the students see themselves in the mirror but do not know they are being watched from the other side. Another example is when the director of an agency systematically calls the agency's help line as a "customer" to verify the time it takes to get through, the courtesy of the employee, and the accuracy of the information provided. A variation is participant observation, when the researchers participate in an activity without anyone else knowing they are observing; they appear to be just like everyone else. For example, the researchers might participate in a training program where the instructors are being assessed; the instructors, however, do not know they are not like the other students.

When engaging in unobtrusive observation, the researchers must carefully avoid any ethical violation. No one should be harmed because of the research. The participants should not be identified or identifiable and their privacy rights must be protected. When in doubt, researchers should seek legal advice. For example, to determine whether minorities are being discriminated against in obtaining housing, both white and nonwhite researchers posing as renters approach apartment owners or rental agents. The actions of the owners and rental agents are being observed unobtrusively. While they might appear to be violating the law by offering the apartment to a white renter rather than to a black renter, the owner or rental agent may, in fact, not be discriminating; it is possible that the white renter had a better credit score or a better recommendation from a prior landlord. On the other hand, it might be discrimination solely based on race. The point here is that researchers can observe behavior but it is hard to determine motivation based on a single action. However, if the researchers see a consistent pattern of white preference, then they would have stronger evidence of housing discrimination. From a research perspective, the researchers are not running a sting operation; they are looking for larger patterns of behavior rather than trying to judge a specific action. The information they gather will let elected officials know whether there is a problem, but it will not be used to bring lawsuits against specific owners or rental agents.

The advantage of using observation is that it collects data on actual behavior rather than people's perceptions about their own behavior. For those who like to kick the tires, it has a directness that is appealing. Although observation might feel unfiltered because of its directness, it is potentially unreliable since different people might observe the same things and interpret them differently. Most of us have had the experience of being surprised when talking with others who had been at the same meeting to learn they heard things differently than we did.

The reality is that everyone tends unconsciously to look at the world through particular frameworks or paradigms. These frameworks can be blinders that make it hard to see things that do not fit expectations. Organizational consultant Joel Barker asked a small group of people to identify eight cards pulled from what appeared to be a normal deck (Barker 2001). The cards were turned over very quickly and the people were asked to recall them. Most were able to recall the normal cards—the black ace of clubs, the red queen of hearts, and so on. But there were a few rogue cards—a black ace of hearts and a red jack of clubs. Most people had difficulty recalling these untypical cards even after several runs through the deck, demonstrating how hard it is to recognize things that are outside the normal card deck paradigm.

It is also true that observation alone might not be sufficient to answer the research question. Researchers can observe the downtown-parking situation, but that does not provide the information needed to understand why citizens do not shop downtown. To answer that question, the researchers have to ask the citizens.

THE DESIGN MATRIX

The research design process is a funnel, moving from general concepts to specific details. Clearly, collecting data is at the narrow end where the careful attention to detail is essential, especially in the structured data collection approaches. There is a danger here—it is easy to get so lost in the detail that the purpose of the research is forgotten. At this point in the process, it is important to step back and make sure that the data collection approach connects to the research questions and measures.

Application 7.2
Participant Observation
Nickel and Dimed

"How does anyone live on the wages available to the unskilled?" asks Barbara Ehrenreich (2001). In her book *Nickel and Dimed: On (Not) Getting By in America*, she says that she got the idea for this research while sitting at an upscale restaurant and being served by people who earned a lot less per hour than she paid for her lunch. She decided that if she wanted to really understand whether people could live on low wages, she needed to get out from behind her desk and become one of them; and that is what she did.

She set some ground rules. She would not rely on her skills or college education to get a job. She would take the highest-paying job offered and do her best to hold it. She also was determined to take the cheapest accommodations she could find, despite some concern about safety and privacy.

Ehrenreich left home with a few personal items and some money, determined to find a place to live and a job from the classified ads of the local paper. She worked as a waitress in Key West; a dietary aide in a residential center and a maid in Maine; and as a Wal-Mart sales clerk in Minnesota. She did not invent a whole new identity, merely modifying what she told the people she met. She introduced herself as a divorced homemaker reentering the workforce after many years. Her book captures her experiences as a participant observer.

Her objective was to see if she could live on the wages earned by the working poor. While she had some sense of the struggle, she could not really know what it was like because, as she notes, she always knew she would go back to her middle-class life and her health insurance. She also makes no claim that her experiences reflected anyone's situation other than her own. Still, being a participant observer provided insights that statistics cannot fully convey. Can people live on low wages? Yes, she concludes, if they worked two jobs and seven days a week or lived with a working spouse. While those she met lived lives largely invisible to the general public, she was able to get this story before the public because of her status as a known writer.

Ehrenreich's research is an example of a semistructured approach to participant observation. She kept notes but had no check-a-box form to be completed every day. She reports the factual information about her wages and her costs for food, rent, and transportation. Her impressions and recall of conversations are based on her field notes.

The researchers should revisit their answers to the following questions:

- What do they want to know?
- How will they measure it?
- Where do the data reside?
- What resources are available to gather data?
- Will the data enable the researchers to answer the questions they have asked?

A handy tool is the design matrix (available in Appendix E on page 263). For readers of research results, the design matrix provides a way to break a study into its component parts so the basic structure of the research can be seen. Using this approach, it is possible to map exactly what the researchers did and how they did it to make sure everything connects.

For researchers and managers of research projects, the design matrix provides a visual way to make sure that every question is addressed in each step of the planning process and to track all the tasks necessary to answer each question. Since researchers do not have all the information needed at the start of the project, it will be necessary to revise some of their initial ideas and approaches as things become clearer.

Designing a research study is a process that requires both flexibility and creativity. In the early phases, the design matrix helps keep track of issues and concerns so they do not get forgotten. Once all the issues are settled, researchers should have a clear plan for collecting the data needed to answer every research question.

CONCLUSION

Researchers make choices about the degree of structure they will use to gather data. The choice should be the best option available given, the research question, the concerns of the requesters, the location of the data and the amount of time, money, and staff available. This choice gets us back into the quantitative-qualitative debate. It is important to remember that neither is inherently better. The choice about the degree of structure is driven by the situation. The quality of the research is driven by the attention to detailed planning and the researchers' efforts to minimize bias and error.

Using information that is already available makes sense if it will answer the research questions. When considering using available data, the researchers must ask whether the data are valid, reliable, and accurate. This means that the researchers must assess the quality of the methods used in the prior study. If original data collection methods were flawed, then the researchers will have to go to Plan B to collect the data.

As researchers root through files, records, and reports, data collection instruments will standardize the data collection. The equivalent is used in making structured observations. They require attention to detail and everyone on the team needs to be trained to ensure that data are gathered reliably; it is important to test for inter-rater reliability. The standardized data will be easy to analyze.

Semi-structured observations are useful when situations are complex, when rich data are desired, when much is unknown, or when the data do not suit a check-a-box format. The research team members need to be sure that they fully understand the research objectives and are clear about the data they should collect. This narrative data will be challenging to analyze but might yield great insights.

One takeaway lesson is that data collection requires meticulous attention to detail. The second is that it takes time to nail everything down. Last but not least, while data collection is presented here as a single step, in practice it is interwoven with decisions about the measures and sampling.

EXERCISES

1. What are your personal concerns about qualitative and quantitative methods? Do you have a preference? Explain.
2. Some citizens have complained that there is not enough time to walk across the busiest intersections before the traffic light changes in the downtown area How might you go about researching this issue?
3. The city manager has received complaints that people calling the city offices often are greeted rudely, put on never-ending hold, or that the calls are just dropped. How can the city manager find out if this is true?
4. Pick one of the following research situations, develop a short data collection instrument, and test it out. Summarize your conclusions and then reflect on the process. How well did it work? What happened that you did not anticipate and what kind of changes would you make if you were to expand your work into a large research project?
   a. Is there too much violence in children's TV programs? First define what you mean by violence. Then develop a DCI to measure the amount of violence on children's programs. Randomly select three different Saturday morning shows and complete a DCI for each show.
   b. Are prices higher at a grocery store in a middle-income neighborhood compared to a grocery store in a low-income neighborhood? First develop a shopping list (DCI) for the basic foods people eat. Then compare prices for those items at two grocery stores, one that serves middle-income people and one that serves low-income people.
   c. Who holds the power at meetings? Consider how power is demonstrated at meetings. Attend three meetings and consider such things as where people sit, who speaks, and who interrupts. How can you observe without being noticed?
   d. What do the cartoons posted on the walls, doors and cubicles in your place of work say about the organizational issues and concerns of the employees? Develop a data collection instrument to systematically observe the cartoons and test it out on five offices. What did you discover?
5. What are three demographics that describe your neighborhood, city, town, or county? Write a short memo to the elected officials. Cite the sources. As a side note, reflect on how hard or easy it was to obtain this data.

Data Collection II

Interviews and Focus Groups

OVERVIEW

The only way to learn about people's thoughts concerning public issues, their experiences in using public services, or their perceptions about their community is to ask. Researchers also sometimes ask people to self-report about their behavior. While the responses may not be accurate, asking people is often the easiest way to collect such data. For example, to find out how much time adults spend playing video games, researchers will have to ask them. While it is not impossible to create some sort of cyber-monitoring program, it would be costly and not foolproof.

After deciding that people can provide the desired data, researchers turn their attention to data collection options. Each has its advantages and disadvantages depending on the situation. Each also has some specific elements that researchers must take into account.

Because there are so many choices for collecting data from people, these methods will be presented in two chapters. This chapter focuses on the big issues in deciding which method to use to collect data from people and discusses the key elements for collecting data through interviews and focus groups. Chapter 9 will focus on the different survey approaches and structured questionnaires.

GENERAL GUIDELINES ABOUT CHOOSING THE APPROPRIATE METHOD

Researchers have different methods available: face-to-face interviews or focus groups, or surveys via telephone, e-mail, the Internet, mail, or in a group setting. Each method has strengths and limitations (see Exhibit 8.1). The choice partly depends on whether the intention is to gather quantitative or qualitative data. For example, a structured mail survey is best used to gather quantitative data while a semi-structured focus group is best for qualitative data.

One key factor is whether the questions are sensitive. People are far more likely to report honestly about illegal drug use, sexual activity, or cheating on taxes when

Exhibit 8.1 **Choices: Collecting Data From People**

Option	When to use	Characteristics	Strengths	Limitations
Structured interviews	Opinions and attitudes	Structured, fixed script	Personal	Time-consuming to conduct
	Complex questions	Closed-ended questions: check-a-box	Easy to analyze	Can be expensive
	When people cannot read	All interviewers ask exactly the same questions	Allows for clarification	Requires trained interviewers
			Forgiving of mistakes	Need to control for interviewer bias
				Not good for sensitive questions
Semistructured interviews	Stories and perceptions	Interview guide: a handful of broad, general questions	Personal	Time-consuming to conduct and analyze
	Complex topics	Open-ended questions	Rich data	No counts: limited to themes and patterns
	Complex processes		Allows for probes and clarifications	Expensive
	Exploratory research: when not sure what to ask		Can veer off script	Requires skilled interviewers
			Does not limit responses	Potential bias
			Long interviews	Not good for sensitive questions
			Easy to develop	
Focus groups	Stories and perceptions	Protocols guide the discussion	Personal	Can be time-consuming if many are done
	Complex topics	A handful of broad, general, open-ended questions	Rich data	Difficult to analyze
	Complex processes	Small groups	Quick to do	No counts: limited to themes and patterns
	Exploratory research: when not sure what to ask		Easy to develop	Costs: location, incentives, food
	When researcher wants to elicit different perspectives		Flexible and adaptable	Requires skilled facilitators
			Does not limit responses	Potential for bias has to be managed
			Allows for cross discussion	Not good for sensitive questions
			More cost-effective than interviews	
Mail survey	Opinions and attitudes	Structured	Reach large sample	Impersonal
	Many people	Easy to fill out	Relatively inexpensive	Time-consuming to create
	Dispersed locations	Should take less than thirty minutes (shorter is better)	Easy to analyze	Can take months to get all the responses back
	Moderately complex questions		Comparable data	Unforgiving of mistakes
	Sensitive questions		Can determine response rate	Response rate may be low

(continued)

(Exhibit 8.1 continued)

Option	When to use	Characteristics	Strengths	Limitations
E-mail or online survey	Opinions and attitudes	Structured	E-mail is inexpensive; web-based survey may have associated costs	Impersonal
	Many people Dispersed locations	Easy to fill out Should take less than twenty minutes	Easy to analyze Rapid completion	Time-consuming to create Includes only those with known e-mail addresses; list-serves can be very unreliable, with out-of-date addresses or which go unread
	Moderately complex questions Sensitive questions		Comparable data	Unforgiving of mistakes Computer access and literacy required Need to have privacy controls in place Difficult to determine response rate
Telephone survey	Opinions and attitudes	Structured	Quick	Useful when questions are simple
	Many people	Should take less than fifteen minutes	Easy to analyze	Not good for sensitive questions
	Dispersed locations		Use random digit dialing	May not include all segments of the population
	Simple questions		Rapid completion	Need to make many calls to reach quota
			Lower cost than interviews	

using a self-administered survey than in a telephone survey or in-person interview, in which they are likely to tell the interviewer what they think the interviewer wants to hear or what they believe they "should" say. This is called the social desirability response problem.

The literacy of the intended audience is another factor to be considered in choosing an approach. If the target population has limited reading ability, then a structured interview is better than a self-administered survey.

ENCOURAGING PARTICIPATION

Gathering data from people always depends on the willingness of people to participate. Researchers can do a few key things to encourage people to participate.

It is important to stress that the respondents' opinions matter and that the researcher truly wants their frank opinions. People are more likely to participate if they do not have to worry about any negative consequences from their answers. If researchers promise confidentiality, they must make sure that no individual's response can be identified.

Researchers should also provide full disclosure, explaining who is conducting the research, what its purpose is, how the information will be used, and how the subjects were selected. A contact person and phone number should be provided in case someone wishes to verify the legitimacy of the study. Researchers should give an accurate estimate of the amount of time needed to participate in the study; if it is short, people may be more willing to participate. They are also more likely to participate if it is easy; asking difficult questions, creating an overly complex and slow online survey, or asking for information that requires people to go through their personal or work files are all likely to cause them to say "no thanks."

The interview and focus group questions must be appropriate to the respondents and deal with familiar topics so they can offer an informed opinion. The best way to find out if the questions are on target is to pretest them with a few people from the intended audience. It is therefore essential to leave enough time to pretest the data collection methods before going live.

To encourage participation, researchers sometimes offer small incentives, such as a promise of a copy of the report, a discount shopping coupon, or an entry in a drawing for a prize. It is common for researchers to pay focus group participants for their time; sometimes transportation or childcare are provided or paid for as well.

IN-PERSON INTERVIEWS

Face-to-face interviews can be structured, semistructured, or a combination. The degree of structure generally reflects the intention to do qualitative or quantitative research. It also reflects the situation and the specific research question. It is difficult to capture all the possible variations of a fluid or complex situation in a structured format. For example, it is easier for researchers to interview various local officials responsible for handling a weather emergency about lessons learned from the last flood than to develop a questionnaire that covers the experiences of the entire community.

From a participant's perspective, it is far easier to talk to someone than write long, in-depth answers to open-ended questions in a written survey (see Application 8.1). With interesting questions on a topic that matters, people often are willing to be interviewed for an hour or more. It is unlikely they would spend that much time filling out a questionnaire, whether it is open-ended or closed-ended. However, the amount of time people are willing to spend in an interview can vary tremendously; high level officials, for example, may be only willing to spend 20 to 30 minutes; researchers need to adjust the interview guide so only the most essential questions are asked. It is important to provide the interviewees with an accurate estimate of the amount of time the interview will take when scheduling the meeting. The researcher should be prepared to stay within that limit unless the interviewee decides to go beyond the scheduled time.

In certain situations, structured, in-person interviews are needed. For example, in the United Way's 2002 Community Assessment, the research team wanted to make sure to include the viewpoints of the immigrant population. The team decided to work with groups that provided services to immigrants, such as the immigrant center and local churches. It was assumed that some immigrants would not be able to read the English questionnaire, so volunteers were available to translate the questions during an interview so the surveys could be completed.

Structured interviews might also be used when the questionnaire is very complex or long with many different sections that not everyone will answer. A researcher trained

Exhibit 8.2   **Guidelines for In-Person Interviews**

- Identify who you are, why you want to interview the respondents, how they were selected, and how the information will be used.
- It might help to send a letter explaining all this before calling to set up an appointment; you may want to include a copy of the interview guide as well.
- Keep the questions as simple, clear, and direct as possible.
- Respect the respondents' time and attention span. Let them know ahead of time about how long the interview will take and stick to that estimate; if the interview goes longer, ask if they want to continue and, if so, how much more time they can give. An in-person interview typically can take up to an hour, even two hours if it is really interesting to the interviewee.
- Obtain permission to use a tape recorder and give respondents permission to turn it off whenever they wish.

in the intricacies of the survey, who knows how to go through the maze of questions without getting lost, can most effectively elicit accurate responses.

Face-to-face semistructured interviews require clarity, good communication skills, and the ability to establish rapport. In some cases, it helps to send the interview guide (the exact open-ended questions that will be asked) in advance. Sending the questions in advance reassures the interviewees that the researchers are not trying to play "gotcha." Some basic guidelines for in-person interviews are presented in Exhibit 8.2.

It is also a good idea to offer the interviewees an opportunity to review the final report, especially if they will be quoted. Sometimes a quote is technically correct but the placement distorts the meaning, so it is not really accurate. Offering this option builds trust by giving interviewees a sense of some control over how they will be portrayed. They may be far more willing to be interviewed and to speak freely if they feel they will be treated fairly.

While the researchers should be prepared to adjust quotes that the interviewees feel were taken out of context, the conversations may be more challenging when an interviewee disagrees with the interpretation of the information or the conclusions. The researchers should be open to considering whether they have made a mistake. However, if they feel the interpretations are based on solid evidence and are essential to the integrity of the report, then the best they can do is explain their rationale. Chapter 16 will provide more guidance in handling reporting inconvenient truths in highly political situations.

FOCUS GROUPS

A focus group is a qualitative method to collect data from people in a small group setting (Krueger and Casey 2008). People are brought together to discuss specific topics of interest to the researchers. The group process tends to elicit more information than individual interviews because people engage in a dialogue with one another. The basic elements of the focus group methodology are described in Exhibit 8.3.

When invited to participate, focus group members are told who is doing the research, what its purpose is, and how they were selected. Focus groups should be held in a neutral setting but sometimes it is more important to choose a location that is easily accessible. To facilitate conversation, participants sit around a table or in

Application 8.1
Interview Guide
The First Generation of Women Governors

Although American women received the right to vote when the Nineteenth Amendment to the U.S. Constitution was ratified in 1920, it was not until 1974 that Ella Grasso of Connecticut became the first woman elected governor without having been preceded by her husband. In the twenty years that followed, only eight more women governors were elected. They are the first generation.

Little is known about this first generation of women governors because their stories have not been told. I began this research because I wanted to learn about their experiences, the factors that enabled them to seek a political life, and the challenges they faced and overcame might inspire other women to lead political lives. Four recent presidents—Jimmy Carter, Ronald Reagan, Bill Clinton, and George W. Bush—were all former governors, making governorships an important political steppingstone.

I am still working on this research project. The initial data collection of this research focused on reviewing news stories, as well as speeches, and official documents in the state archives. That material provided the context for interviews with the first generation governors who were still living. Appointments were made and the governors received a copy of the interview guide prior to the interview. The standard interview guide was adapted to reflect issues specific to each governor's term in office.

Standard Interview Guide

1. What led you to politics?
   a. Beliefs, volunteer activities, supports?
   b. What helped, what hindered?
2. What was it like to be the governor?
   a. Major activities, "typical" day, greatest joys, greatest challenges, greatest frustrations?
   b. Of all your accomplishments, which ones give you the greatest sense of satisfaction?
   c. What would you have done differently? Lessons learned?
   d. What difference, if any, did it make that you were the first woman governor of your state?
3. It takes a great deal of courage to step out into politics and even more to seek the state's highest position. What enabled you to seek a position that no woman had ever held?
   a. How did you find a way to take risks and not let fear stop you?
4. What advice or insights can you offer about how to handle the intense visibility and criticism inherent in political life while remaining open to the public?
5. What was your experience with the press? How did you deal with the images and caricatures, especially those you felt were distorted?
6. How did you maintain a positive sense of self in the face of criticism?
7. As you look toward the future, what are the significant changes in American culture that may make it easier or harder for the next generation of women in politics?
8. What advice can you offer the next generation of women in politics?
9. What do you feel is important for the next generation of women in politics to know about you and your experience that is not covered in these questions?

Exhibit 8.3 **Guidelines for Focus Groups**

- Use small groups (six to twelve people).
- Use diverse groups, with the exception that people of a different status (i.e., students and teachers, employees and supervisors) should not be in the same group.
- Provide monetary incentives.
- Provide transportation and child care arrangements.
- Provide comfortable, safe surroundings.
- Offer refreshments.
- Tape-record the sessions and, ideally, prepare a verbatim transcript.
- Make sure that a skilled moderator guides the process, keeps the group focused, and allows all group members to voice their views. A second person should take notes, manage the tape-recording, and handle any unexpected events.
- Begin with a very clear explanation of the purpose of the research, the rules of the process, what is a focus group, and why and how participants were selected.
- Follow a script (sometimes called a protocol) containing the questions asked. Few questions are asked: all are open-ended, moving from an easy, conversational opening question to the more serious questions and ending with a wrap-up question.
- Emphasize the key rule: "What is said in this room stays in this room."

chairs arranged in a circle. It is possible for a few observers to be present in the room while the focus group is conducted; they should be introduced at the beginning of the session.

A moderator facilitates the conversation while another person takes notes and handles anything that happens that might distract the moderator or disrupt the focus group. The moderator welcomes all participants, introduces the members of the research team present and their roles, discusses the purpose of the research, and provides an overview of the focus group process. All ground rules should be covered in the introduction. There also should be an opportunity for participants to ask questions about the process. The intent is to create a friendly, supportive environment so people feel comfortable. The introduction sets the stage and should not be rushed (see Application 8.2).

The moderator's instructions, known as the protocol, contain the set of prepared questions. The questions should be open-ended and phrased to indicate that all points of view are welcome. They should also be balanced; asking a question about what works should be balanced with a question that asks about what does not work. The set of questions is fluid and the moderator can improvise with probes or additional questions as warranted by the situation. The flow of conversation is not necessarily linear; participants may bring up new information or different perspectives at any time. Sometimes the participants will answer a question before it is even asked. The moderator then decides whether to ask it again according to the protocol, ask a follow-up question, or skip it altogether.

One key task of the moderator is to make sure everyone gets to speak. While not everyone will answer every question, it is important that everyone weigh in at some point. This means encouraging the shy people while managing those who would dominate the conversation if given the chance. I tend to intervene at various points, saying, "Let's hear from someone who has not spoken yet."

The moderator's main task is to manage the conversation so that it stays on target. The moderator needs to judge when to let the conversation roll and when to bring it back to the next question. While the tangents might be interesting, the goal is to work through the questions within the available time—the moderator needs to pay careful attention to the clock. Focus groups, like interviews, should start and stop on time. It helps to have the questions memorized so they appear conversational. One of the greatest challenges for the moderator is to be totally present and responsive to each participant while avoiding nodding and other body language that can send a signal that some answers are more preferred than others. It is a delicate balance.

What people say matters so it is important to capture it accurately. Ideally, each focus group is audiotaped and each tape is transcribed verbatim. If taping is not possible, a second note taker should be present because people talk faster than anyone can write. Sometimes taping is possible but getting the tapes transcribed is not feasible. In this case, the note takers should expand their original notes after listening to the tapes several times. Both moderators and note takers are often surprised to discover how much they missed during the actual focus group. Writing in-depth notes based on the tapes can easily take eight hours for each focus group. The notes should be written as soon as possible after the session because memory can provide some context. For example, the fact that someone intended a statement as a joke may not be clear from the tape-recording. The moderator and note taker should review each other's notes as one way to provide some quality control.

While focus groups are generally set up as a conversation around a table, some researchers find that using flip charts to capture information helpful in eliciting more information from the participants. I have seen it used most effectively for the last question of the focus group session—such as, what are the major messages we should take back to Congress, what would you tell the program director are the major actions that should be taken to improve the program, or what are the most important things you heard here today.

It is not unusual for several focus groups to be scheduled in a single day. This can be very fatiguing for the moderator because it is difficult to be truly present and listen for several hours. While there will not be time to do extensive notes between these sessions, it is essential to capture at least the major themes and anything that is noteworthy before going on to the next session. It is all too easy for the sessions to blend together.

There is no fixed rule about the number of focus groups to conduct for a single research project. The general rule is to do them until the same themes emerge or until no new information emerges. This usually happens after three to six focus groups. However, sometimes it is necessary to do more to meet other requirements, such as covering a variety of groups in an organization or neighborhoods in the city. We are back to the idea of face validity mentioned in the discussion of case studies in Chapter 6. If only three focus groups are held, the research might be suspected as biased. By conducting focus groups across all parts of the organization or community, the researchers can elicit results that appear to be more valid since many different groups were included.

In research projects where many focus groups will be conducted, it is not unusual

Application 8.2
Focus Groups With Social Service Clients

The director of social services wants to explore clients' perceptions of services and their experiences with the agency. In particular, she wants to understand the different experiences and explore possible reasons for those differences, as seen from the clients' perspectives. The researchers suggest conducting a few focus groups so the differences can become the topic of discussion. The director agrees.

The researchers select a small number of current or recent clients and invite them to a focus group session. They decide to provide transportation, childcare, and a small monetary incentive in order to increase participation. Although the agency is a familiar and accessible location, the researchers weigh these assets against the clients' comfort level: will they feel comfortable saying negative things at the agency? The researchers decide to hold the focus groups at the neighborhood library instead.

The researchers develop the set of questions (with probes) to use in each of the focus groups. The director and the management team review these. After discussion, the protocols look like this:

Welcome and Introduction

- Thank you for coming to this focus group. My name is Sally Smith and I will be facilitating our discussion today. John Jones will be taking notes.
- The director of the social service center is seeking to understand how clients view the services they received. She wants to know what you think about the services, what works well, and what needs improvement. Your views are very important, and everything that is said here is confidential. Only the overall views will be reported; no one will be identified with specific comments.
- Have any of you ever participated in a focus group? A focus group is a way for a small group of people to share their views, to surface differences in perspectives, and explore the reasons for those differences. There are no wrong answers. We expect that people will have different experiences and different opinions, and we would like to hear from everyone. I will ask a series of questions and will encourage each of you to speak. While not everyone has to answer every question, I would like everyone to contribute to the discussion at some point in our time together.
- We will be tape-recording this session since we think your views are valuable and there is no way to take notes fast enough to capture everything that is said. The focus group will last for one hour. We have some refreshments so please feel free to help yourself.

The Ground Rules

- What is said in this room stays in this room. No one's comments or information will be shared with anyone outside this room. Everyone should feel safe in speaking his or her mind.

- Only one person should speak at a time. Everyone will get a chance to speak but the tape recorder cannot handle several people speaking at once.
- Any questions before we get started?

Discussion

- First, let's do introductions. Please tell us your first name and the names and ages of your children.
- We would like to find out about your experiences with this agency. Let's begin with the positive experiences.
  - What are the most positive experiences you had with this agency? Probe: Most positive experience with the social workers?
  - What made those experiences so positive? Probe: What factors made those positive experiences happen?
  - How did those positive experiences benefit you?
- Thank you. Now let's look at the other side. What does not work so well for you?
  - What are some of the not-so-positive experiences you have had? Probe: Not-so-positive experiences with social workers?
  - What made those experiences not positive? How did those experiences affect you?
  - (If there are different viewpoints, set up the discussion: There appears to be differences in experiences. Why do you think people have different experiences?)
- What message would you give to the director about the services?
  - What should she not change?
  - What should she change?

Wrap-up

- Of all that you heard today, what do you think is the most important for us to tell the director?
- Other comments?
- Thank you so much for your willingness to share your views. Your views will assist the director in making the agency more helpful and effective in providing services.

to maintain a core set of questions at every focus group while alternating a set of optional questions to highlight narrower issues. It helps for the research team to debrief after every focus group so decisions can be made about adding, deleting, or changing the questions in subsequent focus groups. This adaptability is one of the strengths of focus groups.

Focus groups have several other advantages as well. They are generally faster, easier, and less costly than conducting separate in-person interviews with the same number of people while still enabling the researchers to get a first-hand sense of the intensity and passion people feel about specific issues. In addition, the dialogue allows different perspectives to surface and be discussed. Focus groups give the researcher flexibility to make changes in the process and questions as new information emerges. Lastly, they are fun to do!

However, focus groups have some downsides. For one thing, it takes time to set them up and it can be difficult to find a time and place that works for everyone. Making sure people show up can also be challenging. Solid organization around logistics and providing incentives are essential.

There is also a risk that the focus group conversations might not yield good information. The dialogue may fall flat if the moderator is unskilled or unable to create a sense of comfort and safety. There is also the possibility that the moderator or dominant members of the group might influence the dialogue. Another limitation is that because focus groups include relatively few people, the results are not considered representative of the larger community. Lastly, analysis is time-consuming and there is a high risk of bias creeping in as the researchers interpret the data.

However, despite the limitations and challenges, focus groups generally work very well and yield useful information as the primary data collection approach. They are also helpful in the planning phase to help the researchers figure out the issues and in the reporting phase where they can be used to help make sense of the survey findings. The insights and examples drawn from a focus group can be used in the final report to provide more information to complement survey results.

CONCLUSION

When the research question is about people's opinions, perceptions, and experiences, then the researchers have to gather the data from people.

Data can be gathered in a highly structured way or in a semistructured way. While interviews can be structured using a check-a-box format, as in the National Longitudinal Survey of Youth, interviews are more often guided by a series of open-ended questions. This format allows researchers greater freedom to explore statements in greater detail by asking additional questions that are not on the interview guide.

Focus groups have a few advantages over interviews. It takes less time to conduct a focus group of ten people than it does to conduct ten individual interviews. More importantly, focus groups provide for cross-dialogue that can move the discussion to a deeper level as people explore their different experiences and opinions.

Both interviews and focus groups provide rich understandings that are not possible with structured surveys. They can be used with other data collection methods as well as in the planning and reporting phases of survey research; focus groups can help researchers develop a questionnaire or make sense of survey results. Although the amount of data generated can feel overwhelming, these are energizing data collection approaches.

EXERCISES

1. You have been asked to find information about the public leaders in your community so that others may follow in their footsteps.
   a. Who are some likely people you would interview?
   b. Develop a short set of open-ended question that you would want to ask.
2. The city is concerned about the growing numbers of homeless people and the capacity of the nonprofit service providers, faith communities, and service organizations to meet the needs as the economy gets worse. City officials would like to conduct at least three focus groups with the key players most involved in this issue. What five questions would you suggest for the focus group sessions?

9 Data Collection III
Surveys

OVERVIEW

A March 2007 Pew Research Center poll reported that Jon Stewart of *The Daily Show* tied with Tom Brokaw, Brian Williams, and Dan Rather as the "most admired journalist." I am not sure what it means when a comedian is seen as one of America's most admired journalists, but other polling data might give public administrators pause. By the end of 2008, 72 percent of Americans reported being dissatisfied with the way things are going in this country, as compared to 35 percent in 2001. This tracks with the low approval rating for both the president and Congress; in 2008, President George W. Bush had an approval rating of less than 30 percent while Congress had a mere 11 percent approval rating (Pew Research Center 2008).

Polls provide a window into the opinions and perspectives of citizens. Do citizens know as much as—or more than—the officials they elected? Should elected officials' votes reflect the views of the citizens? This question takes us into the debate about whether polling data should influence public policy. From a philosophical perspective, the debate centers on the degree of representative or direct democracy the United States should have. From a research perspective, this issue is simply whether polling data are credible.

This last chapter in the data collection section focuses on surveys. Researchers who opt to administer a survey face two challenges. One is making sure a high percentage of the people participate. The second challenge is developing closed-ended questions that work. Writing these is harder than it might seem at first, so this chapter provides a fair amount of detail about how to write questionnaire questions. Even though managers themselves are not likely to develop surveys, they are very likely to use survey results, so it helps to know what good survey questions should look like.

BASIC METHODS

Researchers have some degree of choice about how to administer a survey. While a telephone survey might also be considered an interview because the researchers administer the survey, I have included it here with the other survey approaches that are typically self-administered.

Self-administered surveys can be structured, semistructured, or a combination. Data can be gathered by phone, Internet, mail, or in person (Dillman et al. 2008). All these methods typically consist almost entirely of closed-ended questions because it is much easier for participants to check a box than write answers. From a researcher's perspective, the check-a-box format means less chance of losing data due to indecipherable handwriting or unique spelling. It also makes data analysis easier because the data is easily coded to create an electronic database.

Researchers typically include one or two open-ended questions. These open-ended questions enable respondents to express their views more fully and may provide insightful information, including things that were not asked in the survey. These questions also may provide quotable quotes that might be used in the report to highlight the key findings. Limiting the number of open-ended questions minimizes the respondent's burden to complete the survey. Since researchers rely on people's goodwill, it pays to be mindful that people will not complete the survey if it takes too long or is too much work.

Self-administered questionnaires should be short, requiring no more than thirty minutes to complete. Of all the methods used to gather data from people, self-administered questionnaires are the most likely to elicit honest responses to sensitive questions. If respondents have to give their answer directly to another person, they may opt to say what they think is the right thing to say rather than what is true for them.

Which is the best method to administer surveys? While not definitive, one group of researchers did a small study comparing three methods of gathering data from college students about tobacco use: a postal mail survey, a web-based survey, and an in-class survey (James et al. 2005). The in-class survey had the highest response rate (66 percent). The mail survey had a 23 percent response rate, and the web-based survey had 10 percent. It is hardly surprising that the method involving a captive audience had the highest response rate. The lesson here is that if you want a high response rate, about tobacco use among college students, gaining access to them through college classes makes sense. It may work in other situations where people are gathered together.

RESPONSE RATES

Whether surveys are distributed to everyone or a random sample (to be discussed in Chapter 10), the proportion completing the survey matters. This is called the response rate. When only a small proportion of those who are asked to complete a survey actually do, the low response rate creates a volunteer sample. Chapter 5 discussed the problem of having people volunteer to participate in the stress reduction program. It is the same problem here: the volunteers might be different from the population as a whole and that difference alters the results in some way.

For example, suppose an organization conducts an employee attitude survey by e-mailing questionnaires to all 1,000 employees but just 200 actually complete the survey. This is a 20 percent response rate. If the most dissatisfied employees were motivated to answer the survey while those who were satisfied did not, the results will show a higher percentage of dissatisfied employees than would have been the case if everyone had responded. It would be a mistake to make decisions based on these results from a low response rate without getting some verification of how representative the respondents were of the larger population.

What is a good response rate? There is no agreed on absolute benchmark in social science, other than that higher is better than lower. When I worked at the U.S. Government Accountability Office (GAO), the aim was to get at least a 60 percent response rate. At this level, the researchers are reasonably certain that they have a fairly accurate representation of all who were asked to participate. However, 60 percent is difficult to obtain; it is not unusual for a mail survey to achieve only a 20 percent or 30 percent response rate.

While the results from a survey with a low response rate may still be interesting and/or important, researchers must limit the discussion of the results only to those who responded, resisting the temptation to conclude that these results represent anyone other than those who actually participated. However, if the results track with other similar surveys, it makes the results more believable. If the demographics of those who answered generally match those of the larger population, that also adds to the credibility of the results.

Whatever the response rate, the researchers should report the number of people (or units, such as organizations) surveyed, the number who responded, and the response rate. The sophisticated reader will then be in a position to decide how much credibility to give the reported results and any conclusions.

TELEPHONE SURVEYS

In a sense, telephone surveys are like interviews because the researcher asks the questions, so it is not self-administered. However, phone surveys are generally considered a survey method. Some "how-to" guidelines are presented in Exhibit 9.1.

Telephone surveys should be narrowly focused, simple and short—the shorter, the better. It is wise to make them less than fifteen minutes to complete. Telephone surveys, therefore, are not a good approach to explore complex topics. They are useful for simple topics, like voting preferences, which is one reason why pollsters use them. Telephone surveys typically have mostly structured questions and limited opportunities for open-ended comments. Answers to open-ended questions take more time and are hard to capture because people talk faster than researchers write.

Until recently, telephone surveys were touted as an approach with a high response rate. However, telephone surveys have also become a way for organizations to solicit donations and a marketing ploy for some businesses. It now takes many phone calls to reach the necessary number of respondents. Telephone surveys rarely report the total number of calls made or response rates.

A few strategies can boost participation. In a small community, publicity announcing the telephone survey may increase participation (see Application 9.1). It may also help to use a familiar, reputable organizational name so people know that the telephone interviewers are not trying to sell something. In some situations, it might be possible

Exhibit 9.1   **Guidelines for Telephone Surveys**

- Keep the survey as simple as possible.
- Identify who you are, why you want to talk to the respondents, how they were selected, and how the information will be used.
- Put important questions up front because respondents may hang up before the end of the call.
- Time how long the survey takes during the pre-tests. Aim for not more than fifteen minutes.
- Whatever the amount of time, be sure to tell participants what to expect and stick to it.
- Be mindful that many words sound the same but have different meanings: check how the questions sound when read.
- Develop guidelines and a script for the telephone interviewers.
- Provide training for the team.
- Think about when to call: calling homes during the day is likely to reach a different demographic than calling in the evening.
- Have interviewers keep a careful record of call attempts; decide how many callbacks to use before giving up on that number.

to send a letter to the participants ahead of time to describe the purpose of the survey and give a rough time frame when someone will be calling. For example, I received a letter from the U.S. Department of Agriculture saying I had been randomly selected to participate in a survey. As a result, I did not hang up when the researcher called because I knew he was not trying to sell me something.

When planning to conduct telephone surveys with organizational or political officials, it helps to call ahead of time and schedule an appointment for the phone survey.

Researchers who frequently conduct telephone surveys use Computer Assisted Telephone Interviews (CATI), which is software that allows the interviewer to enter responses directly into the computer file, thus eliminating transferring information from paper. The computer can be programmed to automatically check for errors as data are entered so they can be corrected on the spot.

While skip questions can be used in any survey method, the computer makes it easy to handle skip questions. For instance, if the researchers want to know if people have been satisfied with their dealings with city hall, it first is necessary to ask something like: "Have you called city hall in the past six months?" Those who answer "yes" can then be asked a series of questions about the nature of the call, the quickness of city hall's response, and their level of satisfaction with the resolution. The computer will automatically skip those who answer "no" to the next general question. Maybe the next general question would be whether respondents have used the city library in the past six months. Those answering "yes" would then be asked several specific questions about services and satisfaction, while those answering "no" would skip to the next question.

Typically, random digit dialing is used in telephone surveys to obtain a random sample of the population. This is what polling firms use. When the geographic area of interest matches the area codes, random digits are generated for the calling list and even those with unlisted phones have an equal chance of being included. When the area codes do not match the geographic area of interest, then the researchers have to screen the respondents. For example, suppose the researchers are only interested in the views of people who pay city taxes but the area code includes people who live outside the city limits. The researchers would begin the telephone survey by asking whether the respondent lives within the city limits or not. Only those within the city limits would continue with the telephone survey.

As a side note, there is increasing concern about the impact of cell phone users on the reliability of telephone surveys (Thee 2007). One problem is that people are less likely to agree to participate in a survey because cell phone users pay for incoming calls. It is also harder for the researchers to call cell phones; unlike landlines, auto dialing is not allowed. As a result, if there are specific demographics associated with cell phone users, these people will be systematically excluded. However, it is uncertain how cell phones impact surveys, especially the ubiquitous political polls. The fact that cell phones are part of modern reality is noted in the description of a recent poll by the Pew Forum on Religion and Public Life: "The survey was conducted by telephone—both landline phones and cell phones—from July 31–August 9 among a national sample of 2,905 adults" (2008b).

MAIL SURVEYS

Questionnaires sent in the mail include a cover letter, the questionnaire, and a stamped self-addressed envelope for returning the questionnaire. Because the questionnaires typically have a unique identifier matched to a specific participant, it is easy to target the nonresponders with follow-up postcards and/or a second questionnaire package in an effort to increase the response rate. Exhibit 9.2 presents guidelines for mail surveys that should increase the response rate.

If a questionnaire is asking very sensitive questions, the researchers may want to go beyond confidentiality; they may want to use an anonymous approach. For example, in GAO's study on discrimination related to the Immigration and Reform Control Act of 1987, the questionnaire asked businesses if that law caused them to discriminate against people who looked or sounded foreign. Since such discrimination is illegal, the research team opted for an anonymous mailing approach. There were no unique identifiers on the questionnaires. Instead, the packet included a stamped postcard addressed to GAO with the identifier on the back. Participants were asked to send the postcard back separately from the questionnaire, which was to be sent back in the stamped self-addressed envelope. While it was possible for people to just send back the postcard without completing the questionnaire so they would be left alone, the number of postcards and returned questionnaires was about the same. This strategy allowed GAO to do the necessary follow-up to non-responders to obtain a high response rate while guaranteeing anonymity.

CYBER-RESEARCH: E-MAIL AND WEB-BASED SURVEYS

The use of e-mail and web-based surveys has increased over the past decade. Like snail-mail surveys, they tend to be closed-ended, so the questions need to be clear and the intended audience needs to be literate. In addition, the intended audience must have access to the Internet.

E-mail surveys are sent directly to the recipients, either as part of the e-mail itself or as an attachment. Completed surveys can be returned via e-mail. E-mail can also

Application 9.1
United Way Telephone Survey

In 2002 the decision was made by the Community Partnership to conduct a telephone survey of residents of Thurston County, Washington, for United Way's Community Assessment. A polling organization was contracted to provide 3,000 random phone numbers within the Thurston County area code. At the time, it seemed ridiculous to me that it would take so many phone numbers to get 400 respondents, even allowing for nonworking numbers. Students from the local Master of Public Administration program agreed to make the calls and were trained. Several organizations allowed them to use office phones in the evenings and weekends.

Even though the local paper announced the telephone survey and encouraged residents to take part in this community assessment, it was a challenge to get people to participate. Many people screen their calls, but a message was left in hopes that they might be willing to participate when the researcher called back. Of those who did answer the phone, many hung up before the telephone interviewers could get through the introduction. The 400 participants were obtained within four weeks of calling, using up most of the 3,000 random numbers in a very labor-intensive effort. The responses were entered onto forms that were electronically scanned into a database.

All interviewers were given a script to use, including this introduction:

Good evening (afternoon/morning).

My name is _____ and I am volunteering to conduct a short telephone survey that will gather information to help shape the future of Thurston County. This survey to gather information is being sponsored by the United Way along with the Community Partnership of Thurston County. This survey was reported in *The Olympian*—maybe you heard about it?

Your opinions about the quality of life in Thurston County are important—you are one of only a few hundred people who are being called. Your phone number was randomly selected and your views are confidential. Your views will be combined with the views of the other people who participate in this survey and a report will be prepared that will help service providers and local government shape future decisions.

We would like your honest opinions and views—there are no right or wrong answers. We would greatly appreciate your taking about fifteen minutes to answer the questions on our survey.

Would you be willing to participate in our survey?

Exhibit 9.2   **Guidelines to Increase Response Rates for Mail Surveys**

- Make the survey look professional: printed, maybe in booklet form or on colored paper.
- It should be error-free.
- Include the name of a person respondents can call if they have questions.
- Use the cover letter to induce people to participate by identifying who is conducting the research, what its purpose is, and why their participation is important.
- Make it personal. Personally address the letter and envelope. Sign the letter in blue ink.
- Assure respondents confidentiality and mean it.
- Never, ever ask people to identify themselves on a survey. Do not ask for names, identifying Social Security numbers, or other identification numbers on the survey. Include a 3 x 5 card or postcard for respondents to provide contact information if they want a copy of the final report or want to participate in follow-up interviews or focus groups.
- Always provide a self-addressed, stamped envelope.
- Be prepared to do at least one follow-up; two or three are not unusual. To save money, a postcard reminder could be sent rather than duplicate surveys to everyone. Allow about two weeks between follow-ups.

---

be used to invite people to participate in a web-based survey. Web-based surveys can also be posted on a website; this work well when the intention is to survey organizations with a subscriber membership.

For example, *The Scientist*, a magazine of the life sciences, posted a web-based survey in 2007 to find out what its readers thought were the best places to work. E-mail invitations were sent to readers of *The Scientist* as well as to those registered for the magazine's online version, TheScientist.com. The magazine advertised the survey on its website and other electronic promotions. The survey was accessible for two months and received 2,072 usable responses.

Having stuffed and licked envelopes for more surveys than I care to recall, the ease of using e-mail and websites is a definite benefit of cybersurveys. They can also be cheaper than surveys on paper, although a lot depends on the host site. One downside is that this e-mail may be treated as spam.

The major downside is that e-mail surveys require cyberspace addresses, which limits this method to people with known e-mail addresses, such as people who are part of work, social, professional, or volunteer organizations or listservs. It should be noted that list-serves might not be all that accurate; the e-mail addresses might be incorrect or be an address that is rarely read by the recipient.

Cybersurveys do not meet the definition of "random sample" used in social science (discussed in Chapter 10), although whether it is close enough to random is a hot debate among statisticians and social scientists.

Another negative is that web-based surveys can be distorted when people get their friends to take the survey. By having people who share the same views "vote" for a particular candidate, they can easily warp online polls conducted by newspapers and TV stations. For example, in 2007 a cable news station reported that 87 percent of the people taking its online survey wanted President Bush impeached. Was this an accurate reflection of "we the people"? No. The cable news station had an audience with a particular demographic and some people sent e-mails to their friends encouraging them to vote for impeachment. These polls are purely for entertainment and have no research credibility. Serious polls do not operate like *American Idol*.

DEVELOPING CLOSED-ENDED QUESTIONS

While managers generally do not conduct research themselves, they may either ask staff or hire consultants to develop a questionnaire. Managers and staff need to be aware that writing closed-ended questions is harder than it appears—it is as much an art as a science—and takes more than a week. In my experience, it can take several months if the survey deals with complex topics. There are many possible questions and many shades of meaning based on wording choice. The English language can be problematic because the same words can mean different things.

There is no way to cover here every detail that skilled survey designers need to know, but there are some basics that will help researchers and managers requesting a survey avoid some common mistakes. A few tips based on my experience are presented in Exhibit 9.3.

It is essential that the questions be understandable to respondents because self-administered questionnaires provide no way for participants to ask for clarification. If people do not understand a question or can interpret it in more than one way, they essentially will be responding to different questions. Vague, poorly worded questions create the ultimate elastic measuring stick. Even worse, they may generate so much frustration that people throw the survey away.

Biased questions that clearly suggest the right answer are to be avoided. For example, "Don't you think it is wrong to vote against a woman running for political office solely because she is a woman?" is a biased question. Another one I recently received in a mail survey asked, "Don't you think it is a bad idea to have government bureaucrats administer health insurance?" Double-barreled questions that embed two questions in one are also ineffective. "How satisfied or dissatisfied are you with the number of classes, teams, etc. offered by the Parks Department?" is an example of a double-barreled question. Maybe some people are satisfied with the number of teams but not the number of classes. How can they answer this question?

Since poorly constructed questions cannot be saved in analysis, prevention is the best strategy. Managers should make sure that the staff or consultants leave plenty of time to have survey reviewed and pretested. If using self-administered surveys, have the pretesters actually complete the survey rather than just read it over. I do not understand why the feedback is so much more helpful when pretesters actually fill out the questionnaires, but it is. When a questionnaire is just reviewed, typos are found but whether a question is actually answerable is missed. The pretesters should consider these key points:

- Is each question clear?
- Are any odd or unfamiliar words or phrases used?
- Is there a better way to ask each question?
- What questions did the pretesters expect to see but did not?

USING ONE-WAY AND TWO-WAY INTENSITY SCALES

The hallmark of a closed-ended question is its check-a-box format. Sometimes it takes the form of a list. For example, a question might list ten city services and ask people

---

Exhibit 9.3   **Writing Questionnaires**

- *Use an existing questionnaire as a guide*: modify as needed to fit the situation. It is easier to modify than it is to create from scratch.
- *Use a logical order*: ask general questions first, then the specific questions, and then demographic questions. The last question should be an open-ended question, such as "Any comments or anything else you want to say?"
- *Keep it short*: use as few questions as possible. It is sometimes helpful to identify which questions are essential, which ones are nice to include if there is room, and which ones are really not needed.
- *Plan the analysis*: this helps eliminate unnecessary questions and is also a check to make sure everything needed has been asked.
- *Use simple, clear language*: keep it appropriate for the respondents and avoid jargon.
- *Make the questionnaire easy to complete*: provide boxes that respondents can check and ask for information they can recall without having to look it up.
- *Provide clear instructions*: for example, "Check only one," "Check all that apply," "If yes, then go to question 5."
- *Avoid double-barreled questions*: ask only one question in each question.
- *Signal acceptance*: write questions so that all people feel their responses are acceptable. Use the lead-ins to show a range of responses: "To what extent, if at all . . ." or "How important or unimportant are . . ."
- *Avoid "yes" or "no" responses for opinion questions*: when asking a factual question, like "Are you pregnant?" a yes-or-no response set makes sense. However, when asking for an opinion about something, there are shades of intensity that a yes-or-no response set misses.
- *Use five-point or seven-point scales rather than a simple yes or no response set*: these provide a way to gauge the intensity of the respondents' feelings.
- *Avoid memory decay*: ask questions about the current situation because accurate recall fades with time; embed a time limit into the question. For example: "How frequently have you seen a doctor in the past three months?"
- *Use appropriate response categories that are mutually exclusive*: for example, if asking age groups, use categories such as 20–30, 31–40, 41–50, 51+, so each respondent can check only one category. If the categories are set up like this—20–30, 30–40, 40–50, 50+—some people will fit into more than one category.
- *Use accurate skip questions*: make sure all skip questions lead people to exactly where they are supposed to go.
- *Avoid absolutes*: soften the end of the scales when asking about how frequently people do things. Use "Always or almost always" at one end of the scale and "Never or almost never" at the other end of the scale.
- *Leave exits*: these include "No basis to judge" and "No opinion" categories. If respondents do not have an exit, they may make meaningless responses in the scale.
- *Ask only the demographics that are absolutely necessary*: be sensitive that some people can be identified by demographics; if they do not feel safe, they may not answer honestly.
- *Review the questions*: have your draft questions reviewed by experts and the final version reviewed by a "cold reader."
- *Pretest the questionnaire*: have a typical respondent answer the questionnaire rather than just read it. Then go back through each question to get the respondent's opinion about what worked and what did not. Ask for suggestions about questions and wording. Build in the time and do as many rounds as are needed.

---

to indicate which ones they used in the past six months. This makes sense when it is a factual question and the intention is just to obtain counts.

When asking people their opinions, it is best to use intensity scales that capture a range of possible feelings. These scales come in two types. The first type is a one-way scale that moves along a single dimension from least to most. The second type is a two-way scale, which has an equal number of positive and negative responses on either side of a neutral middle. The classic format is the Likert scale, developed

Exhibit 9.4 **Example of a Five-Point Likert Scale Matrix**

Do you agree or disagree with the following statements about the course you just completed:	Strongly agree	Agree	Neither agree nor disagree	Disagree	Strongly disagree	No opinion
a. There were sufficient opportunities to participate in class discussion.	1	2	3	4	5	N/O
b. The course provided engaging learning experiences.	1	2	3	4	5	N/O
c. The course material is useful in the work setting.	1	2	3	4	5	N/O
d. The course material was current.	1	2	3	4	5	N/O

Exhibit 9.5 **Example of a Seven-Point Scale**

Strongly agree	Moderately agree	Slightly agree	Neither agree nor disagree	Slightly disagree	Moderately disagree	Strongly disagree	No opinion
1	2	3	4	5	6	7	N/O

by Rensis Likert, which asks people how strongly they agree or disagree with a particular statement. In the jargon, this type of scale is called a five-point scale, because there are five options, excluding the "No opinion" box. This format lends itself to asking a series of questions on a specific topic embedded in a matrix such as the one shown in Exhibit 9.4.

Sometimes researchers add more descriptors to create a seven-point scale, as shown in Exhibit 9.5. It is important to maintain an order to the viewpoints, with three positive and three negative responses on either side of a neutral middle.

Including a "No opinion" option in addition to the uneven scale provides an "exit," an appropriate box to check for people who have no opinion because the question does not apply to them. For example, a question asking about the usefulness of course material in the workplace is unanswerable for MPA students who have no significant work experience. They need an exit, such as "No opinion," "No basis to judge," or "Don't know."

I recommend using a five-point or seven-point scale (not counting the exit category) because some people do not like to admit that they "don't know" and will look for a middle category. I have actually had people tell me during pretests that they did not have an opinion but then said, "I'll give it a three." That was the middle category of the five-point scale, neither agree nor disagree. Analyzing middle categories and exits is discussed in Chapter 12.

Questions can also be asked using a more specific descriptor. For example, if what the researchers really want to know is how satisfied or dissatisfied students are, they need to ask, as shown in Exhibit 9.6.

Note that in these matrix formats, the lead-in question is framed in terms of the scale ("agree-disagree" or "satisfaction-dissatisfaction"). All the subquestions should make sense given the lead question and the scale used. The lead-in question always provides

120

CHAPTER 9

Exhibit 9.6 **Example of Satisfied-Dissatisfied Scale Matrix: Student Satisfaction**

Considering all the courses you have taken to date, how satisfied or dissatisfied are you with each of the following?

	Very satisfied	Generally satisfied	Neither satisfied nor dissatisfied	Generally dissatisfied	Very dissatisfied	No opinion
a. Number of opportunities to participate in class discussion	1	2	3	4	5	N/O
b. Extent to which you are learning new information	1	2	3	4	5	N/O
c. Extent to which you are learning useful information	1	2	3	4	5	N/O
d. The currency of course materials	1	2	3	4	5	N/O

the range of acceptable answers. Asking "How satisfied or dissatisfied" sends a signal to the respondents that it is acceptable to the answer on either side of the scale. If the wording were "How dissatisfied are you?" it would send a signal that the respondents are expected to be dissatisfied. This is an example of a biased question.

There are other two-way intensity scales besides "agree-disagree." A few examples are shown in Exhibit 9.7. You will note that there is an implied order, going from very positive to very negative, with a neutral middle.

It is also possible to use one-way scales—that is, scales that gradually measure a single characteristic. Grades are a good example. The English descriptors, however, might differ (see Exhibit 9.8). For example, the English descriptors that I use for each grade are more positive than what other instructors may use. Descriptors for scaled items are more like metaphors than mathematics. They provide a relative narrative sense of things. What is important to note is that the middle category is not neutral; it contains information.

Survey researchers want to get as much distribution across the scale as possible, so the end points should invite people to choose those categories rather than be so specific that only a very few will choose them. Having very few people answering on the extreme ends of the scale defeats the purpose of having a scale in the first place.

Exhibit 9.7 **Examples of Two-Way Scales Used With Closed-Ended Questions**

Type of scale	Scale categories					Exit
Effectiveness scale	Very effective	Generally effective	Neither effective nor ineffective	Generally ineffective	Very ineffective	No opinion
Helpfulness scale	Very helpful	Somewhat helpful	Neither helpful nor unhelpful	Somewhat unhelpful	Very unhelpful	No opinion
Yes/no scale	Definitely yes	Probably yes	Unsure	Probably no	Definitely no	No opinion
Likelihood scale	Very likely	Somewhat likely	As likely as unlikely	Somewhat unlikely	Very unlikely	No opinion

Exhibit 9.8 **Letter Grades and Descriptors**

My descriptors	Other descriptors
A = Excellent	A = Outstanding
B = Very good	B = Good
C = Good	C = Average
D = Minimally acceptable	D = Poor
F = Failing	F = Failing

For example, I almost never watch TV but it would not be true to say that I never do. If the last category on a scale said "Never," I would choose "Occasionally" as the better descriptor given the options even though it is not really accurate. However, if the last category were "Never or Almost Never," I would choose that as the most accurate descriptor. Do not use absolutes such as "always" or "never" as the anchors to intensity scales; they will work better if they are softened to "always or almost always" at one end and "never or almost never" at the other end. Three common one-way scales are presented in Exhibit 9.9.

RANKING QUESTIONS

Ranking questions appear to be a good choice for surveys, but looks are deceiving. I do not recommend using ranking questions because (1) they are difficult for people to answer when there is not much difference between items, (2) they become extremely annoying if the list is too long, and (3) they are a nightmare to analyze.

Let us examine how a question about the perceived usefulness of various MPA courses could be answered using a ranking structure versus an intensity scale. The question asks students to rank five courses in terms of their usefulness in preparing the respondents for their first job after graduation. They are to rank the most useful course as 1, the least useful as 5, and the rest in numerical order, with no ties allowed. Two students rank the five MPA courses in exactly the same way:

A. <u>5</u>   Public Management Statistics
B. <u>1</u>   Human Resources Management
C. <u>3</u>   Introduction to Public Administration
D. <u>2</u>   Organizational Theories and Behavior
E. <u>4</u>   Public Budgeting

Exhibit 9.9 **Three Common One-Way Scales**

Type of scale	Scale categories					Exit
Extent scale	Very great extent	Great extent	Moderate extent	Some extent	Little or no extent	No opinion
Frequency scale	Always or almost always	Mostly	About half the time	Occasionally	Never or almost never	No opinion
Goldilocks scales	Much more	Somewhat more	Just about right	Somewhat less	Much less	No opinion

Exhibit 9.10   **Comparing Intensity Scales Ratings**

Respondent A's ranking of the usefulness of each course:

Courses	Very great extent	Great extent	Moderate extent	Some extent	Little or no extent
a. Public Management Statistics			X		
b. Human Resources Management	X				
c. Introduction to Public Administration		X			
d. Organizational Theory and Behavior	X				
e. Public Budgeting			X		

Respondent B's ranking of the usefulness of each course:

Courses	Very great extent	Great extent	Moderate extent	Some extent	Little or no extent
a. Public Management Statistics					X
b. Human Resources Management		X			
c. Introduction to Public Administration				X	
d. Organizational Theory and Behavior				X	
e. Public Budgeting					X

In this ranking, the human resources course was the most useful and the public management statistics course the least (no surprise there). But what might the results look like using intensity scales? Exhibit 9.10 shows how the answers might have looked. While the two students' rankings are exactly the same, their ratings on the intensity scale are quite different. Respondent A had two courses that she rated highly but she was forced to rank them. Her second choice, however, was still highly valued. Respondent B also ranked Organizational Theory and Behavior as his second choice in the ranking format but did not value it as highly as Respondent A. The takeaway lesson is that ranking questions can be misleading.

CONCLUSION

Public administrators need to maintain a steady stream of feedback in order to find out what matters to citizens, clients, customers, and employees. Ensuring the quality of research results when collecting data from people is doable but time-consuming. Gathering data from people takes time and writing good survey questions is harder than it appears at first.

Surveys provide a way to gather data from a large number of people in a relatively cost-effective way. Surveys by phone, mail, or cyberspace have characteristics that make them more appropriate in some situations than others. All typically use closed-ended questions, which must be simple, clear, and unambiguous. They take time to develop but are easier to analyze than data gathered using open-ended questions. Keep in mind that no matter which approach is used, collecting data directly from people is always about collecting their perceptions, including their perceptions about how they behave.

When asking people about their opinions, it makes sense to ask closed-ended questions that use an intensity scale to capture the range of feelings. One-way or two-way intensity scales are commonly used. It also makes sense to allow people to say they have no opinion. Ranking questions should be replaced with intensity scales. One or two open-ended questions might capture additional information that was not asked about and will provide respondents with an opportunity to elaborate on their answers.

The exact questions should be presented in the report. This can be done in a chart or table that graphically shows the results. In a long report, the results can be overlaid onto the questionnaire and presented in an appendix. Full disclosure allows readers to see the exact wording.

It is essential that the plan for the data collection and the actual questions be tested before going live. However, it is not unusual for planning to take longer than expected and pretesting is usually what gets cut. It is therefore important to set realistic schedules so there is time to pretest surveys. Mistakes in survey research are often unrecoverable and pretests help avoid many errors.

EXERCISES

1. Critique these survey questions. The problem could be with the question, the responses, or both. Identify what is wrong and fix it.

   a. Do you read books?
      1. ___ Yes   2. ___ No

   b. To what extent do you agree that children should be exposed to conflicting and different religious beliefs? (check only one)
      ___ Strongly agree
      ___ Somewhat agree
      ___ Agree
      ___ Disagree
      ___ Strongly disagree

   c. Given that women are very greatly underrepresented in elected office, would you vote for a woman to correct this unfair imbalance?
      1. ___ Yes   2. ___ No

   d. Social scientists are highly trained in conducting research. In general, to what extent do you think research results are important and useful and should dictate public policy?
      ___ A very great extent
      ___ A great extent
      ___ Some extent
      ___ Little extent
      ___ Absolutely no extent

e. Overall, how helpful are these exercises? (mark along the scale)

Very helpful   Not useful at all
(1)   (5)   (10)

_____

f. Do you think the economy is much better under the current administration?
   ___ Much stronger
   ___ About the same
   ___ Much weaker

g. To what extent, if at all, do you feel empowered in the current management paradigm?
   ___ Very great extent
   ___ Great extent
   ___ Moderate extent
   ___ Some extent
   ___ Little or no extent
   ___ No opinion

h. What is your income? _____

i. How old are you?
   ___ less than 20
   ___ 20–40
   ___ 40–50
   ___ over 50

2. In the following scenarios, which data collection option—interviews, mail surveys, telephone surveys, Internet surveys, focus groups, available data, or observation—would be best given the situation? Explain your choice.
   a. You want to gather information about how the five most senior program officials see the strengths and weaknesses of their program.
   b. You want to find out what the residents of the largest city in the county think are the major social and economic problems that need attention.
   c. You want to find out what high school students see as the greatest supports and barriers to prevent pregnancy and sexually transmitted diseases among teens.
   e. You want to find out if there is less flooding after major rainstorms in the areas surrounding the new drainage dams.
   f. You want to find out what knowledge, skills, and abilities businesses are looking for when they hire college graduates.
   g. You want to find out what current MPA students in an online program think are the major challenges facing public administrators in the coming decade.

3. Go to Portland's Citizen Survey posted on the city auditor's website: www. portlandonline.com/auditor/auditservices/residentsurvey2007/.
   a. View the survey form. In what ways does this survey follow the guidelines presented in this chapter? In what ways is it different? How would you rate the ease of completion on a scale from 1 (hardest) to 10 (easiest)? Explain your judgment. What improvements would you suggest and how will they help?
   b. Critique the methodology. What worked and what did not? Explain.

4. You have been asked to develop a closed-ended survey to find out what the directors of food banks and homeless shelters in your state have observed in the last three months of the economic downturn, what the greatest challenges they face as service providers are, and what could be done to help them. Develop a questionnaire of ten closed-ended questions and one open-ended question.

10 Sampling Demystified

OVERVIEW

Planning research is an intricate dance between choosing the research questions, identifying the likely measures, and developing a sampling strategy that fits with the data collection. While each of the steps gets its own chapter, the actual planning process is not linear. Indeed, it can be both messy and frustrating because it goes round and round for a while. This is normal. It takes time to get all the pieces aligned.

As the researchers consider the likely measures and data collection strategies, they also wrestle with how much data to collect. Is it is possible review every file, observe every street, or talk to every person in their class? Collecting data from the whole population makes it possible to accurately report the qualifications of every teacher in the school system, the views of all the students in the class, or the quality of all the roads in the city. However, collecting data from every file, street, or person often requires too much time and money. Instead, researchers opt to gather the data from a subset of the entire population—that is, they work with a sample.

This chapter explains sampling jargon, types of samples, and how to determine the right sample size. Confidence levels and confidence intervals are presented along with a discussion of nonsampling errors. The takeaway lesson is that random sampling can be very powerful, but there is also an inherent potential for error when working with sample data.

SAMPLING JARGON

Sampling has some particular language that researchers and sophisticated users of research results need to know. Here are the primary terms and concepts:

Population: While population typically means all the people inhabiting a specific geographic area, the meaning is broader in social science. The population could be students at the university, news stories about the 2008 presidential candidates, the streets in the city, or applications for a zoning variance in the past year.

Census: A count of the entire population. This could mean every student in the university, every news article about the 2008 presidential candidates, every street in the city, or every application for a zoning variance in the past year.

Sample: A subset of the population.

Sampling frame: The list of all members of the population of interest, with the specific characteristics needed for the research. For example, the sampling frame could be all the students in a school, all the students in the school who are majoring in science and engineering, or all the undergraduate students who are majoring in science and engineering at all the state four-year colleges and university.

Sample design: The method of sample selection. Most broadly, there are random or nonrandom sampling methods. Within each of these two large categories, there are options.

Statistic: This very narrow meaning is defined as a characteristic in the population based on sampling results. For example, the average salary of the population is estimated to be $35,000. This is also called the point estimate.

Parameter: This is the inference made about the likely range of the statistic. For example, the average salary in the population is estimated to be between $33,000 and $36,000. This is also called the confidence interval.

RANDOM AND NONRANDOM SAMPLES

In the world of science, a random sample enables researchers to do two very important things. First, random sampling minimizes selection bias because the selection of who is included in the study is taken out of the researchers' hands. Researchers cannot select only those people that look like them or who share a particular viewpoint. A random sample should be representative of the population as a whole.

Second, random sampling enables researchers to make mathematical estimates about the population based on the sample's results. The jargon shorthand for this ability to infer what is true about a population based on the results of a random sample is called generalizing the results. Researchers must use random sampling if they want to make general statements about the population as a whole based on their results.

We are all familiar with blood tests. The lab workers do not take all a patient's blood. They take only a sample and assume it to be an accurate reflection of all the person's blood. They then infer, draw conclusions, or make generalizations about the patient's health based on that sample. The idea of drawing a sample for research is the same.

Random, as scientists use the term, does not mean "whatever." It has a very narrow definition that reflects its grounding in probability theory. A random sample means that every unit in the population of interest—whether it is a population of people, files, classrooms, or streets—has an equal chance of being selected.

Random selection should not be confused with random assignment used in experimental designs. While both random selection and random assignment serve to reduce bias, in the language presented in Chapter 5, random assignment enhances internal validity while random selection enhances external validity. For example, much of what we know about social psychology comes from experiments using college freshmen randomly assigned to treatment or control groups. However, those freshmen were not randomly selected from the larger population and therefore are not representative of everyone in the population.

When a nonrandom sampling method is used, the magical power of inference is lost. A nonrandom sample, however, is frequently used because it is the best option given the situation (see Application 10.1). For example, if researchers want to understand why a few communities are considered leaders in sustainable growth, there is no intention to generalize to all communities engaged in sustainable growth. In this kind of best practices research, a nonrandom sample of a few communities recognized as leaders in sustainable growth makes sense. The research approach here is basically a case study.

Nonrandom sampling is often preferable in situations where only a small group will be observed, interviewed, or surveyed. It is also used when researchers do not have all the information necessary for random sampling. For example, researchers are likely to talk with a small number of homeless people in their community that have been nonrandomly selected because the entire homeless population is unknown. Lastly, nonrandom sampling is useful when researchers are doing exploratory work to learn about the issues as the initial step in designing a much larger study.

While the random and nonrandom sampling designs are presented as if they are an either/or choice, in reality they can be used in combination with different data collection strategies within the same study. With a combination of random and nonrandom selection procedures, the results might be more focused on a specific group that cannot be reached through just random sampling alone.

Whether researchers use a random or nonrandom sample, they should provide a clear statement about the sample used and their rationale for selection. It also helps if the researchers gather and report demographic or other essential information so the readers can make an independent assessment about how similar the sample is to the population.

NONRANDOM SAMPLES: THE OPTIONS

Researchers have several choices in nonrandom sampling methods: quota, judgmental, accidental, convenience, and snowball.

Researchers use a quota sample to make sure specific numbers of members of different subgroups are included. For example, researchers decide to interview ten women and ten men at a health clinic. They approach men and women and accept the first ten in each group who agree to participate in the interviews. Another example is a telephone survey that is designed to include fifty Republicans and fifty Democrats. The researchers call until they have filled the quota; if they get fifty Republicans fairly easily, they must keep dialing for Democrats until they get fifty.

A judgmental sample, which is sometimes called a purposive sample, shares the goal of ensuring that the different subgroups of the population are included. However, selections are based on very specific, predetermined criteria that make sense given the research question and the situation. For example, if researchers are interested in understanding why some elementary schools are successful as measured by high student scores on standardized tests, they may decide to interview the principals of the schools with the five highest scores. How is this different from a quota sample? A quota sample would accept the first five principals who raise their hands at a conference to volunteer to participate. In a judgmental sample, the principals are selected on specific criteria and are named.

An accidental sample is the classic "person on the street" sample, sort of like the *Tonight Show*'s "Jay-walking" although probably not as funny. Accidental does not mean random in the narrow statistical sense. If researchers stand outside one supermarket on Saturday to ask people to fill out a survey, only those shopping at that time and place have a chance of being selected. Not every person in the community has an equal chance of being selected, thus violating the definition of random sample: every unit of the population of interest must have an equal chance of being selected. A reasonable assumption is that the people shopping at this time and place are not representative of the community as a whole.

A convenience sample is similar to an accidental sample in that not everyone has an equal chance of being selected. For example, it is convenient for an MPA professor to ask her students to complete a survey about public service motivation. However, these students are not representative of all public service employees, of all MPA students across the country, or even of all students in that particular MPA program. As long as the reported results stay within the limitations of the sampling approach used, the survey results can be useful. This type of sampling approach is a good starting place for exploratory research.

A snowball sample is used when researchers do not know whom to include and rely on others to tell them. For example, if researchers are trying to determine the informal power structure in an unfamiliar community, they probably will not know with whom they should talk. The researchers would begin with the people most likely to have the desired information about power in the community. At the end of the interview, they will ask, "Who else should I talk with?" Ideally, they would continue this snowball process until no new names are suggested. At that point, they will feel fairly certain that they interviewed all the key people knowledgeable about this issue.

Application 10.1
Teenage Mothers on Welfare

Unmarried teenage mothers received particular attention in the run-up to major welfare reform in 1996. From a policy perspective, welfare reforms aimed at unwed teen parents were thought to make sense. If the laws could change their behavior, then fewer teenagers would become parents outside of marriage. Although they represent a relatively small group on the welfare rolls, teen mothers are likely to receive welfare benefits for a number of years.

One relationship the researchers wanted to explore was whether the availability of welfare caused teenagers to have babies. In addition, the researchers wanted to understand the teenagers' views on various welfare reforms targeted at teenage mothers and what they saw as the consequences of ending welfare for teenage mothers. Lastly, the researchers wanted to understand why the teens made the choice to have a baby and their ideas about pregnancy prevention for teenagers (Johnson 2001).

The first plan was to send surveys to a random sample of teenage mothers on welfare. However, neither a national listing of all teenage mothers on welfare nor a listing of teenage mothers within state welfare agencies existed. With no reasonable way to do random sampling, the researchers went to plan B: a qualitative study using focus groups with a nonrandom sample.

A decision was also made to recruit participants from programs that provide services to unwed parents or programs that serve a broader population, such as Job Corps. The researchers selected sites that would include a diverse set of teenage mothers on welfare: whites, Hispanics, African-Americans, and Native Americans living in urban or rural settings. The researchers also wanted to capture respondents' views based on different ages. Participant groups were organized by age: those under seventeen, those between seventeen and nineteen, and those in their early twenties who were teenagers when they became parents.

Over ninety teenage mothers participated in a total of nine focus groups. All the participants had to agree to take part in the focus groups and minors had to have the permission of their parent or guardian. This is one way to document informed consent and ensure that all participants were there voluntarily.

Given the situation, a judgmental nonrandom sample made sense to obtain the views from a diverse group. While the results are not generalizable to all teenage mothers in those locations or the nation, this study provided insight into the policy debate as seen from the perspective of those who would be most affected by the proposed reforms.

RANDOM SAMPLES: THE OPTIONS

Random samples (also called probability samples) mean that every unit in the population has an equal chance of being selected. In order to select a random sample, the researchers need a complete listing of every unit in the population, although there are a few approaches that can be used when there is no complete list. Random sampling techniques range from simple to complex. This section will focus on four categories: simple, systematic, stratified, and cluster samples.

SIMPLE RANDOM SAMPLE

Researchers establish a sample size (discussed later in this chapter) and then randomly select that number of people, files, roads, whatever from the population of interest. For example, researchers plan to interview fifty clients from the local social service agency. The researchers have a list of all 300 clients from the past five years. They assign each client a number from 1 to 300. To make their selection, they use a random number table, such as the one found on the National Institute of Standards and Technology's website (listed in Appendix C on page 261). Picking any three-digit column from the random number table, the researchers select the first fifty numbers that are from 1 to 300. Those fifty numbers are matched to the client names and will constitute the sample of clients to be interviewed.

Selecting phone numbers from a phone book using this technique, however, is never a random sample. It is considered a biased method because some people do not have landline telephones and others are unlisted. A report by the U.S. Department of Housing and Urban Development states, "In most areas up to 30 percent of the households do not have their telephone numbers listed; in large metropolitan areas, this proportion approaches 50 percent" (2000, 7).

SYSTEMATIC RANDOM SAMPLE

How can simple random sampling be done when there is no list of all the files kept in boxes stored in a basement of a government building? Researchers would not want to spend the time numbering all the thousands of files in order to use a random numbers table. Instead, the researchers can use a systematic sampling technique. This involves taking a random start and pulling every kth file until researchers have enough.

For instance, supposing closed welfare case files are located in a basement in no particular order and the researchers want to select a random sample of 200 files. The researchers would select a random number from the random numbers table as the starting point. Suppose their random start number is 65. They would count the files to 65 and begin there. They then have to determine the interval they will use to actually select the files. This will depend on their estimate of how many files there are and what it will take to get through all the files. If there are relatively few files, they might choose to select every thirtieth file. If there are a large number of files, they might choose to select every hundredth file. They would systematically select the files until they have the desired sample of 200. A systematic selection with a random start is acceptable because it constrains the researchers from making personal choices, thus limiting selection bias.

STRATIFIED RANDOM SAMPLE

There are two basic situations in which a stratified random sample is needed. One is when researchers want to guarantee inclusion of members of relatively small groups within a much larger population, groups that might be missed if simple random sampling is used. However, in some situations this problem can be corrected by merely increasing the sample size.

The second situation is when researchers intend to compare data from these relatively small groups to the data from the predominant members. It is crucial that the sample size for each group (called stratum) be sufficiently large to make statistically valid comparisons. For example, a simple random sample of chief executive officers (CEOs) would probably not include enough women or minorities to make meaningful statistical comparisons because so few are CEOs.

To select a stratified sample, researchers must divide the population into strata based on some meaningful characteristic. The researchers would have a listing of each unit within each stratum and then draw a random sample. In a way, the procedure is like drawing multiple simple random samples.

Sometimes people confuse stratified random samples with a judgmental sample. It is true that stratification is based on a judgment—that is, a decision to divide the population of CEOs into groups based on gender and race. However, there is an element of randomness in the selection along with choosing a large enough sample to do statistical analyses. In a nonrandom judgmental sample, it is possible to make the final selection randomly to eliminate bias, but this is rarely done. The key point is that the judgmental samples are more typically nonrandomly selected but in either case are so small that no inferences can be made.

There are two basic types of stratified samples: proportional and disproportional. While the descriptions presented below to illustrate these approaches are relatively simple, it is important to keep in mind that stratified samples can get complex.

PROPORTIONAL STRATIFIED SAMPLE

The key feature of a proportional stratified sample is that the sample maintains the same proportion of the different groups as in the population. For example, say there are 800 male and 200 female senior managers in a large federal agency. In a proportional sample of 80 male and 20 female managers, the proportion of men and women remains exactly the same as it is in the population (see Exhibit 10.1). This makes sense when the intention is to obtain a sample that will give a reasonable estimate of the population as a whole but not if the researchers want to make statistical comparisons between the men and women.

DISPROPORTIONATE STRATIFIED SAMPLE

If the researchers want to make comparisons between the men and women, they will use a disproportionate stratified sample. This means that the researchers will deliberately randomly select a larger number from the smaller groups relative to their proportion in the population. This is disproportionate sampling.

Suppose the researchers want a 50/50 split between the male and female managers in the federal agency. The sample size is still 100, so the researchers will select 50 men and 50 women (see Exhibit 10.2). In the jargon, the researchers will oversample the women.

The stratification can get complex. For example, if the researchers want to compare the views of white men, minority men, white women, and minority women, they

Exhibit 10.1 **Senior Managers in a Federal Agency: Proportional Sample**

	Population	Percent distribution	Sample	Percent distribution
Men	800	80	80	80
Women	200	20	20	20
Total	1,000	100	100	100

Exhibit 10.2 **Senior Managers in a Federal Agency: Disproportionate Sample**

	Population	Percent distribution	Sample	Percent distribution
Men	800	80	50	50
Women	200	20	50	50
Total	1,000		100	

would have four strata. However, if the number of all minority men, white women, and/or minority women were small, the researchers might select all of them and then select a random sample of the white male CEOs. This would still be considered a disproportionate stratified sample.

When the U.S. Government Accountability Office (1990a) decided to survey businesses across the country to determine the extent of discrimination related to the Immigration Reform and Control Act, it chose a disproportionate random sample design. The rationale was that the opportunity to discriminate against people who look and sound foreign would vary based on the industry and area of the country. Given these factors, almost 10,000 businesses were randomly selected with a disproportionate technique using fifty-six strata.

Analyzing Disproportionate Samples

Having sufficient numbers in each of the strata makes sense so that the results can be compared. However, this creates some problems when generalizing to the larger population. The stratum that was oversampled distorts the aggregate results unless it is corrected in the analysis. Disproportionate stratified samples need to be weighted so that the proportions of the strata in the sample are the same as the proportions in the population.

Let us look at a dramatic example of the results of a disproportionate sample when it is unweighted and weighted. These are fake data; it is unlikely that real life would have anything so dramatic.

Researchers have taken a disproportionate stratified random sample of 400 graduate students from a population of 4,000. They also selected 400 undergraduates from a population of 16,000 students. One survey question asks how satisfied or dissatisfied the students are with the university. The results are displayed in Exhibit 10.3. If the researchers are only going to refer to the separate strata and not combine them, they could accurately state that 100 percent of the undergraduates were satisfied while 100 percent of the graduate students were dissatisfied.

Exhibit 10.3   **Satisfaction With School: Analysis With Unweighted Data**

	Graduate students	Undergraduate students	Total
Satisfied	0%	100%	50% n = 400
Dissatisfied	100%	0%	50% n = 400
Total	n = 400	n = 400	n = 800 100%

Exhibit 10.4   **Satisfaction With School: Analysis With Weighted Data**

	Graduate students	Undergraduate students	Total
Satisfied	0	100% N = 16,000	80%
Dissatisfied	100% N = 4,000	0	20%
Total			N = 20,000

However, if the researchers wanted to give an overall picture of all students at the university, the unweighted summary would be misleading. Based on the unweighted data, the researchers would conclude that half of all the students are satisfied. This is because the unweighted sample has a disproportionate number of graduate students relative to the population of students and their dissatisfaction distorts the generalized results to all students.

Weighting the data means putting the groups back into the proportion as they exist in the population. Each graduate student in the sample represents ten students (calculated: 4,000/400). Each undergraduate in the sample represents forty students (calculated: 16,000/400). Multiplying the 400 graduate students who reported being dissatisfied by 10 totals 4,000. For the undergraduates, multiplying the 400 respondents who report being satisfied by 40 totals 16,000.

The correctly weighted data show that 80 percent of all students report being satisfied as compared to 20 percent who report being dissatisfied (see Exhibit 10.4). If this were real data, the university officials should be concerned about the views of the graduate students, but when generalizing about all students, it is accurate to report an 80 percent satisfaction level. The takeaway lesson is that the weighted and unweighted results can be dramatically different. Therefore, researchers must use weighted data to generalize results to the whole population if they are working with a disproportionate stratified random sample.

CLUSTER SAMPLE

Cluster sampling is a multistep approach to select a random sample when a complete listing of the population does not exist (see Application 10.2). It is particularly useful when working over a large geographic area. For example, researchers who want to find out MPA students' future plans after graduation will quickly find that there is no national list of all students. To locate students, the researchers would have to contact every program in the country. However, if there are not enough resources to contact every program but they still want to do a random sample, they will use a cluster sampling approach.

To do a cluster sample, the researchers would first obtain a listing of all MPA programs in the country. They would randomly select maybe twenty programs and contact them in order to obtain the names of all the students. It is unlikely, however, that the schools would give out the names because of privacy laws. The school officials might, however, let the researchers administer surveys in classes. The researchers would randomly select classes likely to be attended by those closest to graduation.

One drawback of the initial selection is that the twenty schools may not reflect all MPA programs or all the students because it is a relatively small number. While random selection reduces research bias in selection, it is possible to wind up with schools all located in large metropolitan areas on the east and west coasts. The study's results might not be representative of all MPA students. However, it may be a limitation that the researchers are willing to live with given the resources available. This is the kind of limitation that must be stated in the reported results.

Alternatively, the researchers could make the initial school selections judgmentally. For example, they might choose five schools from different regions of the country: the northwest, southwest, northeast, southeast, north central and south central. One takeaway lesson is that it is possible to combine elements of random and nonrandom selection within a single study.

DETERMINING SAMPLE SIZE

Sample size is not a concern when working with nonrandom samples. Whether they are large or small, they are never "generalizable" to the larger population. However, sample size is a huge issue for random samples, which need to be large enough so researchers can determine how likely the results are a fairly accurate reflection of the population.

How do researchers decide on how large a random sample should be? The decision is based on three factors. One is the size of the population, which is a given. The second factor is how sure the researchers want to be that sample results are a fair representation of the population; this is called the confidence level. The social science standard is to set the confidence level at 95 percent. In the world of statistics, this translates to a statement that says: If the researchers selected 100 different samples, only 5 percent would be very different from the population. Put more simply, this means that the sample results have only a 5 percent chance of being wrong. Those are good odds.

If researchers drop to a 90 percent confidence level, there is a 10 percent chance of being wrong and the needed sample size will be smaller than at the 95 percent level. If researchers want to be 99 percent confident, there is only a 1 percent chance of being wrong and researchers will need a larger sample. There is a trade-off between sample size and the amount of risk of having a sample that is not a good representation of the population.

Application 10.2
Estimating Iraqi Deaths

Sampling methodology can become the center of the storm on politically charged issues. The *Lancet*'s 2006 study estimating the number of Iraqi civilian deaths is a good example (Burnham et al. 2006). The study team was based at the Johns Hopkins University.

Determining the number of civilian deaths in any war is difficult because there is no reliable official count. Wars also tend to have mixed support and the research results are likely to get caught in the political spin cycle. Those opposed to the war in Iraq quickly grabbed the *Lancet* estimate and stated it as fact. Those supporting the war just as quickly dismissed the research out of hand.

The study estimated that there were over 600,000 Iraqi deaths because of the war. The *Washington Post* provided context: "It is more than 20 times the estimate of 30,000 civilian deaths that President Bush gave in a speech in December. It is more than 10 times the estimate of roughly 50,000 civilian deaths made by the British-based Iraq Body Count research group" (Brown 2006). It should be noted that neither of those estimates was based on death certificates; one relied on what the military counted and the other relied on what was reported by the media. Both were likely to be undercounts.

From a research perspective, the essential question is whether the researchers used an appropriate sampling methodology.

"The technique, called 'cluster sampling,' is used to estimate mortality in famines and after natural disasters," the *Washington Post* explained. It is hard to say how many readers had a clue about what cluster sampling is; the *Post* did not describe the actual methodology.

The study published in *Lancet* described the cluster sampling procedures. Briefly, fifty clusters were randomly selected from sixteen governates (which are subdivisions of a country). Within each of the governates, the researchers randomly selected the main streets from a list of main streets; they then randomly selected the residential streets from a list of all residential streets that crossed the main street. Once the researchers got to the randomly selected street, they randomly selected a house as the starting point. They then interviewed the adjacent households, continuing in this fashion until they reached forty households. Having eliminated three clusters because of problems, the researchers used forty-seven clusters containing data from 1,849 households. The researchers did not ask demographic questions in order to assure the participants that they could not be identified.

This looks pretty much like a textbook description of cluster sampling, but the political debate was intense. "I don't consider it a credible report," President George W. Bush stated. Army general George Casey, commander of ground forces in Iraq, also told a reporter he did not find the estimates credible (MacQuarrie 2006). Steven Moore, a political consultant with ties to the Republican Party, called the study "bogus" in a *Wall Street Journal* op-ed article published on October 18, 2006. His primary criticism was that the researchers used too few clusters to be credible. The results, he opined, were "crazy" and not likely to be representative of all the Iraqi people. If the demographics of the survey respondents were similar to those of the population, he stated, it would give the study more credibility. However, Moore stated, "without demographic information to assure a representative sample, there is no way anyone can prove—or disprove—that the Johns Hopkins estimate of Iraqi civilian deaths is accurate." Gilbert Burnham, who headed the Hopkins' research team, responding in the *Wall Street Journal* in a letter to the editor, stated that whether researchers used 47 clusters or 470 clusters, the method was unbiased.

There is something strange in seeing sampling methodology debated in the Wall Street Journal. However, the controversy emphasizes that the details of the research methods can indeed have a significant impact on the debates about policy issues.

The third factor in deciding the size of the sample is precision: how precise do the researchers want to be in making estimates about the population based on the sample results? Precision is sometimes presented in terms of sampling error.

For example, polling data are reported in terms of the margin of error. National polls set their standard at plus or minus 3 percent. A poll might report that 49 percent plan to vote for the Republican candidate and 51 percent for the Democratic candidate, with a sampling error of plus or minus 3 percent. In statistics language, this means that the pollsters are 95 percent certain that if they had surveyed everyone, the true likely vote for the Republican candidate would be between 52 percent (49 percent plus 3) and 46 percent (49 percent minus 3). Similarly, the true likely vote for the Democrat would be between 54 percent and 48 percent (51 percent plus 3 and 51 percent minus 3). When the sampling errors overlap, as they do in this fake example, it means that the election is too close to call.

When working with real numbers (interval and ratio level data), the precision is presented in terms of the confidence interval (not to be confused with the confidence level, explained above; this is yet another example of similar terms with different meanings that make us all crazy). Researchers use confidence intervals when they want to estimate the range of the actual number or average in the population based on the sample results—in sampling jargon, when they want to estimate the parameters.

For example, if the average salary in a sample is $20,000, this becomes the point estimate in the population. The computer then calculates the confidence interval; it is $18,000 at the low end and $22,000 at the high end. The researchers would state that they are 95 percent certain (this is the confidence level) that the true average salary of the population is between $18,000 and $22,000 (this is the confidence interval). In the Iraqi mortality study discussed in Application 10.2, the *Lancet* researchers reported that they were 95 percent certain that the true number of deaths was somewhere between 393,000 and 943,000; the researchers are reporting the confidence interval.

The key point is that sample size is affected by the choices of desired precision and confidence levels. At the social science standard of 5 percent precision and a confidence level of 95 percent, the researchers need a sample of 384 if the population is 250,000. However, if the researchers wanted to be very precise plus or minus 1 percent, they would need a sample size of 9,248 for a population of 250,000.

It is also important to note that the smaller the population, the higher the proportion of cases needed. If the population is 200, the sample size will be 132 (see Exhibit 10.5). At 700, the sample will be 248. When the population is larger than 100,000, 385 are needed. These are based on a 5 percent precision and a 95 percent confidence level.

The last factor in calculating sample size is the proportion of the characteristic in the population. The population proportion means that if the researchers were looking at the gender variable, they would assume there would be a 50/50 split between men and women. The most conservative estimate is .50, meaning that the characteristic is found in 50 percent of the population. It is considered a conservative measure because it results in the largest sample size to meet the social science standards of 5 percent precision and a 95 percent confidence level (Krejcie and Morgan 1970). If the researchers were considering a population consisting of managers and non-managers in an organization, the population proportion might be 10 percent managers and 90 percent non-managers. Statisticians would calculate the precise sample size based on

Exhibit 10.5   **Guide to Sample Size**

Population size	Sample size
10	10
50	44
100	80
200	132
250	152
500	217
700	248
1,000	278
3,000	341
50,000	381
100,000+	385

Source: Krejcie and Morgan, 1970.
Note: These are based on the social science standard of 5 percent precision and 95 percent confidence level.

all these variables using the formula in Appendix A (see page 230), but the sample sizes in Exhibit 10.5 provide useful conservative estimates.

It is important to remember that these sizes are minimums. A researcher may want to select a sample size somewhat larger if the data collection is not likely to receive a 100 percent response rate. In order to compare strata, researchers should select sample sizes for each stratum based on the population and desired degree of confidence and precision so they can obtain statistically valid comparisons.

While samples are used to keep down the costs of data collection, my advice to any researcher is to try to gather data from the whole population. If an organization has 100 employees, it is best to survey them all rather than just eighty. However, if the population is just too large and a sample is needed, researchers should select as large a sample as they can manage. There is nothing more frustrating than doing all the work involved in research only to be unable to draw conclusions because the sample was too small. Do not skimp on sampling!

NONSAMPLING ERRORS

Research results may have errors that have nothing to do with the probabilities of error associated with random samples. These nonsampling errors refer to possible problems with how the data were collected. A major nonsampling error is a low response rate. Even when the researchers select a large enough random sample, if few people respond, the researchers are left with a volunteer sample: those who chose to participate in the survey might be different from the rest of the population.

Other nonsampling errors can come from the questions and responses. When interviewers ask different people slightly differently questions, the data are no longer reliable and create a nonsampling error. Nonsampling errors can also occur when people do not give truthful answers. For example, people may say what they believe the researcher wants to hear or what they think is the socially desirable response. "Of course," someone might say to a woman interviewer, "I would vote for a qualified woman for president." Whether that is a truthful answer, however, is unknown. Asking if people use illegal drugs runs the risk of people saying "no" because they believe it is safer.

Researchers should do what they can to minimize nonsampling error and acknowledge it as a possible limitation of their study. In the Iraq mortality study (Burnham et al. 2006), for example, the researchers attempted to minimize nonsampling errors in a variety of ways. The researchers attempted to minimize response bias by having equal numbers of men and women on the teams. All interviewers were medical doctors, fluent in Arabic and with prior survey experience. To ensure that the teams conducted the interviews in the same way, all interviewers participated in two days of training before starting the study. The teams were required to carefully document how they approached each household and how the counts were made. The teams were instructed to encourage honest answers by assuring the respondents that the interviews were confidential. No identifying information was gathered, although the lack of demographic data was criticized later.

However, even with these preventive measures, the researchers acknowledged a variety of possible nonsampling errors in their discussion. For example, large-scale migration in the clusters could have affected the population estimates. The researchers also noted that the number of deaths might have been underreported: infant deaths might have been underreported or families might not have revealed the deaths of household members who would be considered enemy combatants. It is also possible that deaths could have been misattributed to coalition forces.

Clearly, the danger in conducting a survey in a war zone impacted the study design, including using very small teams, selecting few clusters, and reducing the amount of time spent in collecting data. However, the researchers stated that their approach followed the standards developed over time by epidemiologists.

The takeaway lesson is that the potential for error is just part of the research. Researchers should do what they can to limit errors and be honest about what they did. By reporting likely errors, they give readers information they can use in assessing the credibility of the researchers' conclusions.

CONCLUSION

The decision about whether to use a sample depends on the context. Sometimes it makes sense to include everyone in the population for reasons other than research requirements. For example, a manager might want to survey all the staff members, rather than a sample, so everyone feels included. When sampling is required, the choice of whether to use nonrandom or random samples depends on the intention of the research and the situation.

Random samples are used when the population is too large to be included in the study but the researchers intend to draw general conclusions about the population. The sample size is based on the researchers' desired confidence level and precision.

The researchers should present all the information about their sampling frame, their rationale for choosing the type of sample, and the sample size; if surveys are used, then response rates should also be reported. Lastly, they should reveal both sampling and nonsampling errors and discuss their implications for drawing conclusions.

It is generally wise to select a somewhat larger sample than the minimum required. It is frustrating to be unable to draw conclusions because the sample was too small! My best advice is to include the entire population whenever it is reasonable and possible, and if you have to sample, then sample large.

The key takeaway lesson is that random samples minimize bias and allow researchers to make inferences to the larger population based on the sample results. Once researchers use random samples, they must use inferential statistics (see Chapter 15); they go hand in hand.

EXERCISES

1. For each of the following situations, identify the likely data collection approach and then identify your sample: the population of interest, the type of sample, and the sampling procedures you would use. Explain your rationale and any known limitations given the situation.

   a. There has been increasing concern about the ability of the federal government to attract college graduates as employees. Your team has been asked to determine what image college students have about working for the federal civil service. However, there is no listing of all college students, and privacy laws prohibit the colleges from giving out their addresses.

   b. Your organization's diversity task force wants to find out the attitudes of managers and frontline workers about diversity. The task force would like to conduct an attitude survey and asks you for advice about the sample.

   c. What sampling strategy would you use to determine the number of potholes in the city?

   d. The director of the child welfare agency is interested in the length of time that families receive protective services. She asks you to provide information regarding the number of treatment hours received by these clients. The data are not in a computer, so you will have to look at closed files. The agency has been in operation for twenty years and has served over 100,000 clients.

   e. The city council wants to find out the citizens' views about the challenges facing the city in the next two years.

11 Qualitative Data Analysis

OVERVIEW

The research process consists of three major phases: planning, doing, and reporting. Data analysis occupies the central position because it is interwoven with both the planning and reporting phases. In fact, researchers typically consider analysis options in the planning process when considering measures and data collection approaches. Good research proposals will include an analysis plan to ensure that the right data are collected to conduct the desired analyses. The analysis flows into the reporting phase, where the major findings are presented in a user-friendly way.

Chapters 11–15 focus on data analysis. Researchers have already decided whether they need qualitative or quantitative techniques. Do the researchers want narrative or numbers? Semi-structured observations, open-ended interviews, analysis of written documents, and focus group transcripts all require the use of qualitative analytical techniques. Qualitative analysis is labor-intensive and while it should be systematic, the potential for bias is always a concern.

This chapter provides some basic guidelines for analyzing qualitative data. The major concern is with bias. Even the most scrupulous researchers have to be mindful of honest bias, meaning bias that creeps in without any conscious intention. It is perfectly possible that different people can look at the same scene or hear the same words but come away with very different meanings. Analyzing qualitative data takes a great deal of time and attention to detail. Although qualitative data are seen as weak, when done well they can yield important information that cannot be obtained through quantitative approaches.

ANALYZING QUALITATIVE DATA

Although qualitative research has a reputation of being easier than quantitative research, it is actually more challenging and time-consuming than quantitative techniques. Easy-to-use software is available for quantitative data analysis, but the software packages available for qualitative analysis are not yet in the easy-to-use category. The analysis typically uses low-tech approaches. Despite the challenges, many researchers find qualitative research richer, more interesting, and more satisfying than quantitative techniques.

As mentioned previously, researchers collecting qualitative data want to capture as much information as possible. In addition to interview write-ups and verbatim focus group transcripts, the researchers will want to capture other information about what was happening in separate notes. Observations about the setting or the dynamics of interviews may prove helpful. Lastly, the researchers' initial reactions and sense making may be useful to capture the moment; things tend to blur together over time.

When analyzing qualitative data, researchers look for common words, themes, and patterns. Electronic documents can be searched for specific words or phrases, but researchers also use the low-tech process of making notes of words, issues, themes, and patterns as they go through the material. The process is a content analysis, which was described in Chapter 6 as a research approach; the difference here is that the content analysis is applied to transcripts from focus groups, interview write-ups, and responses to open-ended questions.

Researchers begin with an initial scan of their notes, interview write-ups, open-ended responses in a survey, or focus group transcripts in order to get a sense of what is there before developing a general framework for analyzing the rest of the data. Once a general framework of common words and themes has been developed, the researchers go through all the data to identify the themes and their frequency. It is not uncommon to discover other themes as the analysis proceeds; researchers often find themselves going back to recode earlier material based on insights that emerge halfway through the analysis. In addition to uncovering common themes, researchers also want to capture context, additional issues raised by the participants, and variations in themes and views, so the themes can be presented with some degree of complexity. It is useful to identify potential quotes that can be used in the report to highlight specific aspects of the various themes.

Some researchers use a spreadsheet to capture the common themes and their locations in the transcripts or notes. Other researchers use note cards or develop elaborate color-coding schemes using highlighters on the printed material. It is also possible to use the cut and paste functions of word-processing software to create thematic files. No matter which method is used, however, it is important to have a system in place so that the researchers know exactly where the source data are located. This is necessary to verify quotes or the context.

Bias is the major concern in this process. One way to limit possible bias in the analysis is to have two people analyze the same set of data and then compare the results. People rarely see things in exactly the same way, but the results should be similar. If not, comparing the two analyses will result in a deeper conversation about the data. New themes or different ways of understanding the data may emerge, capturing a broader view; this broader view eliminates the narrow view that can be biased.

IDENTIFYING THEMES AND QUOTES

Ideally, several researchers are involved in analyzing the data. The affinity diagram process is a good way for the research team to quickly identify the common themes; it was developed in the 1960s by Jiro Kawakitain according the American Society for Quality (ASQ). The ASQ describes the affinity diagram process as an idea generation tool that can be used by research teams to identify common ideas or themes. With this process, everyone's ideas are considered and there is less ownership of a single idea. No one has to sit out as the facilitator of the discussion. It is a quick way to develop an organizing structure for the analysis and final report. The team walks through the process as described in Exhibit 11.1.

The process begins with each member of the team reviewing a portion of the written material. Each might each read a different focus group transcript if focus groups were used to collect data. If interviews were used, the researchers would each read two or three different interview write-ups. If the researchers were going to analyze the open-ended responses in surveys, they would each read several different dozen surveys. Selecting different portions of the written material helps the researchers discover whether a wider range of topics were discussed; if the researchers only read a single interview transcript, for example, they would have a limited awareness of the range of topics that might have been discussed in the other interviewees. In addition, the team members will review their own notes jotted down during the data collection phase.

This collaborative process begins in silence. This rule is important because it keeps people focused on the process and limits distracting conversations or arguments. The process requires a room with a large empty wall where people can stick notes, index cards or paper with a light adhesive so papers will stick; it is important that the notes or cards can stick but also be easily moved around.

Once the basic framework is established, the team reviews all the material and identifies places where they see each of the themes. As with content analysis described earlier, there is the question of whether to report counts or themes. In qualitative analysis, it makes sense to keep track of the occurrences of the various statements that reflect the major themes. However, counts do not make sense. Why not? When responding to an open-ended question, for example, people choose which issue they want to talk about. Some responses may be very idiosyncratic while others may reflect a somewhat more common sentiment. Without surveying all the respondents, the researcher might not be able to gauge whether those few are the only ones that feel that way or not. It is also easy to get distracted by the vehemence of a few articulate people who care passionately about an issue that was not very important to others.

For example, a number of people answered an open-ended question asking about "other concerns" by complaining about a particular failure in one aspect of a training program on one survey I conducted. As it turned out, there was a closed-ended question on that aspect of the training program and 85 percent of the respondents state that they were satisfied. If that closed-ended question had not been asked, it would have been easy to assume that this failure was a common theme and therefore important.

Exhibit 11.1   **The Affinity Diagram Process**

1. In silence, all team members identify ideas or themes that they observed in the data and write each one down on a large self stick notepaper or index card. It is important that *only one* idea, concept, or theme be written on each note.
2. In silence, the team members place their ideas on a wall in no particular order.
3. In silence, each person on the team begins to sort the notes so that similar ideas are placed together. It can get a little chaotic as people move notes around but it is important to maintain silence.
4. Once it appears that the notes have been sorted into general themes, the team members discuss the groupings.
5. The initial groupings are not fixed: new groupings can be made and ideas can be shifted.
6. The team members discuss names for each of the large themes.
7. The team can then develop the framework based on the large themes to use in analyzing all the data, being mindful of themes and issues that do not fit into the framework; these can be tracked separately and developed into a new theme if necessary.

However, most people were satisfied with that aspect of the training program; for the few who were dissatisfied, it was a strong pain point.

Another challenge is determining when a topic is a common theme. If mentioned only twice, is it a common theme? What if it is mentioned ten times? What if it is the main topic in three focus groups but not in the other three? Deciding when a topic is a common theme is a subjective judgment made by the researchers. If it is mentioned in every interview or focus group, then it can be easily defined as common. But that does not always happen. Since there are no agreed upon rules about how to define common themes, researchers get to improvise. Sometimes the research team will analyze the data separately and if each member identifies the same theme, it will be determined to be a common theme. Alternatively, the researchers might select the five themes mentioned the most often and call them the common themes. Another option is to count a topic as a common theme if it is mentioned in a majority of the interviews or focus groups. A key point to remember is that this is a time when the researchers need to explain the basis for determining a common theme. The researchers also need to remember that reasonable people can—and likely will—disagree on what constitutes a common theme.

It is also true that the researchers might decide to highlight an isolated idea or perspective that is clearly not common. It may just be an interesting idea. Alternatively, the researchers may believe that it is an important issue for people with specific experiences that were underrepresented among the participants. For example, suppose that the issue of racial discrimination emerged in only one of several focus groups discussing employment opportunities in various communities. After much discussion, the researchers analyzing the data decide to highlight the topic. It might be the tip of an iceberg, they reason, or it might be a problem only in that one community. In their report, they suggest that more research should be done to determine the extent to which discrimination is a problem in these communities.

Another aspect of qualitative research is the use of "quotable quotes" that capture what the participants said in their own words. These words have power and should be selected carefully to reflect the major themes and the diverse viewpoints about each theme. While quotes add interest to the research reports, the risk of bias does creep in here. A wise researcher will present the diverse perspectives about the same themes that exist in the data. Including a range of quotations will provide a balanced view of the data and reduce the appearance of bias.

However, the researchers should be mindful that in the interest of making the report appear to be fair and balanced, an unintentional distortion could be introduced. For example, suppose many people in all the focus groups spoke against a particular policy and a few spoke in favor. If the researchers report one quote in favor and one quote against, it will appear that the opinions were evenly shared. Presenting balanced views is important, but the researchers need to clarify that some views were held by only a small proportion of those participating. This can be done easily by introducing the quotes with something like the following wording: "While many of the participants opposed building a parking garage, a few favored it." Then the quotes are placed into context. The different views are presented but without the distortion.

WORKING WITH QUALITATIVE DATA

Analyzing qualitative data has its own challenges that can sometimes make the analysts wish they had used a check-a-box format. One challenge is the process of making meaning of the data. Another is to keep it all organized. Lastly, the sheer amount of data generated from qualitative data collection can be overwhelming. An hour interview can generate ten pages of single-spaced notes, and a verbatim transcript of a single focus group can generate even more.

Exhibit 11.2 shows a very small segment of a focus group transcript. A few points are notable here. First, the participants are identified not by name but by number. This protects their privacy but allows the researcher to determine whether different people mentioned a particular theme or whether one person talked a lot about a single issue.

Second, a number of issues emerge that are not specific to the question itself but will contribute to the larger themes. For example, one theme that emerged across all nine focus groups in this research was unplanned pregnancies. Note the last statement in this excerpt: "It just happened." It was a common theme. Thematic statements can occur anywhere regardless of the actual question being asked.

Making sense of all the data in the transcripts from nine focus groups is a slow process. Having a clear set of guiding questions helps researchers maintain focus without getting lost. At the same time, it is important to stay open to surprising and unexpected information.

It takes a few drafts to summarize the major themes before writing the final report. Generally, researchers report qualitative data in terms of "common themes" or "a number of people said." A general statement might be made about the theme, followed by a quote to illustrate the point. Exhibit 11.3 is an example of a summary that tried to capture the themes about why teenagers become parents; this summary is based all the focus group rather then the snippet shown in Exhibit 11.2. Note the use of "some people said" or "others said" to try to capture the range of points made without tying it to frequency counts.

While it is fairly easy to develop a handful of open-ended questions (as opposed to closed-ended questions) and gather data, analyzing qualitative data takes a substantial

146

Exhibit 11.2 **Transcript Excerpt: Focus Group With Teenage Mothers**

MODERATOR: Let me focus one minute on the idea of being teenagers. What do you think maybe you needed raising children as teenagers that other mothers don't need?

PARTICIPANT 1: Support.

PARTICIPANT 6: You really need support.

MODERATOR: What kind of support?

PARTICIPANT 6: Any kind of support from anywhere. If you don't have that support, like most teenagers—I was fourteen years old. Thank the Lord my mother did not put me out on the streets. That's the support you need. You need someone to be there for you. That's the main thing, support.

PARTICIPANT 4: I feel like everybody needs support, you know, from the youngest to the oldest. But I think that teenagers need for somebody to go through it with them more so than somebody older. You know, I think they need somebody right there by their side. It's a lot of emotional wear and tear on your body.

MODERATOR: Raising the baby?

PARTICIPANT 4: No. Being pregnant and having a baby and raising a baby. You know, seeing yourself like, I'm a mother and your friends that don't have kids, you talk to them and they can't relate to what you're going through. You have to sit up and talk to other teenagers that have kids.

MODERATOR: Okay. Good point. What else do teenagers need?

PARTICIPANT 1: Help but it is hard. Now, my mother she's a big support in my life, but me and my mother only get along on the understanding that we don't stay together. We get along better because we are not together, because we so much alike. . . . That's the one thing I dislike about my family is when they try to throw things in my face that they had done for me.

PARTICIPANT 3: That's what makes you want to have your own.

MODERATOR: Tell me a little bit more about that, about how that makes you feel.

PARTICIPANT 3: It makes you feel—if you're going to do something for somebody, why talk about it?

PARTICIPANT 1: Especially if you didn't ask. You can't turn it down, because you need it.

MODERATOR: So I hear you say that support is great, but don't put strings to it? Don't tell me how to run my life.

PARTICIPANTS: Yeah.

PARTICIPANT 4: I think that when a young person has a baby, people feel like you're irresponsible. You know, that's not the case, because in my situation nobody ever took me to the—you know, nobody ever took him to the doctors. I always did that. I caught buses in the snow. I did all of that. But everybody gets in a bind sometimes. I think they think because you're a teenager and you get in a bind, you just the most irresponsible person in the world.

PARTICIPANT 8: And they think you're stupid.

PARTICIPANTS: Yeah. Um-hum.

PARTICIPANT 9: You're so stupid for having a baby at a young age. I didn't plan to have a baby, it just happened.

Exhibit 11.3   **Initial Write-up of Focus Groups Results**

The focus group participants offered a wide range of reasons to explain why teenagers become pregnant and parents. Lack of contraception was one reason, which included the lack of information, lack of access to birth control, contraceptive failure, and/or failure to use birth control. "I knew about condoms and birth control but I didn't know where to get them. I couldn't ask mom where to get birth control. My God, she would kill me." Others said they did not have money to buy contraceptives and could not ask their parents for the money.

Finding a clinic was a challenge for some. In both urban and rural areas, participants reported that getting to a clinic located in a different neighborhood or town was not easy.

Still others said that some girls do not use contraception either because they were "too scared to go tell their moms even though their mom tells them if you want it, tell me" or because their "boyfriend won't use condoms."

Another reason for teenagers to have a baby stems from a desire to have someone to love and/ or someone to love them. One participant put it this way: "Their mom and dads aren't around and they just want someone to love them." For others, having a baby stems from a wish to please their boyfriends.

While many said the pregnancy was not planned, that "it just happened," others admitted that they planned to have a baby, believing that it would cement their relationship with their boyfriend. One young woman stated, "I thought he would love me more if I had a baby for him."

For others, having a child is sometimes part of a fantasy: "When you're pregnant you think the dad's going to be around and you're just going to be with this big whole Walton family."

amount of time, which needs to be built into the plan. For managers contracting for qualitative research, it typically takes more time to analyze qualitative data than to gather it. The researchers should be realistic and plan enough time to do it well.

CONCLUSION

Qualitative data is precious; every attempt should be made to ensure the most accurate transcriptions of interviews and focus groups. The amount of data can be overwhelming, so researchers must have a good system in place to keep track of it all. Having an analysis plan can provide the necessary structure so researchers do not lose their way. The original research questions provide the anchor. Lastly, adequate time should be given to this very step-by-step analysis, although a deadline also helps the analysts reach the finish line.

Qualitative data analysis tells a narrative story that serves to put a human face on a public issue. It requires a systematic process and an awareness of how easily bias can creep into the analysis. It is necessary to develop some quality control procedures, such as having several people analyze the data or check early analysis of the same data to ensure that all the researchers are interpreting the data in a similar way. Researchers working with qualitative data must be disciplined in stepping back and asking whether their interpretation is supported by evidence. It helps to have a neutral person review the final report to check for bias.

The choice of the approach depends on the situation rather than the researchers' preferences. Qualitative analysis is harder to do than quantitative analysis in my experience and takes longer as well. However, qualitative data can be very powerful and more illuminating than those limited check-a-box surveys in some situations. Although decision-makers may say they want just the facts, they are often persuaded by the human story. Qualitative research can be very persuasive.

EXERCISES

1. Below is an excerpt from a focus group transcript in which teenage parents offer advice to other teens. What do you see as the major themes that emerge from this data?

MODERATOR: Well, let me ask you this. If you could pass on some advice to other teenagers who don't yet have a baby, what would you tell them?

PARTICIPANTS: Wait. Wait.

PARTICIPANT 6:   My advice would be, finish school, try to get a—for a baby, you have to be mentally prepared, too.

PARTICIPANT 8:   You do. You have to be mentally prepared.

PARTICIPANT 6:   My advice would be, wait till you've finished school, because I didn't finish school and now I'm finishing. I feel in order for my kids to go to school, I've got to finish school to try to teach them a lesson. Wait. That's it. Wait.

PARTICIPANT 3:   Emotionally it is hard. I had to take him to the doctor one day and it was cold, it was real cold and I had to catch the bus. It was like, nobody had a car and he was crying when I was walking down the street because I had a long way to get to Seven Mile and he was just a crying and I'm crying right with him.

MODERATOR: That was one of those tough times, huh?

PARTICIPANT 8:   My advice would also be to wait, because it's not fair to bring a child into an impoverished family, a family with no father, you know, a father that's not in the home. It's just not fair to the child.

MODERATOR: Okay.

PARTICIPANT 7:   My advice would be also to wait, too. Wait till you have something going for yourself. If you don't, if you end up having a baby at a young age without finishing school, it is hard. You have to be strong and be there for your child. Take care of him or her.

PARTICIPANT 4:   Finish school. Don't matter how hard it be, the obstacles that come in your way. Like this is my last year of school. And it seems like through all my high school years, nothing ever, you know, stopped me—and, you know, nothing ever stopped me from going to school. I used to mess up in school. But then when I had my baby, I could not go to school. I paid day care for a while, and then I couldn't pay day care any more. You know, I had problems at home and I had to move and then I was missing a lot of school. Now, I go to school. This school provides day care while I am at school. So I am playing catch-up and busting my brains so I can try and graduate. Because if I don't go to school and then go to college, I'm not ever going to be able to give him anything. You know, just keep going to school. It's hard but you have got to keep going to school.

12 Data Analysis for Description

OVERVIEW

It is hard to avoid descriptive statistics, even if we wanted to. They describe much of our world. How many miles of road were repaired last year? What percent of the people in the state are without health insurance? How satisfied is the public with the performance of elected officials? How has the crime rate changed over time? What is the percentage change in the number of women graduating from medical school this year as compared to the number thirty years ago?

Conceptually, descriptive statistics describe the way things are—sort of "the state of the state." The basis for some statistics is complex, but when stripped of the jargon and the mathematics, it loses much of its mystery.

Within quantitative data analysis, there are two big categories: descriptive and inferential statistics. In the narrowest definition, descriptive statistics are used only with census or nonrandom sample data. More generally, however, descriptive statistics are used to describe data from any source and that is how I present the topic here.

This chapter focuses on descriptive statistics, such as ratios, rates of change, and distributions as well as means, medians, modes, and standard deviations. Chapters 13 and 14 discuss statistics used to explore relationships. Chapter 15 covers inferential statistics that are used with random sample data. The focus here is on interpretation, but a few books listed in Appendix C (see page 256) present the nuts and bolts of statistical techniques (Klass 2008; Meier et al. 2008).

SIMPLE DESCRIPTIVE STATISTICS IN PUBLIC ADMINISTRATION

Simple descriptive data can paint compelling pictures. On "each day in America," for example, according to the Children's Defense Fund (2008a), four children are killed by abuse or neglect, five children or teens commit suicide, eight children or teens are killed by firearms, and seventy-seven babies die before their first birthday. The organization translated data into a context of "every day" to make the statistics concrete. Similarly, the World Health Organization talks about the deaths of children

Exhibit 12.1 **Federal Budget: Surplus and Deficit Over Time, 1974–2009**

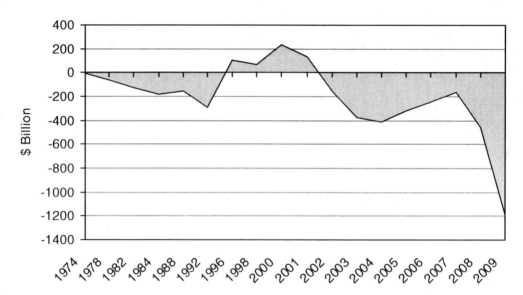

from malaria, a treatable disease, in terms of time: a child dies of malaria every thirty seconds in the world (McLennan 2005). In the two minutes it takes to read this page, four children died of malaria.

Simple descriptive statistics can be used to paint pictures about complex phenomena. Those who argue against antipoverty programs use descriptive statistics. For example, one critic pointed out that "last year, the federal government spent more than $477 billion on some 50 different programs to fight poverty. That amounts to $12,892 for every poor man, woman, and child in this country" (Tanner 2006). Another example concerns the federal budget deficit and surplus over time. The trends shown in Exhibit 12.1 are clear. In every year between 1974 and 1998, the federal government spent more money than it took in (U.S. Office of Management and Budget 2009). There were dramatic increases in the annual deficit from 1980 to 1992 (growing from $74 billion to $290 billion) and again from 2002 to 2006 (growing from $158 billion to 248 billion). There was a short-lived downward trend in 2007, with a deficit of only $162 billion. However, it skyrocketed to $455 billion in 2008 and is estimated to be $1.2 trillion in 2009, assuming no additional spending legislation is passed (U.S. Congressional Budget Office 2009). For the most part, the big deficits took place when Republicans lived in the White House.

The deficit began to get smaller starting in 1993 and actually crossed over into a surplus in 1998, for the first time in decades. Fiscal year 2000 saw a surplus of $236 billion, the highest ever. Democrats lived in White House during that time.

One interpretation would suggest that maybe it is a mistake to label Democrats as the "big spenders." However, before drawing any conclusion, it would be necessary to look at other factors—like the economy and which party controlled Congress—as rival explanations.

While the federal budget calculates the annual deficit or surplus, the national debt is the running total. It was $10 trillion at the start of 2009. In concrete terms, this means that every American owes about $33,000. The national debt is conservatively projected to rise to $16 trillion in ten years (U.S. Congressional Budget Office 2009). These are simple descriptive statistics that tell an important story about the looming nightmare for our grandchildren.

COMMONLY USED DESCRIPTIVE STATISTICS

Commonly used descriptive statistics are counts, percents, rates, ratios, rates of change, distributions, means, medians, and modes, and standard deviations. Sometimes they are used alone but more often in combination.

COUNTS

A good place to look for counts of "how many" is the decennial census. The U.S. Census Bureau attempts to enumerate every person in the country. The census is a function of government because every person counts in creating elective districts and calculating some transfer payments from the federal government to states and localities. While some data are collected through a mailed survey, census workers go to some dwellings to gather further data in person. The count is not perfect—how are homeless people counted, for example? Still, the decennial census is the best count available of the U.S. population.

When counting money over time, it is important to pay attention to whether the budget analysts are reporting actual (current) dollars or dollars have been adjusted to a standard year (constant dollars) to control for inflation. Dollars today have much less buying power than they did in 1960. Using constant dollars makes the buying power equivalent, which is useful when comparing dollars across time.

For example, Exhibit 12.2 shows the differences in median income of men and women over time, using both current and 2006 constant dollars (U.S. Census Bureau, Table P-36). The difference measured in current dollars is dramatic, but when the dollars for the earlier years are adjusted to reflect the buying power in terms of 2006 dollars, the differences are less dramatic. Women still earn less, though. The choice to use current or constant dollars will affect how the results appear; depending on the situation, this might be important to know.

PERCENTS

"Percentage of" can be very effective in presenting a snapshot of a situation. A good example is women's earnings as a percentage of men's earnings. Based on full-time workers fifteen years of age and older, the U.S. Census Bureau found that women earned 59 percent of what men earned in 1970. By 1990, women earned 70 percent of what men earned and 77 percent in 2006 (Table P-40). These figures could be expressed more concretely: for every dollar men earned, women earned 77 cents in 2006 as compared to 59 cents in 1970.

Exhibit 12.2   **Median Income by Gender for Full-Time, Year-Round Workers**

	Men		Women	
	Current dollars	Constant 2006 dollars	Current dollars	Constant 2006 dollars
2006	$44,958	$44,958	$34,989	$34,989
2000	38,891	45,534	29,123	34,098
1990	28,979	45,337	20,591	30,793
1980	19,173	44,667	11,591	27,003
1970	9,184	41,644	5,440	24,667
1960	5,434	31,611	3,269	19,174

Source: U.S. Census Bureau, Table P-36 Full-Time, Year-Round All Workers by Median Income and Sex: 1955 to 2006, www.cenus.gov/hhes/www/income/hisinc.p36ar.html

Sometimes, however, a percentage of another measure does not tell the full story. For example, the federal government typically reports the federal debt as a percent of the gross domestic product (GDP), The GDP, which is the total amount of goods and services produced in the United States in a year, was $14.2 trillion in 2008. The U.S. Congressional Budget Office (2009) reported that the national debt held by the public was 41 percent of the GDP in 2008. However, this percentage was based on the "debt held by the public," which is only part of the federal debt. In 2008 the public debt held was over $5 trillion. The other part of the debt is "intergovernmental holdings," meaning money owed to other governmental entities, such as the Social Security Trust Fund. That added more than $4 trillion, bringing the total debt to just under $10 trillion at the end of 2008. The total federal debt as a percentage of the GDP was more than 70 percent, the highest it had been in more than fifty years. Clearly, it helps to know how researchers define their measures.

If the economy picks up and the GDP increases at a faster rate then the federal debt, the proportion of the federal debt will appear smaller over time. This is the "bigger pie" distortion; when the pie grows much faster than a slice, the slice will be proportionally smaller. In this case, it could create the illusion of a smaller debt. However, the debt will continue to grow if no actions are taken to reduce it.

RATES

We see rates all the time: crime rates, infant mortality rates, birth rates, and so on. Rates are presented in terms of the number of occurrences "per" something: debt per person, crimes per 1,000 people, output per 100 staff years, or accidents per 100,000 miles driven. Rates create an apples-to-apples comparison that is especially useful when the units being compared vary in size.

For example, a comparison of the number of crimes in two cities is not particularly useful when the cities have different populations. The larger city is likely to have more crimes just because it has more people. By presenting crime in terms of "per 1,000 people," large and small cities can be compared using the same standard. In Exhibit 12.3, even though city C has a higher number of crimes, its crime rate is lower than the two smaller cities.

Exhibit 12.3 **Crime Rates of Three Cities**

	City A	City B	City C
Population	200,000	400,000	1,000,000
Number of crimes	20,000	30,000	60,000
Crime rate	100/1,000	75/1,000	60/1,000

RATIOS

Ratios are another way to standardize data to make comparisons. If small class size is a measure of a school's quality, then schools with few students per teacher will be deemed of high quality. Looking at the student-teacher ratio enables parents to easily compare schools of different sizes. If school A has 1,500 students and 45 teachers, and school B has 2,000 students and 50 teachers, which one has the fewest students per teacher?

These ratios are easy to compute: divide the number of students by the number of teachers. So 1,500 students divided by 45 teachers equals 33 students per teacher, a student-teacher ratio of 33 to 1. In contrast, school B has a student-teacher ratio of 40 to 1. If parents had a choice, they would probably want to send their children to school A because it has the lower teacher-student ratio, all else being equal.

RATES OF CHANGE

The rate of change is used when public administrators want to show how much change there has been between two points in time. For example, an administrator might want to show how much the budget has changed from the prior year. If the budget increased from $10 million in fiscal year 2007 to $12 million in fiscal year 2008, it increased 20 percent.

Calculating a rate of change is a technique I learned in my first job in the federal government. It is a good thing to know. Calculating a rate of change is a three-step process.

Step 1.   Divide the newest data by the older data; this is the initial result.
Step 2.   Take that initial result and subtract 1; this is the second result.
Step 3.   Multiply the second result by 100 to get the percentage change.

Using the federal deficit data mentioned above, the rate of change between 1980 and 1992, when the deficit increased from $74 billion to $290 billion, is calculated as follows:

Step 1. $290 billion (FY 1992 deficit) divided by $73.8 billion (FY 1980) = 3.93.
Step 2.   3.93 minus 1 = 2.93.
Step 3.   2.93 multiplied by 100 = 293 percent.

Exhibit 12.4   **Distribution of Respondents by Educational Degree**

	Number	Percent
High school diploma	33	33
Bachelor's degree	50	50
Graduate degree	17	17
Total	100	100

The results for other years would very different. For example, the rate of change between 1982 and 2002, when the deficit was $128 billion and $178 billion respectively, is 39 percent, a relatively small increase in the deficit.

Each rate of change calculation is correct. However, as the storyteller, a public administrator can emphasize the 300 percent increase or the 39 percent increase, depending on the spin desired. If readers did not see the trend line over time, they would not know that while the analysis might be technically correct, the choice of which figure to use might reflect a political agenda.

DISTRIBUTIONS

Frequency distributions are counts of all the choices (or values) within a single variable. If the variable is educational degree obtained, the values might be high school, bachelor's, or master's degrees. For example, the distribution of the education levels of the 100 people in an organization might be as follows: 33 have a high school degree, 50 have a college degree, and 17 have a master's degree or advanced degree.

Another way to describe a single variable is by the percent distribution. For example, of the 100 people in this organization, 33 percent have a high school degree, 50 percent have a college degree, and 17 percent have a master's or advanced degree (see Exhibit 12.4).

If the percents in this distribution had decimal places, they could be rounded to the nearest whole number. Rounding is beneficial for two reasons: whole numbers are easier to remember, and decimal places give a false sense of precision when working with sample data. The rounding rule: if the decimal is .5 or higher, round up, if it is less than .5, round down. If done correctly, the total should never be less than 99 percent or more than 101 percent because of rounding.

ANALYZING SURVEY SCALES

At long last, we come to analyzing survey data. Surveys often ask respondents to give their answers along an intensity scale. Some researchers use a four-point scale, but this discussion reflects my bias for five-point scales discussed in Chapter 9.

Exhibit 12.5 shows the responses to questions about satisfaction with various aspects of a city's recreation programs. It uses a five-point intensity scale plus an exit. Respondents who do not use the programs will check "Don't know." How can the data in Exhibit 12.5 be analyzed?

The first issue in analyzing survey data is how to handle exits: the "Don't know,"

Exhibit 12.5 **Satisfaction With the City's Recreation Program** (in percent)

	Very satisfied	Satisfied	Neither	Dissatisfied	Very dissatisfied	Don't know
Easy to get to	25	40	10	10	10	5
Affordable	50	20	10	20	0	0
Open at convenient times	20	35	0	25	20	0
Good variety of programs	20	50	15	15	0	0
Adequate number of classes, teams, etc.	15	30	5	30	20	0

"No opinion," or "Not applicable" responses. Leave in or exclude? There is no firm rule. If the percentage of respondents using the exit is relatively small, they can be included or excluded; in either case, the percentage distributions will not change much.

If substantial number of respondents took an exit, however, the analysts need to figure out why. If the question was part of a skip sequence, then it makes sense to report on only those who answered. For example, a citizens' survey might ask respondents to rate various city services. Those who did not use the services of the zoning department, for example, would hopefully check "No basis to judge." Whenever the exit responses are excluded from the analysis, the report should state, "of those who gave an opinion."

If it seems reasonable that a high proportion of the respondents do not use the program, then the exit did its job. However, if it is not clear why so many people took an exit, it might indicate that the question is flawed. The analysts need to figure this out before deciding whether to use the data from this question.

A second decision is the benchmark for identifying important findings. Again, there is no fixed rule. My strategy when analyzing survey data is to first identify where a majority responded positively or negatively.

Related to the benchmark decision is whether to combine categories. If so, how should they be combined? In my initial analysis, I look at the combined percentage of the two positive categories and the two negative categories. The neutral middle always stands alone. I then apply my benchmark to identify the questions where a majority reported that they are "satisfied or very satisfied" or "dissatisfied or very dissatisfied."

APPLYING THE DECISION RULES

Let us work with the citizens' perceptions about the city's recreation program shown in Exhibit 12.5. If the decision rule is to combine the "satisfied" and "very satisfied" categories and we use 50 percent as the benchmark, then the results might be presented this way: "A majority report being satisfied or very satisfied with four of the five factors related to the recreation programs: easy to get to (65 percent), affordable (70 percent), open at convenient times (55 percent), and good variety of program (70 percent). Just under half (45 percent) are satisfied with the number of classes and teams available."

It also is acceptable to report data from the dissatisfied side of the scale. In this case, the write-up might look this way: "Fifty percent report being dissatisfied or very dissatisfied with the number of classes, teams, etc." Although this is not a well-written question (because it is double-barreled—and what does "etc." mean?), an analyst might highlight this as an issue to be considered.

If a majority of the respondents are satisfied or very satisfied with most of items, the analysts might want to do an "extreme" analysis to identify the most important items. This means looking only at the extreme end of the scale and identifying the questions that had the highest percentage in the "very satisfied" column or the "very dissatisfied" column. It is important to note that if only a three-point scale was used in the survey, there would be no way to do an extreme analysis.

Again, a benchmark is helpful. I tend to use 50 percent as the initial benchmark because it is unusual to get that high a percentage in the extreme end of any scale. In Exhibit 12.5, half the respondents report being very satisfied with the affordability of the recreation program. This would be highlighted in the report.

While the extreme analysis is clear, confusion and some distortion can occur if the analysts report only the "satisfied" column without reporting the "very satisfied" column as well. For example, half the respondents (50 percent) are "satisfied" with the variety of recreation programs. In contrast, just 20 percent are "satisfied" with program affordability. The reader thus gets the impression that more people were satisfied with the variety than with the affordability. However, 50 percent of the respondents are "very satisfied" with affordability in contrast to 20 percent being "very satisfied" with the variety of programs. While both have a 70 percent combined "satisfied" and "very satisfied" rating, the conclusion based on the extreme analysis is that there is greater satisfaction with affordability than with variety.

HANDLING THE MIDDLE CATEGORY IN ONE-WAY INTENSITY SCALES

One-way scales change in intensity over the whole five-point scale and the middle category might actually contain opinion information. For example, the Goldilocks scale reads: Much more, somewhat more, about right, somewhat less, much less. If 55 percent of the students report that the number of required research courses in the master's program is "about right," it is useful information signaling that the students see no need for change; it is not a neutral middle category as is the case in two-way intensity scales.

However, it can be tempting to combine the categories of one-way scales to get very different results. For example, Exhibit 12.6 presents the results of a survey of employees' perceptions about the behavior of the managers in department A. The analysts initially adopt decision rules to combine the "great" and "very great" categories and report results using a benchmark of 50 percent or greater. The analysts find that of the five behaviors, only "meets frequently to share information" is rated as "great" or "very great" by a majority (55 percent) of the respondents. This does not look so good for the manager of department A.

However, a more positive result can be achieved by including the "moderate" column in with the "great" and "very great" columns. Now, the analysts can report that

Exhibit 12.6 **Department A: Employee Survey Results** (in percent)

To what extent, if at all, does your manager exhibit the following behaviors?

	Little or no extent	Some extent	Moderate extent	Great extent	Very great extent
Provides clear expectations	15	15	30	20	20
Provides frequent feedback	25	20	35	10	10
Meets frequently with staff to share information	5	10	30	30	25
Seeks staff input before making major decisions	15	25	35	15	10
Trusts me to do my job without close supervision	25	20	25	20	10

Exhibit 12.7 **Department B: Employee Survey Results** (in percent)

To what extent, if at all, does your manager exhibit the following behaviors?

	Little or no extent	Some extent	Moderate extent	Great extent	Very great extent
Provides clear expectations	15	15	10	30	30
Provides frequent feedback	25	10	5	20	40
Meets frequently with staff to share information	5	10	15	20	50
Seeks staff input before making major decisions	15	10	15	25	35
Trusts me to do my job without close supervision	25	5	5	10	55

the majority of respondents say that the manager of department A engages in all five behaviors to at least a moderate extent. Now, the manager looks pretty good.

If the "some extent" column is added—leaving only "little or no extent" on its own—the analysts could accurately state that at least 75 percent of the employees in department A say that their manager exhibits each of these five behaviors at least to some extent. Now, the manager looks really good!

How do employees in department B rate the behaviors of their manager? Exhibit 12.7 shows that if the analysts use the combination rule that adds the "some extent" column to the "moderate," "great," and "very great" columns, the results for department B's manager look the same as those for department A's manager.

However, if the analysts stick to the original decision rule to combine only the "great" and "very great" categories, substantial majorities report that the manager of department B engages in each of the five behaviors. If the analysts do an extreme analysis, a higher proportion of employees in department B report their manager engages in these five behaviors to "a very great extent" than those in department A. In fact, 55 percent report that the manager in department B "trusts me to do my job without close supervision" to a very great extent.

Given a choice based on the ratings of these two managers, which one would you prefer to work for, all else being equal?

The takeaway lesson here is that warning flags should go up when analysts combine too many of the response categories and most especially when they combine the middle category with one side of the scale or the other. The middle category stands alone.

Exhibit 12.8   **Guidelines for Analyzing Survey Data**

- Decide on decision rules and apply them consistently.
- Do *not* combine the middle category with either side of the scale.
- Focus on one side of the scale or the other initially.
- If there is little difference in the data, do an extreme analysis that focuses on the ends of the scale: "very satisfied" or "very dissatisfied."
- Do not report an "agree" category without also reporting the "strongly agree" category.
- Anchor narrative statements, like "some" or "most," with the actual percentage in parentheses.
- Provide the total number of respondents for an anchor if needed.
- Round percentages to the nearest whole number.

Analysts make decisions about how to interpret the data. While there are no fixed rules, some guidelines might make the job easier (see Exhibit 12.8). Sophisticated users of research results should understand the researchers' choices in analyzing the data and reporting the results. As always, the tough question is: Are the data being reported accurate and unbiased?

MEASURES OF CENTRAL TENDENCY

While distributions provide detail, sometimes managers want a single measure that provides a bottom-line summary of the distribution. What they want is a measure of central tendency.

Measures of central tendency look at the distribution as a whole and provide a single number that best describes the center of the data. I call the options the 3-Ms: mode, median, and mean. They provide slightly different summaries of the distribution. A mode describes the most frequent response or value. The median is the midpoint of the distribution; half are above, half are below this point. The mean is the average.

Averages are mentioned in the news all the time. For example, CBS (2007) reported a study that stated that children who played video games "played an hour on the weekdays and 1.5 hours on weekend days on average." How does this compare to time spent on homework? MissouriFamilies.org reported research that found that "on average, elementary school students spend 63 minutes on homework, and the middle/junior high students spend 77 minutes per day" (Gosche 2007). While we would want to know more about how these studies were designed before drawing firm conclusions, comparing averages gives an overall sense of which activities might get more attention by young people.

Since averages often include fractions or decimals, it sometimes seems to make more sense to use the whole numbers described by a mode. For example, people may be puzzled by news reports that the average number of children in U.S. families is 2.3. In this case, the mode might be the better measure to use: the most frequently reported number of children is 2.

WHICH MEASURE TO USE?

As with so many things in statistics, analysts working with measures of central tendency have choices. One constraint is the variable's level of measurement (see

Exhibit 12.9   **Analysis Choice Determined by Type of Data**

Type of data	Choice
Nominal data	Mode
Ordinal data	Mode or median
Interval/ratio	Mode, median, or mean

Exhibit 12.9). If analysts are working with nominal data, the only measure that can be reported is the mode. Analysts cannot calculate an average on religion because it is not possible to look at the number of people reporting to be Catholic, Muslim, and Jewish and combine it into an average. The analysts could, however, present a percent distribution of the religious preferences of the survey respondents or they could report the mode. When working with ordinal data, analysts can report either the mode or the median. When working with interval or ratio data, analysts can choose mean, median, or mode.

Sometimes the situation influences the choice. For example, there are times when the median more accurately captures the center of the data than the mean. Why is that? The mean is most appropriately used when the distribution looks normal—that is, it appears like a bell-shaped curve. In a normal distribution, the mean, median, and mode are very close, if not identical. However, if the distribution has a few very high scores or a few very low scores, the mean will no longer be close to the center. A few extreme scores change the shape of the curve. In these situations, the median will be a better descriptor of the center of the distribution.

For example, analysts may want to compare two sets of student scores (see Exhibit 12.10). The midpoint (the median) is the same in both sets of scores, as is the most common score (the mode). However, the means are different. Why? Look at the ranges. Student scores in group B range from 20 to 90 compared to 60 to 85 in group A. In the jargon, we would say this distribution for group B is negatively skewed: the distribution has extreme low scores that result in the mean being lower than the median and mode.

Some variables, such as household income, are typically reported in terms of the median. The U.S. Census Bureau shows the mean and median household incomes at various points in time (Table H-9). In Exhibit 12.11, the mean is higher than the median in each of the four years. This is because a few families with very high incomes will raise the average, but will give an inaccurate picture of the income in that community. Think of Bill Gates living in your neighborhood. Therefore, the median is used.

SHOULD MEANS BE USED WITH NOMINAL AND ORDINAL DATA?

Simple numeric codes are used to enter survey data because it is faster and much less prone to error than typing "strongly agree" hundreds of times. However, the computer can treat these codes like real numbers, raising the issue of whether to use means with nominal and ordinal data.

How is data coded? In entering survey data, "Strongly agree" is coded as 1 and "Strongly disagree" is coded as 5. Coding for ordinal scales is always arbitrary; it

Exhibit 12.10   **Two Sets of Student Test Scores**

	Group A	Group B
Range	60–85	20–90
Mean	73	66
Median	71	71
Mode	68	68

Exhibit 12.11   **U.S. Median and Mean Household Income**

Year	Median	Mean
2006	$48,201	$66,570
2000	41,990	57,135
1990	29,943	37,403
1980	17,710	21,063

Source: U.S. Census Bureau, *Historical Income Tables, Table H-9*, www.census.gov/hhes/www/income/histinc/h09ar.html.

is just as possible to code "Strongly agree" as 5 and "Strongly disagree" as 1. In a five-point scale, the neutral category "Neither agree nor disagree" is coded as 3. If there is an exit, such as "Don't know," it will be coded too, maybe as 6. If a question is unanswered, it is typically coded as 9. These look like real numbers to the computer.

Means of nominal data do not make sense and should not be used—ever! The survey data might be coded as 1 for Catholic, 2 for Protestant, 3 for Muslim, 4 for Jewish, and 5 for other. How would you interpret a mean of 2.4 for religion? You cannot. Take another example, gender. The survey data is likely to be coded a 1 for male and 2 for female. The computer, seeing numbers, will provide an average if asked. The average might be 1.6. Reporting that the average gender was 1.6 makes no sense. Percentage distributions or modes are the best options to describe nominal data.

What about ordinal data? There is disagreement in the field about whether means should be used. Sometimes using means for ordinal data just makes life easier for the analysts. They can quickly scan the computer results to see which variables have the highest and lowest mean scores. This enables them to focus on a few variables rather than analyzing the distributions of 200 survey questions.

It is also true that using means sometimes make it easier for readers to make quick comparisons. For example, student evaluations of faculty performance typically use ordinal scales and the results are reported as means. It is a quick and dirty analysis that is sufficient for the situation.

As a general rule, however, I prefer to report the results of ordinal scales in terms of percentage distributions when working with survey data. I think they are easier for readers to understand because they are so commonly used. However, if the choice is to use means for ordinal data, it is necessary to exclude the exits and nonresponse data from the analysis. Including them will distort the results because they are typically coded with higher numbers than the scale items. Including them will inflate the mean. If they are coded as zero, they will deflate the mean.

MEASURES OF DISPERSION

Measures of dispersion show how far the data are from the mean. A simple measure of dispersion is the range. Salaries in a public agency might vary from $15,000 to $150,000. Whether the range is too wide, too narrow, or just right is a judgment call.

The most commonly used measure of dispersion for interval or ratio data is the standard deviation. The standard deviation is a measure of how far the scores are from the mean. A low standard deviation means there is little dispersion. For example, if everyone scores 71 on a test, the standard deviation will be 0. In contrast, a large standard deviation indicates there are many scores that are far from the mean. The test scores in Exhibit 12.10 show differences in the amount of dispersion; that is, the range is narrower for group A than for group B.

Assuming that the data look like a normal bell-shaped curve when graphed, these rules apply when working with the standard deviation:

- 68 percent of the variation is within one standard deviation of the mean, in either direction.
- 95 percent of the variation is within two standard deviations of the mean, in either direction.

The standard deviation's importance in statistics has more to do with its use in calculating other statistics than in reporting it as a stand-alone figure, although it is sometimes used that way. For example, if professors wanted to curve an exam, the standard deviation would be used to construct something called a z-score (see Appendix A on page 230 for formula). The standard deviation is also used to calculate the standard errors of estimates based on random samples or confidence intervals.

Ideally, analysts would report the standard deviation whenever they use a mean so that the reader can get a sense of the amount of dispersion in that distribution. However, the standard deviation might be an unfamiliar concept to the average reader. Analysts should consider the preferences of their primary audience when deciding whether to use means and standard deviations to present their results rather than percent distributions of ordinal-level data.

DESCRIBING TWO VARIABLES AT THE SAME TIME

While the initial analysis of survey data focuses on describing a single variable (called univariate analysis), many times it is necessary to analyze two variables simultaneously (called bivariate analysis). If both variables are nominal or ordinal, then cross tabulations, sometimes called contingency tables, are used. If one variable is interval/ratio and the other is nominal, then a comparison of means is used.

Exhibit 12.12 **Respondents' Race and Gender**

Race	Men		Women		Total
	Number	Percent	Number	Percent	
White	50	21	72	31	122
Black	35	15	25	11	60
Hispanic	15	6	14	6	29
Other	18	8	4	0	22
Total	118		115		233

Exhibit 12.13 **Participation in Classes by Gender**

	Hands-on classes		Traditional lecture classes	
	Number	Percent	Number	Percent
Boys	28	55	34	45
Girls	22	45	41	55
Total ($N = 125$)	$N = 50$	100	$N = 75$	100

CROSS TABULATIONS

In describing data, cross tabulations, crosstabs for short, can provide more detail than a percentage distribution of each variable by looking at two variables at the same time. Exhibit 12.12 shows the detail obtained by looking at race and gender together. The table shows that of the 233 respondents, 15 percent are black men, 21 percent are white men, 6 percent are Hispanic men, 11 percent are black women, 31 percent are white women, and 6 percent are Hispanic women. White women constitute the largest proportion of respondents.

Similarly, crosstabs can describe the composition of participants in a classroom. For example, a school has two different teaching approaches: traditional lecture and hands-on application (see Exhibit 12.13). How would the analysts describe the proportion of girls and boys in each type of class? They would write something like this: "Of the 50 students in the hands-on classes, 55 percent are boys, and 45 percent are girls. In contrast, of the 75 students in the traditional classes, 55 percent are girls, and 45 percent are boys." The totals are shown as N, meaning the number of cases (in this example, the number of students). When interpreting and reporting the result of crosstabs, it helps to anchor the percentages in terms of the number on which they are based.

COMPARISON OF MEANS

When one of the two variables is interval or ratio, crosstabs will not be effective because they are likely to provide a long table that is hard to interpret. Comparison of means is a better way to summarize and describe the data.

For instance, analysts want to compare grade point averages (GPA) of men and women in a Master's of Public Administration program. The analysts have permission to access the student data online and compute the GPA's for men and women. The men have a mean GPA of 3.2 and the women have a mean GPA of 3.4. The analysts report that in this MPA program women MPA students have a somewhat higher GPA on average than men: 3.4 as compared to 3.2.

In another situation, the director of human resources of a public agency wants to determine whether salaries are equitable between men and women. He asks the analysts to compute the average salaries of men and women in his agency. The director receives the following descriptive data: the mean salary for men is $45,250 and the mean salary for women is $39,995. The mean salary for men is higher by more than $5,000. Do these data prove discrimination? No. It is possible that other factors besides gender—those pesky rival explanations—could explain the salary difference. More analysis is needed.

CONCLUSION

Descriptive statistics are used to shed light on a situation, provide feedback on performance, inform budget decisions, and persuade others that a course of action is needed. Counts, rates, ratios, percent distributions, and rates of change are all effective analysis tools in describing data. In other situations, means, medians, and modes will do the trick. There are also situations where it is necessary to look at two variables simultaneously to describe a situation.

While sophisticated analytic techniques can dazzle, it makes sense to use the simplest analytical technique that meets the requirements of the situation, keeping in mind the audience's knowledge of and comfort level with statistics. Sophisticated users should understand how the measures are defined. If there are distortions, it is likely to be in the measures, such as calculating the federal debt just in terms of the debt held by the public and ignoring the rest. The math is correct but the results are distorted. It is also important to pay attention to the decision rules used by analysts in analyzing survey data. Do their choices about how things are measured and analyzed result in distortion or bias?

Still, there is always some suspicion of numbers, even simple averages. "I abhor averages," Supreme Court justice Louis D. Brandeis stated. "I like the individual case. A man may have six meals one day and none the next, making an average of three meals per day, but that is not a good way to live."

EXERCISES

1. Data on oil profits were presented in Exhibit 3.3.
   a. What is the rate of change in the total profits (a) from 2003 to 2005, and (b) from 2005 to 2007? Which period had the greatest increase?
   b. What is the rate of change in profits for Exxon Mobil and Conoco-Phillips during those same two time periods?
   c. What is the story that your analysis reveals?

Exhibit 12.14 **Effectiveness of Instructional Approaches** (in percent)

Instructional approaches	Very effective	Generally effective	Neither effective nor ineffective	Generally ineffective	Very ineffective	No opinion
Lectures	34	51	10	4	1	1
Case studies	40	45	13	2	1	6
Class discussions	50	34	10	4	2	0
Student presentations	8	22	17	33	18	29
Group student projects	8	27	16	29	20	0
Exams	6	45	22	23	4	4
Research papers	33	45	15	6	3	2

2. One of the likely data collection instruments in evaluating the MPA program is a survey. Prepare a memo to the director of the MPA program that summarizes the three most important findings from your analysis of students' assessment of the effectiveness of various instructional approaches shown in Exhibit 12.14.

3. United Way's Community Assessment surveyed four different groups: households, minority community members, community leaders, and social service providers. Each group was asked the same questions and Exhibit 12.15 shows their responses in terms of the percentage reporting the issue as "major." Your task is to prepare a brief memo that summarizes your analysis of these responses:

   a. What are the top three issues for each group?
   b. Are there any patterns in which issues are seen as "major" problems for each of the four groups?
   c. What surprised you in these data?
   d. What conclusions do you draw based on these data? Are there any areas that need more research?

4. What are the best measures for the following and why?

   a. Summarizing annual property taxes paid by homeowners in the city last year
   b. Describing the religions of the survey respondents
   c. Summarizing the undergraduate GPA of the entering class of MPA students
   d. The most frequent score on the admissions exam
   e. Summarizing the annual income of families in different neighborhoods in the city

Exhibit 12.15 **Perceptions of Community Issues: Common Themes and Differences**

Extreme Analysis: Percent Reporting "Major Issue"

Issue	Household survey (*n* = 404)	Minority survey (*n* = 163)	Leader survey (*n* = 303)	Provider survey (*n* = 158)
Poverty	24	47	27	47
Hunger	20	42	19	32
Lack of local jobs	39	57	36	45
Lack of career opportunities	29	60	36	33
Illiteracy	11	38	10	10
Unsafe schools	14	21	7	7
Overcrowded schools	34	19	24	25
Water or air pollution	17	14	18	12
Energy or natural resources	22	14	20	22
Land use	41	18	39	41
Alcohol or drug abuse	35	45	37	51
Access to substance abuse treatment	21	48	31	39
Access to or lack of preventive health services	28	31	27	31
Access to or lack of mental health services	38	30	52	62
Access to or lack of medical care	38	31	41	57
Access to health insurance or lack of affordable medical or dental insurance	57	32	63	74
Access to or lack of dental care	44	40	30	49
Shortage of affordable housing	17	64	24	50
Substandard housing	17	18	14	28
Shortage of recreation/entertainment	17	29	14	16
Lack of cultural activities	11	42	11	10
Crime	21	16	12	15
Gangs	9	13	4	8
Panhandling	17	20	21	20
Discrimination	6	31	8	13
Family violence	26	30	25	44
Child and elder neglect	23	18	20	35
Lack of affordable child care	38	58	32	49
Inadequate public transportation	21	27	27	32
Unsafe sidewalks	14	12	13	9
Poor roads or traffic conditions	27	13	26	21
Homelessness	25	19	24	46
Too few shelters for homeless	77	64	57	76
Ineffectiveness of schools	9	2	10	6

Source: Community Assessment, United Way of Thurston County, 2002.

13 Data Analysis

Exploring Relationships

OVERVIEW

Sometimes describing individual variables is enough to answer the research questions. More often, however, public administrators want to know about relationships. Do some neighborhoods have less crime than other neighborhoods in the city? Is the availability of guns related to the declining crime rate? Do children who attend a preschool program perform better than children who do not? Is there a relationship? If so, how strong is it?

At long last, we come to the correlational design with statistical controls mentioned in Chapter 5! This chapter introduces common statistical techniques—crosstabulations, comparison of means, and measures of association—that are used to (1) create comparison groups, (2) control for rival explanations, and (3) determine the strength of relationships between variables.

USING CROSSTABS TO EXAMINE RELATIONSHIPS

When seeking to answer relationship questions, we need to return to the concepts of independent and dependent variables discussed in Chapter 2. Briefly, the independent variable is assumed to cause change in the dependent variable. For example, if there is a relationship between gender and attitudes about the death penalty, gender is the independent variable (it comes first) and attitude about the death penalty is the dependent variable. The working hypothesis is that if women are indeed kinder and more peaceful than men, then they are more likely to oppose the death penalty.

The workhorse for examining relationships between two nominal or ordinal variables (that contain only a few values) is crosstabs. The crosstabs results between gender and the death penalty are shown in Exhibit 13.1. The trick to crosstab analysis is the way the percentages are calculated. In this example based on my analysis of survey data from the National Opinion Research Center, gender (the independent variable) is shown in the rows and attitudes about the death penalty (the dependent variable) are specified in the columns. In this setup, the percentages should be calculated across the rows (that show the death penalty attitudes) and add up to 100 percent.

Exhibit 13.1 **Format 1: Gender and Opinions About the Death Penalty**

	Favor	Oppose	Total
Male	80%	20%	100%
	n = 515	n = 129	n = 644
Female	68%	32%	100%
	n = 508	n = 238	n = 747

Source: National Opinion Research Center, General Social Survey, 1991.

Exhibit 13.2 **Format 2: Gender and Opinions About the Death Penalty**

	Male	Female
Favor	80%	68%
	n = 515	n = 508
Oppose	20%	32%
	n = 129	n = 239
Total	100%	100%
	n = 644	n = 747

Source: National Opinion Research Center, General Social Survey, 1991.

To interpret this data, we look at the percentage of men who favor the death penalty as compared to the percentage of women who favor it. Of the 644 men who responded to the survey question, 80 percent favor the death penalty as compared to 68 percent of the 747 women. Put another way, the difference between the percent of men who favor the death penalty and the percent of women who favor the death penalty is 12 percent. Is this considered a large difference? My personal rule of thumb in analyzing crosstabs is to find at least a 10 percent difference before I will consider whether there is some kind of a relationship. This example meets that minimalist test, but a 12 percent difference is not huge.

Before continuing, it is necessary to talk about how the independent and dependent variables are placed in the crosstabs tables. There are no fixed rules about whether to put the independent variable in the row or in the column. However, some researchers suggest that it is best to place the independent variable in the columns and the dependent variable in the row as shown in Exhibit 13.2. In this set-up, gender (the independent variable) is in the column and views on the death penalty (the dependent variable) in the rows. The percentages should be calculated down the columns and add up to 100 percent. In practicality, the decision about how to set up the table is based on which presentation will best fit on the page.

Although the independent variable can be presented in either the row or the column, there is a rule about how percentages are calculated in crosstabs: every category (or value) of the independent variable is percentaged down or across the dependent variable. Whether gender is in the columns or the rows, the table shows the percentage of women who favor or oppose and the percentage of men who favor or oppose. The sum of the percentages for each category of the independent variable always total 100 percent. The results in Exhibits 13.1 and 13.2 are the same even though the formats look different.

Exhibit 13.3 **Incorrect Analysis: Satisfaction of Gold Lake and Toxic Lake Residents**
(in percent)

	Very satisfied	Satisfied	Neither	Dissatisfied	Very dissatisfied
Gold Lake n = 1,000	94	87	90	85	83
Toxic Lake n = 100	6	13	10	15	17
	100 n = 490	100 n = 230	100 n = 100	100 n = 130	100 n = 150

Exhibit 13.4 **Correct Analysis: Satisfaction of Gold Lake and Toxic Lake Residents**
(in percent)

	Very satisfied	Satisfied	Neither	Dissatisfied	Very dissatisfied	Total
Gold Lake n = 1,000	50	20	10	10	10	100
Toxic Lake n = 100	20	15	10	25	30	100

What happens when a crosstab table is set up incorrectly? Exhibit 13.3 shows the results from a fake study of citizen attitudes. The independent variable is where people live and level of satisfaction is the dependent variable. The analysts have percentaged down each category of satisfaction and dissatisfaction (which is the dependent variable). Of those reporting to be very satisfied, 94 percent are from Gold Lake. Of those who reported being very dissatisfied, 83 percent are from Gold Lake. These results look goofy. Why?

These goofy results reflect the fact that Exhibit 13.3 is set up incorrectly. Given the names of these locations, we would expect differences in satisfaction based on where the respondents live. The correct analysis would be to look at the distribution of attitudes among Gold Lake residents and compare them to the distribution of attitudes among Toxic Lake residents, as shown in Exhibit 13.4. While this fake data are not nearly as dramatic as might be assumed given the town names, these results show that 50 percent of Gold Lake residents report being very satisfied and 10 percent report being very dissatisfied. In contrast, just 20 percent of Toxic Lake residents report being very satisfied and 30 percent report being very dissatisfied. Setting up the percentages incorrectly is a surprisingly common mistake in crosstabs.

Here are my guidelines for working with crosstabs:

- If you are suggesting that a relationship exists, determine which variable is the independent variable and which is the dependent variable.
- Make sure that the percentages for each category of the independent variable add up to 100 percent.
- Show the total number of respondents for each category of the independent variable since this is the basis for the percentage calculations. Remember, that N is typically used to show the number in the population, while n is used to show the number in the sample.

- Present the data in percents (or percents and counts, but not just the counts).
- Round percentages to the nearest whole number to make the data easy to remember and avoid giving a false sense of precision.

CONTROLLING FOR A THIRD VARIABLE

Sometimes there may appear to be a relationship between two variables, while other times it might appear that there is no relationship. But appearances can be deceiving. It is possible that something else is influencing the results, but has not been detected in the simple analyses of just two variables. Social scientists speak of "controlling for a third variable" to determine whether a seeming relationship disappears or a seeming nonrelationship suddenly stands out. This idea of a "control variable" was covered briefly in Chapter 2.

The choices about which control variables to use will depend on the researchers' understanding of the situation, their awareness of what others have used in similar studies, and the data they have to work with. Previous studies can help determine which variables to include in their study as well as identify variables that have been found to be unimportant. Stakeholders may also have particular variables they want included in the analyses.

When researchers statistically control for a third variable, they are trying to determine whether the original relationship remains the same. If the original relationship remains the same, then the control variable is not a factor. Sometimes a stronger relationship emerges once a factor is controlled. For example, people's attitudes might not be very different based on income but when educational levels are controlled for, differences in views may appear. On the other hand, if the original relationship disappears, the researcher will conclude that the original relationship is spurious. We are back to the bogus relationship between ice cream sales and drownings discussed in Chapter 2.

Controlling for a third variable is fairly typical in analyzing data. This is one way to control for rival explanations. It is useful to go through a few examples here so this analytical technique makes sense (see Application 13.1 on page 171).

Suppose a mayor who has been working to ease racial tensions for the past year wants to find out whether there are differences in satisfaction with city services based on race. The results of a crosstab between race and overall satisfaction with city services are shown in Exhibit 13.5. Based on these results, the analysts might conclude that differences in satisfaction based on race do exist and that the mayor's equity program has not worked. But a quick conclusion like this might be incorrect. Are there other factors that might affect the original relationship? These other factors become control variables.

It seems possible that where people live might be a rival explanation. Maybe those who live in upscale neighborhoods are more likely to report being satisfied than those living in poorer neighborhoods. So neighborhood becomes the control variable and, for simplicity, the city is divided into two types of neighborhoods: poor and nonpoor neighborhoods. The analysts rerun the data controlling for neighborhood; the results are shown in Exhibit 13.6. In essence, there are now two crosstabs looking at race and satisfaction with services: one for poor neighborhoods and one for nonpoor neighborhoods.

Exhibit 13.5 **Differences in Satisfaction With City Services Based on Race** (in percent)

	Satisfied	Neither	Dissatisfied	Total
White	75	20	5	100
Nonwhite	50	20	30	100

Exhibit 13.6 **Satisfaction With City Services by Race, Controlling for Neighborhood** (in percent)

Poor Neighborhoods

	Satisfied	Neither	Dissatisfied	Total
White	30	20	50	100
Nonwhite	30	20	50	100

Nonpoor Neighborhoods

	Satisfied	Neither	Dissatisfied	Total
White	75	20	5	100
Nonwhite	75	20	5	100

The relationship between race and satisfaction disappears when income level of neighborhood is controlled, meaning that the initial relationship was bogus (or more technically, spurious). People of both races living in poor neighborhoods are less satisfied with city services than people of both races living in nonpoor neighborhoods. Of course, these are fake data that I can manipulate to create dramatic results; it is unlikely that results would be quite so dramatic in real life. The takeaway lesson, however, is that sometimes things may appear to be related but are really not. Statistical controls can bring this out.

EXPLORING RELATIONSHIPS: COMPARISON OF MEANS

Different statistical techniques are used when one of the variables is interval or ratio data. If researchers wanted to determine whether men and women are paid the same, they can compare averages. According to data from the National Opinion Research Center's 1991 General Social Survey, the average salary in the United States was $35,738. The analysis shows that men earned $38,965 on average, as compared to an average of $31,135 for women.

But is there something besides gender itself that can explain that apparent difference? One likely variable is education. Maybe men have higher levels of education than women, so it is education rather than gender that explains the difference in salaries.

The researchers do a second analysis to examine the relationship between income and gender, while controlling for education. Exhibit 13.7 shows the results from the General Social Survey. These data show that although women earn less than men on average, education appears to make a difference; the gender gap in salaries lessens as education increases until it disappears at the graduate level.

The next question is how strong is this relationship?

Application 13.1
Explaining Support or Opposition to Antipoverty Programs

Advocates for antipoverty programs are developing a lobbying strategy for the new legislative session. The advocates' strategy is to educate those who are not likely to support antipoverty legislation. The advocates have a hunch (hypothesis) that urban legislators are more likely than rural legislators to support an antipoverty bill. They ask their student interns to gather and analyze past legislative data to see if there is a relationship between the home regions of the legislators (urban or rural) and their votes on social welfare legislation. The interns prepare the following table.

Support or opposition for social welfare bills by location

	Urban		Rural	
	N	Percent	n	Percent
Support	75	63	48	37
Oppose	45	37	82	63
	120	100	130	100

Based on this analysis, it appears that urban legislators have been more likely than rural legislators to support social welfare legislation in the past. The advocates could, therefore, tailor their educational efforts to the new rural legislators. However, is the urban/rural variable really the key factor? What else might explain attitudes toward antipoverty programs? What are possible rival explanations?

The interns suggest that maybe political party identification plays a role. Controlling for political party identification means separating legislators in the urban and rural areas by political party and then looking at votes on antipoverty legislation in the past. The interns do a second analysis, shown below.

Difference in support or opposition for social welfare bills based on political identification

	Urban		Rural		Total	
	n	Percent	n	Percent	n	Percent
Democrats						
Support	72	80	40	80	112	80
Oppose	18	20	10	20	28	20
	90	100	50	100	140	
Republicans						
Support	3	10	8	10	11	10
Oppose	27	90	72	90	99	90
	30	100	80	100	110	

When political party is controlled, the initial urban/rural relationship disappears. Clearly, Democrats are more likely to support social welfare legislation, regardless of whether they are from rural or urban areas. Republicans are less likely to support social welfare legislation, regardless of whether they are from rural or urban areas. Based on this analysis, the advocates might want to focus on meeting with the new Republican legislators regardless of their geographic location.

(continued)

(Application 13.1 continued)

Once again, I am using fake data so I can make the effect of controlling for a third variable dramatic. What would these fake data look like if political party made no difference? The analysis in the table below shows that about two-thirds of the Democrats and the Republicans from urban areas have supported social welfare legislation in the past, while Democrats and Republicans from rural areas have tended not to support this legislation.

Little difference in support or opposition for social welfare bills based on political identification

	Urban		Rural		Total	
	n	Percent	*n*	Percent	*n*	Percent
Democrats						
Support	60	67	20	40	80	57
Oppose	30	33	30	60	60	43
	90	100	50	100	140	100
Republicans						
Support	20	67	20	25	40	36
Oppose	10	33	60	75	70	54
	30	100	80	100	110	90

In this scenario, the original relationship between geographic area and support for social welfare legislation did not change when controlling for political parties. Based on these results, the advocates may want to stick to the original plan of focusing on new rural legislators.

MEASURES OF ASSOCIATION

Analysts can use a variety of measures of association to determine the strength of any apparent cause-and-effect or impact relationship. These statistics are based on complex math that software programs can calculate in a nanosecond. Despite their mathematical differences, they all get interpreted in a similar way, which is a plus for us.

All measures of association are reported in terms of a scale from 0 to 1. Zero means there is no relationship and 1 means that the relationship is perfect. For example, if the relationship between height and weight is perfect, I could predict how much people weigh simply by knowing how tall they are. However, if there is no relationship between height and weight, the measure of association will be 0. The closer a measure of association is to 0, the weaker the relationship; the closer to 1, the stronger the relationship.

However, there is no firm agreement in the social sciences about the English descriptors beyond the absolutes of a "perfect relationship" or "no relationship at all." A measure of association of 0.5 could be considered strong, 0.3 as somewhat or moderately strong, 0.2 as weak or somewhat weak, and 0.1 as very weak or virtually no relationship. Because it is difficult to find strong relationships in the kind of

Exhibit 13.7 **Comparison: Average Income of Men and Women, Controlling for Education**

	Male	Female	Total (mean)
Less than high school	$22,767	$13,607	$18,021
High school diploma	35,556	31,586	33,188
Associate's degree	44,949	38,295	41,129
Bachelor's degree	50,490	47,706	49,034
Graduate degree	62,088	62,275	62,275
Total mean	38,965	31,135	35,738
Number of respondents	609	755	1,364

Source: National Opinion Research Center, General Social Survey, 1991.

Exhibit 13.8 **Guidelines for Interpreting Measures of Association**

0 to 0.1 = no apparent relationship
0.1 to 0.2 = weak or somewhat weak
0.3 to 0.4 = moderate, somewhat strong, or moderately strong
0.4 to 0.5 = moderately strong or strong
0.6 to 0.8 = strong or very strong

research done in public administration, 0.3 is generally respectable in my view and worth talking about.

The last detail is the sign, whether it is plus or minus. Some measures of association are calculated to show the direction of the relationship (as discussed in Chapter 2), using a positive or negative sign; some measures, however, are not concerned about the direction and are reported only in terms of 0 to 1. Briefly, a measure with a positive sign means that the variables have a direct relationship: both variables change in the same direction. They both go up or they both go down. A negative sign indicates an inverse relationship: as one variable increases, the other decreases. The guidelines still apply: 1 is a perfect relationship and 0 is no relationship. If the measure is a 0.5 or –0.5, it is still a strong relationship. The signs indicate direction: 0.5 indicates a moderately strong direct relationship and –0.5 indicates a moderately strong inverse relationship.

Exhibit 13.8 presents some general guidelines for describing measures of association. These are really ballpark descriptors. Given the lack of agreement among social scientists, it is best for analysts to report the actual measure of association so readers can make their own judgment about which descriptor is most appropriate.

There are a few qualifications. First, a low association may mean that there is no relationship but it could also mean that the relationship is being suppressed by another variable or that the relationship is not linear. More research or other statistical techniques may be needed.

Second, it is rare to get measures of association above 0.8. In fact, analysts and sophisticated users would want to look very closely at any results that show a measure of association higher than 0.8 because there might be something wrong with the way the variables are being measured or it might be that the two variables are really two different ways of measuring the same thing. Sometimes analysts eliminate outliers that are very different from the rest of the data. By getting rid of these variations, however, they risk obtaining a high measure of relationship that is misleading.

How do measures of association work? Suppose a public university's admissions committee is trying to determine if there is a relationship between how well students do in high school and their performance in college. The best measure of academic performance, in the committee's opinion, is the grade point average (GPA). The research question is: Is there a relationship between high school GPAs and college GPAs?

To visualize how this works, imagine that ten people in a college class arrange themselves according to their high school GPA. In this scenario, they are ranked relative to one another. They all receive a number indicating their place in the hierarchy: the person with the highest high school GPA receives a 10, while the person with the lowest GPA receives a 1. They then rearrange themselves according to their current college GPA. Again, the person with the highest college GPA receives a rank of 10, while the lowest receives a 1. If there is a very strong relationship between high school GPA and college GPA, then the person with the highest high school GPA (rank of 10) should have a rank of 10 (or near 10) for college GPA. The person with the lowest high school GPA (rank 1) should have a rank of 1 (or near 1) for college GPA.

Exhibit 13.9 shows what the rankings would be like if the relationship was a perfect direct relationship, a perfect inverse relationship, or if there was no relationship. In the perfect direct relationship scenario, those who did best in high school did equally well in college. In the perfect inverse relationship, each person has the exact opposite rank: people who did worst in high school do the best in college. The last column shows that ranking in high school GPA has no discernible pattern in college GPA ranking.

Life would be easy for the admissions committee if it could predict who would succeed in college by using something as simple as a high school GPA or even a standardized test score like the Scholastic Aptitude Test (SAT). The *New York Times* ran a story headlined "College Panel Calls for Less Focus on SATs." "A commission convened by some of the country's most influential college admissions officials is recommending that colleges and universities move away from their reliance on SAT and ACT scores and shift toward admissions exams more closely tied to the high school curriculum and achievement," Sara Rimer reported. After a yearlong study, William R. Fitzsimmons, the dean of admissions and financial aid at Harvard who led the commission, stated, "... no one in college admissions who visits the range of secondary schools we visit, and goes to the communities we visit—where you see the contrast between opportunities and fancy suburbs and some of the high schools that aren't so fancy—can come away thinking that standardized tests can be a measure of someone's true worth or ability" (Rimer 2008).

When a simple test provides inconclusive predictions about how well students will do in college, extracurricular activities, admissions essays, and recommendations have value in the admission decisions.

Exhibit 13.9 **Examples of Relationships**

Perfect direct relationship		Perfect inverse relationship		No relationship	
High school GPA rank	College GPA rank	High school GPA rank	College GPA rank	High school GPA rank	College GPA rank
1	1	1	10	1	5
2	2	2	9	2	10
3	3	3	8	3	7
4	4	4	7	4	8
5	5	5	6	5	2
6	6	6	5	6	9
7	7	7	4	7	3
8	8	8	3	8	1
9	9	9	2	9	4
10	10	10	1	10	6

FREQUENTLY USED MEASURES OF ASSOCIATION

There are many different measures of association but I will focus here on the most common ones used with nominal, ordinal, and interval or ratio data (see Exhibit 13.10). The emphasis is on interpretation rather than the mathematical formulas. The good news is that each gets interpreted within the 0-to-1 rule discussed in the prior section.

Two commonly used measures of association for crosstab analysis using nominal data are phi and Cramer's *V*. Exhibit 13.1 presented data that examined the views of men and women about the death penalty. There was a 12 percent difference between the men and women in support for the death penalty, which just barely met my 10 percent rule. But the measures of association are more precise than my rule of thumb. The measure of association (phi) is .112, which confirms that this is a very weak relationship.

Let us look at another question: are there differences in attitudes about legalization of marijuana based on gender? The results in Exhibit 13.11 show that the majority of people do not favor legalization. However, men were slightly more likely to favor legalization (28 percent) than women (19 percent). This is not a 10 percent difference. What does the measure of association say? Phi is .107, which is pretty close to 0. I would conclude that there is virtually no difference in attitudes toward legalization of marijuana based on gender.

Let us look at one more crosstab using nominal data to determine if there is a difference in employment status based on gender (see Exhibit 13.12). Since there are several categories of employment status, Cramer's *V* is the measure of association needed for this analysis.

The data show that, yes, there are some differences based on gender. Sixty-four percent of the men reported working full-time compared to 40 percent of the women. On the other hand, 23 percent of the women reported keeping house as compared to 1 percent of the men. How strong is the relationship? It is a moderate relationship, with Cramer's *V* registering a .354.

While I have made a difference here between phi and Cramer's *V*, my experience is that there is often very little difference between the two. I have not had phi show

Exhibit 13.10 **Common Measures of Association for Nominal- and Ordinal-Level Data**

Type of data	Measure	Comments
Nominal	Cramer's *V*	Values in the 0.2 to 0.4 range suggest a moderate relationship; values over 0.8 are rare.
	Phi	Phi is used with 2 × 2 tables and Cramer's *V* when working with variables with more than two categories.
Ordinal	Tau *b*	Tau *b* is used for square tables; Tau *b* is considered a conservative measure; therefore the results tend to be small. A Tau *b* of 0.2 or more is respectable.
	Tau *c*	Use Tau *c* for rectangular exhibits; 0.3 suggests a moderate relationship.
Ordinal with interval/ratio	Spearman's rho	Used when interval data are converted to ordinal scale.
Interval/ratio data	Pearson's *r*	Used when both variables are interval/ratio-level data. Shows direction of the relationship.

Exhibit 13.11 **Similar Views of Men and Women About Legalizing Marijuana** (in percent)

	Favor legalizing marijuana	Do not favor legalizing marijuana	
Male	28	72	100 $n = 381$
Female	19	81	100 $n = 549$
Total	23	77	$n = 930$

Source: National Opinion Research Center, General Social Survey, 1991.
Note: phi = .107.

a weak relationship and Cramer's *V* show a moderately strong relationship using the same data. The differences tend to be within the generalities of the English descriptors shown in Exhibit 13.8. So using phi instead of Cramer's *V* is not likely to dramatically alter policy decisions.

When working with ordinal data, the likely choices are Kendall's Tau *b* or Tau *c*. Tau *b* is used when each variable has the same number of categories (or values) so a square table is generated. When the variables have different numbers of categories, a rectangular table is created and Tau *c* is used for this analysis.

For example, what is the relationship between education and views on whether it is necessary to discipline children with a hard spanking? Do those with more education hold different views? Both variables use ordinal scales. Education has five categories while the opinion on spanking has only four. Eyeballing the results in Exhibit 13.13 does not show much difference. There is a 10 percent difference at the higher end of education; those with a bachelor's or graduate degree are somewhat less likely to strongly agree with spanking as a way to discipline children than those with less education. However, there is not a strong pattern here.

What does the measure of association tell us? The Tau *c* is .095. This is pretty weak, confirming what we observed by looking at the data in the table.

Exhibit 13.12 **Differences in Employment Status Based on Gender** (in percent)

	Men	Women
Full-time	64	40
Part-time	7	13
Not working (school, unemployed, retired)	26	22
Keeping house	1	23
Other	2	2
Total	100	100
	$n = 641$	$n = 859$

Source: National Opinion Research Center, General Social Survey, 1991.
Note: Cramer's $V = .354$. This is the test that the computer calculated. It is no different from phi in previous example.

WORKING WITH INTERVAL OR RATIO DATA

Let us look at how measures of association work when the independent variable might be ordinal and the dependent variable is interval or ratio. That is the case when education is measured in terms of highest degree (ordinal data) and income is measured in dollars (ratio data).

Exhibit 13.14 reveals a pattern: as educational degree rises, so does income. Those with less than a high school degree earn $18,021 a year on average; in contrast, those with a graduate degree earn $62,275 on average. Because we are working with both ordinal and ratio data, the measure of association we want is Spearman's rho. Spearman's rho is .480, which indicates a moderately strong relationship. This is consistent with the visual analysis of the data that shows a pattern of income rising as degree increases.

Education, however, can also be measured in terms of the highest year of education completed. This would make it interval/ratio level data. When working with two interval/ratio level variables, researchers have more options. One option is to run a correlation that uses a Pearson's r to measure the strength of the relationship. Using the General Social Survey data for income and years of education, the computer calculates a Pearson's r of .460. The positive sign shows a direct relationship: as years of education increase, income increases. At .460, this is a moderately strong relationship. It is also consistent with the results obtained in Exhibit 13.14, which used slightly different measures.

You will notice, however, that I did not present the results of this analysis of interval/ratio data in the form of a table. Each value would be shown in the table: $23,000 would show up as a separate line and so would $23,025. With over 1,000 respondents, this could be a ridiculously long table.

It is important to add that old data may not reflect the current situation accurately. An article in the *Wall Street Journal* reported that only workers with professional degrees, such as lawyers and doctors, saw "their inflation-adjusted earnings increase over the most recent economic expansion, adding to the concern that the economy has benefited higher-earning Americans at the expense of others" (Dougherty 2008). All other workers, regardless of education, saw their real earnings decline between

Exhibit 13.13   **Effect of Education on Views About Spanking Children** (in percent)

	Strongly agree with spanking	Agree	Disagree	Strongly disagree with spanking	
Less than high school	25	55	15	5	100
High school	26	49	19	6	100
Junior college	26	48	16	10	100
Bachelor's	12	52	29	7	100
Graduate	15	49	23	12	100
Total	23	51	20	7	$n = 997$

Source: National Opinion Research Center, General Social Survey, 1991.
Note: Tau c = .095.

Exhibit 13.14   **Level of Degree Dictates Earning Power**

Degree	Mean	n
Less than high school	$18,021	249
High school diploma	33,188	704
Associate's	41,129	87
Bachelor's	49,034	216
Graduate	62,275	108
Total	$35,738	1,364

Source: National Opinion Research Center, General Social Survey, 1991.
Note: Spearman's rho = .480.

2001 and 2007. Workers with a master's degree saw their earnings decline 3.8 percent and high school graduates' earnings fell by 3.2 percent.

While it is still true that people with higher degrees tend to earn higher incomes, the article points out that in 2000 the average earnings of people with college degrees was roughly double those of workers with high school degrees. By 2004, those college grads earned just 80 percent more. These data are another way to explain the association between education and income.

CONCLUSION

Crosstabs are the workhorse in survey research and any other analyses that compare nominal and ordinal data. If the researchers are looking at a relationship between two variables, the tables should be set up so every category (or value) of the independent variable is percentaged either down or across the dependent variable and adds up to 100 percent.

Measures of association show how strongly variables are related. While they do not prove cause by themselves, a causal relationship cannot even be suggested unless the variables are strongly related. In other words, a strong measure of association is necessary but insufficient in itself to demonstrate causation. Rival explanations still have to be eliminated. Correlational designs using statistical controls are frequently used in public administration research but, as discussed in Chapter 5, they are not as effective in eliminating rival explanations as a classical experimental design. It is also important to remember that variables can be associated but not causally connected.

Assuming a study was designed well, it falls to the analysts to take a careful look at possible relationships. Analysts start off by looking at the relationship between two variables. Sometimes variables appear to be related but the relationship is an illusion, while other variables can appear to be unrelated but their true relationship is being suppressed.

In the article describing the study about race and the death penalty published in the *Houston Law Review* discussed earlier, a critic commented, "It's bizarre. It starts out with no evidence of racism. Then he controls for stuff" (Liptak 2008). Yes, analysts control for stuff—those other possible rival explanations. In fact, the analysts may need to control for several variables simultaneously because it is rare for only one factor to influence or cause something to happen, especially with the complex problems that public administrators and policymakers try to fix.

When reading research results about relationships, my best advice is to exercise healthy skepticism and ask the tough questions before asserting—or believing—that research results showing cause-and-effect relationships are irrefutable facts. When working with data about a relationship, measures of association can help readers make their own determination about its strength.

EXERCISES

1. In this made-up example, the department chairs of three MPA programs agreed to collaborate on a study about differences in the student demographics as well as attitudes about their respective programs. One was a large program within a university, one was a small program within a small college, and one was an online program. The three chairs were curious to see if there were variations in attitudes because of the differences in the programs.

    A random sample was selected from each school. The survey was confidential and all respondents were assured that only aggregate results would be presented. A small incentive was included in the first mail-out: a school key chain. A second survey was sent to those who had not returned the questionnaire one week after the deadline. Three weeks later, the nonresponders were called to remind them to complete the survey. Three weeks later, a final postcard reminder was sent out. This extensive follow-up yielded an overall response rate of more than 60 percent in each school; 170 students responded from the large program, 55 from the small program, and 92 from the online program.

    You have been asked to analyze the following data shown in Exhibit 13.15 to determine whether the students in the three programs differ, and if so, the strength of those relationships. Of particular interest were other factors that might explain differences in the percentages who would strongly recommend their program to others or not. Please write a short memo summarizing your analysis.

2. Strength of Relationships

    a. What is the relationship between undergraduate GPA and graduate GPA?

    $$\text{Pearson's } r = +.375$$

    b. What is the relationship between class size and graduate GPA?

Exhibit 13.15 **Cross-Tabulation Tables** (in percent)

Table A
Does the percentage of students who are the first in their family to pursue a master's degree vary by program?

	First in family to pursue master's degree		
	Yes	No	Total
Large MPA program: University	39	61	100
Small MPA program: College	18	82	100
Online MPA program	50	50	100
Total (n = 317)	39	61	100

Note: Strength of relationship: Cramer's V = .220.

Table B
Does the percentage of men and women vary based on the program?

	Men	Women	Total
Large MPA program	43	57	100
Small MPA program	46	54	100
Online MPA program	36	64	100
Total (n = 317)	45	55	100

Note: Strength of relationship: Cramer's V = .10.

Table C
Do programs vary in terms of percentage of students who receive support from employer?

	Employer pays cost			
	All costs	Some costs	No costs	Total
Large MPA program	9	23	68	100
Small MPA program	2	4	95	100
Online MPA program	30	27	43	100
Total (n = 317)				100

Note: Strength of relationship: Cramer's V = .45.

Table D
Do the programs differ in terms of student employment?

	Not employed	Private sector	Public sector, not military	Military	Nonprofit	Total
Large MPA program	10	8	50	19	13	100
Small MPA program	46	4	27	2	22	100
Online MPA program	10	5	36	46	3	100
Total (n = 317)	16	6	42	24	12	100

Note: Measure of association: Cramer's V = .52.

     c. What is the relationship between gender and graduate GPA?

Spearman's rho = + .422

Note: Gender is coded: male = 1, female = 2.

3. In this made-up data scenario, a welfare-to-work program compared the results for women who participated in the program as compared to those who did not. The women in the program were selected because they had some work

Table E
Does recommendation of program vary?

	Extent of recommendation of program to others					
	Strongly recommend	Generally	Possibly	Generally not	Strongly not recommend	Total
Large MPA program	26	35	26	8	5	100
Small MPA program	16	65	15	4	0	100
Online MPA program	40	50	10	0	0	100
Total ($n = 317$)	30	45	18	5	2	100

Note: Measure of association: Cramer's $V = .29$.

Table F
Does class size affect recommendation of program?

	Extent of recommendation of program to others					
	Strongly recommend	Generally	Possibly	Generally not	Strongly not recommend	Total
Small class (< 20)	27	61	10	3	9	100
Medium class (21–30)	34	42	19	3	2	100
Large class (31 or more)	23	38	25	8	6	100
Total ($n = 317$)	28	45	19	5	3	100

Note: Measure of association: Tau $c = .157$.

Table G
Is the amount of individual attention associated with extent of recommendation?

	Strongly recommend	Generally	Possibly	Generally not	Strongly not recommend	Total
Very satisfied	56	35	8	1	0	100
Generally satisfied	30	60	12	7	0	100
Neither	3	68	20	11	0	100
Generally dissatisfied	5	16	51	19	8	100
Very dissatisfied	0	0	60	10	30	100
Total ($n = 317$)	28	45	19	5	3	100

Note: Measure of association: Tau $c = .46$.

experience already and had first applied for welfare within three months of the start of this new program. One hundred women participated and seventy-five completed the six-month program. Twelve months after they completed the program, the seventy-five women were found to be earning $12 an hour on average while women who had been on welfare during the time of the training program were earning $6 an hour on average. The program director issued a press release declaring that this new welfare-to-work program was a success on the day she was going to lobby the state legislature for more money to double the program.

You work for the chair of the finance committee, who has asked your opinion about this study. Do you think the training program caused these positive results? Why or why not?

Data Analysis

Regression

OVERVIEW

Statisticians have developed mathematical models to explore complex relationships. While similar in some ways to other measures of relationship, regression analysis has some unique features and is commonly used to explain and understand intricate relationships. For example, it can be used to determine what factors are associated with drug use among youth or why the violent crime rate has dropped.

Regression analysis is a powerful analytical technique that enables researchers to do two things. One is to determine the strength of the relationship. The other is to determine how much impact the independent variable has on the dependent variable. This information can be used to make predictions, assuming there is a strong relationship between the variables.

This chapter provides a broad introduction to one common type of regression technique used with interval or ratio data. Regression can be used to look at the relationship between two variables (bivariate regression) or the simultaneous effect of multiple variables (multiple regression). The emphasis here is on interpreting the results. The chapter ends with a discussion about the challenges of explaining complex phenomena in a political environment.

BIVARIATE REGRESSION: KEY ELEMENTS

Regression analysis provides a mathematical estimate of the relationship between variables. It is used to analyze variables where there is a linear relationship that was presented in Chapter 2; there are other techniques used to work with nonlinear relationships that are advanced techniques beyond the scope of this book. The two key elements are: (1) the r-squared value, which is similar to a measure of association, and (2) the regression coefficient, which specifies the precise impact of the independent variable on the dependent variable.

Like measures of association, the r-squared ranges from 0 to 1; the closer to 0, the weaker the relationship, while the closer to 1, the stronger the relationship. However, it is interpreted differently: r-squared means the percent of variation (or change) in the dependent variable that is explained by the independent variable. In the jargon, the concept of relationship is presented this way:

- r = correlation coefficient (overall fit or measure of association, which is also called r, Pearson's r, Pearson product moment correlation coefficient, or zero-order coefficient)
- r^2 = proportion of the explained variance in the dependent variable (also called the coefficient of determination)
- $1 - r^2$ = proportion of unexplained variance in the dependent variable

For example, is there a relationship between SAT scores and college performance as measured by grade point average (GPA)? If SATs are a good predictor of college performance, then they would make it easy for college admission officers to know which students are likely to succeed.

What is a good predictor? We are back to figuring out the strength of the relationship. Suppose the r-squared is 0.3. Researchers would interpret that to mean that the SAT scores explain 30 percent of the variation in GPA. This means that 70 percent (100 percent minus 30 percent) of the GPA variation is unexplained by the SAT score. In this scenario, SAT scores are not a bad predictor of college GPA; it explains something about performance, but the admissions committee should consider other factors as well.

What if the r-squared was 0.75? In this scenario, the SATs explain 75 percent of the variation in college GPAs; only 25 percent in the variation of college grades is explained by other factors. This is very strong: the SAT score would be a key measure in the decisions of the admissions committee.

The key takeaway lesson is that while the math used to calculate the r-squared is sophisticated, the decision about what constitutes a strong relationship is pretty much a judgment call.

The second key result provided by regression analysis is the regression coefficient, which predicts how much change to expect in the dependent variable for every one-unit change in the independent variable. Suppose there was a strong relationship between SAT scores and college GPAs. With regression, the committee would be able to predict how much the GPA score would change for every unit increase in the SAT score.

Visually, a bivariate regression can be graphed using a scatterplot. SAT scores, the independent variable, are plotted on the horizontal axis (also called the X axis). GPA, the dependent variable, is graphed on the vertical axis (also called the Y axis). After the data are plotted, regression analysis mathematically calculates a straight line through all those data points that is said to be the "best fit." This means a line that has the least distance between all the data points. Exhibit 14.1 shows what a strong relationship would look like: there is very little distance between the data and the best line. In contrast, Exhibit 14.2 shows a lot of scatter between the data and the best straight line; this is an example of a weaker relationship, where SATs are not a good predictor of GPAs.

Exhibit 14.1   **Scatterplot: Strong Relationship Between GPA and GRE Scores**

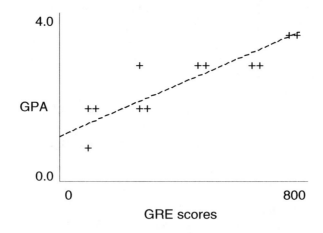

Exhibit 14.2   **Scatterplot: Weak Relationship Between GPA and GRE Scores**

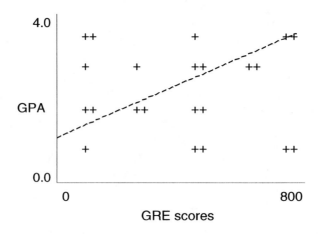

USING BIVARIATE REGRESSION ANALYSIS: SUNSHINE AND TOURISM

A city manager wants to estimate likely sales tax revenue due to tourism. I know nothing about tourism other than having lived in a beach town, but this scenario illustrates how regression can be used and interpreted; the data is a figment of my imagination (see Application 14.1 that was real data).

The question is: What factors are associated with the number of tourists visiting the city? Prior research suggests that sunny days are a major factor. Therefore, the analysts decide to build a model to track twenty years of data measuring the number of sunny days and the number of tourists during the peak tourist season. Once the data are collected, the computer calculates this bivariate regression:

$$Y = 100 + 1,000X$$

The city manager, having forgotten statistics from his MPA course, asks the analysts to explain the formula in the English language. They state:

- *Y* is the dependent variable: the number of tourists
- *X* is the independent variable: the number of sunny days during the peak tourist season
- 100 is the constant, that is, the number of tourists if there are zero sunny days

The number in front of *X* is crucial. In social science jargon, this is the regression coefficient, which is a single measure of how much effect the independent variable has on the dependent variable. In other words, this is the computer's estimate of how many tourists will visit the city for each sunny day. In this example, the regression coefficient is 1,000.

"Suppose the city has fifty sunny days," the analysts tell the city manager. "We can estimate the number of tourists by treating this like an algebra problem." They can make estimates by multiplying the number of likely sunny days by 1,000 and adding the constant of 100. "We expect to see 50,100 tourists if there are fifty sunny days," the analysts tell the city manager. "If there are a hundred sunny days, there will be 100,100 tourists." If every tourist spends an average of $50 on sales tax, the analysts estimate that city would receive $5,005,000 in sales tax revenue if there were a hundred sunny days by multiplying the $50 by 100,100 tourists. What is not explained is how the analysts came up with the estimate of $50 in sales tax per tourist, so a sophisticated user would want to ask that question.

While this is very impressive statistical magic, the city manager might be hesitant to submit a budget that spends this estimated $5 million. Instead, he asks, "How strong is this model?" He is asking about the *r*-squared. If the *r*-squared is high, then the model is a good predictor. If it is low, then there are other factors that explain changes in the number of tourists and the city manager would not want to put too much faith in the predictive powers of this model. If the *r*-squared is 0.6, the city manager could place a fair amount of faith in the model. Sunny days explain 60 percent of the variation in the number of tourists. If the *r*-squared is 0.15, however, the city manager should place little faith in the model because 85 percent of the variation in the number of tourists remains unexplained. When researchers obtain a low *r*-squared, more research is needed and the analysts should continue to build their model, assuming time and resources are available.

MULTIPLE REGRESSION

Building the model means adding additional variables, which brings us to multiple regression. This analytical technique measures several independent variables simultaneously to explain changes in the dependent variable. Multiple regression do four things:

1. It provides the overall predictive strength of the model, known as the *R*-squared value (also called the coefficient of multiple determination). Note that *R* is capitalized in multiple regression and lowercase in bivariate regression.

2. It predicts the dependent variable based on the contributions of all the independent variables, which can be added up.
3. It determines the impact of each independent variable on the dependent variable while controlling for other independent variables in the model (called the partial regression coefficient).
4. It determines the relative strength of each of the independent variables on the dependent variable by using a standardized regression coefficient (also called beta weights).

Continuing with the tourism scenario, what other factors might explain the number of tourists that will visit this summer resort city? One possible variable is the number of dollars spent for tourism advertising; if the city spends money to advertise, the number of tourists might increase. On the other hand, severe weather such as hurricanes might reduce the number of tourists. After discussion with the city manager, the analysts add these factors to the analysis and rerun the data for the past twenty years.

Generally, regression requires that variables be interval- or ratio-level data. However, it is possible to use a dichotomous variable, which is a nominal variable with two values that have been coded 0 and 1. It is also called a dummy variable. In this example, whether the city experienced a hurricane or not has been coded 0 if no and 1 if yes. A better measure would be an actual count of the number of hurricanes experienced in one season, but I want to show how dummy variables work in regression.

Using multiple regressions, the computer gives these results:

$$Y = 150 + 500X_1 + 2X_2 - 20{,}000X_3$$

This equation is not much different from the bivariate regression except that there are more independent variables. The city manager asks for an English translation. The analysts explain:

- Y = the dependent variable, the predicted number of tourists
- X_1 = independent variable 1: the number of sunny days
- X_2 = independent variable 2: dollars spent in advertising
- X_3 = independent variable 3: any hurricanes (no = 0, yes = 1)

The numbers in front of the Xs are the partial regression coefficients (also called unstandardized regression coefficients). These partial regression coefficients give the independent effect on the number of tourists, while the other independent variables are held constant. This is another way of saying "controlling for other variables," which is similar in concept to what we did earlier with crosstabs but using more complicated mathematics.

This equation is interpreted as follows:

- The first number (150) is the constant; that is a given.
- For every increase in number of sunny days (X_1), the number of tourists increases by 500.

- For every dollar increase spent on advertising (X_2), the number of tourists increases by 2.
- If there is a hurricane during the peak tourist season (X_3), the number of tourists declines by 20,000.

One key feature of multiple regressions is that it can be treated like an algebra problem. The partial regression coefficients can be calculated for each independent variable and added to give an overall estimate of the number of tourists. For example, the analysts could estimate the likely number of tourists under different scenarios using these three variables. Assuming a hundred sunny days, $200,000 spent on advertising, and one hurricane, the estimated number of tourists would be found by solving the equation:

$$Y = 150 + 500(100) + 2(200,000) - 20,000\ (1)$$
$$Y = 150 + 50,000 + 400,000 - 20,000$$
$$Y = 430,150$$

Under this set of assumptions, the analysts estimate that 430,150 tourists will visit the city. Assuming this is a highly predictive model, say with an R-squared of 0.75, the city manager could put great faith in these estimates.

BETA WEIGHTS: RELATIVE PREDICTIVE STRENGTH

The city manager then poses another question to the analysts: "Which factor has the greatest impact on the number of tourists?" It is not possible to tell by looking at the partial regression coefficients alone because each of the independent variables uses different measurement scales (number of days, dollars, and yes/no).

Statisticians have therefore provided another tool that enables analysts to determine the variable with the greatest predictive value: standardized beta weights (or standardized beta coefficients). Standardizing allows an apples-to-apples comparison. If the beta weights are 0.3 for sunny days, 0.8 for dollars, and 0.6 for hurricanes, then dollars spent on advertising will be the strongest variable. The city manager might want to increase the advertising budget to boost the number of tourists. If, however, it had turned out that advertising was a weak variable, he would want to rethink the city's advertising strategy.

REGRESSION IN THE NEWS

While most public administrators do not actually conduct this kind of research, they are likely to read about it in newspapers even if the article does not specifically mention regression. For example, a *Washington Post* book review in 1999 reported on the relationship between SAT scores and freshman grades (Bracey 1999). "Correlations between the SAT and those grades generally run around .45 meaning only 20 percent (the square of the correlation) of the grades are accounted for by the test," wrote the reporter. "Fully 80 percent of grades are determined by other factors." When the

Application 14.1
Explaining Income

What does regression analysis look like when using real data? In the previous analysis of the 1991 General Social Survey, gender was not strongly associated with income but education was. What happens if education and gender are analyzed simultaneously to predict income? The computer provides multiple regression results shown below:

Education and gender: impact on income

	Partial coefficients	Standardized coefficients (beta weights)
(Constant)	−5,629	
Highest year of school completed	3,773	.457
Respondent's gender	−5,100	−.099
$R^2 = .222$		

The partial regression coefficients show that for every year of school completed, salary increases $3,773. As gender changes from male to female (this is a dummy variable because there are only two categories, coded 0 for male and 1 for female), salary decreases by $5,100.

The regression equation would look like this:

$$Y \text{ (income)} = -\$5,629 + 3,774 - 5,100$$

To make predictions, we can create various scenarios and solve the algebraic equation. For example, if a man has ten years of education, the model estimates he will earn $32,111. Remember the algebra rule: the result of any number multiplied by 0 is always 0. The equation is solved:

Y (income) = −5,629 + 3,774 (× 10) − 5,100 (× 0 because men were coded 0)
Y (income) = −5,629 + 37,740 − 0
Y (income) = $32,111

What would a woman with ten years of education earn? This model estimates that women with ten years of education would earn $27,011. The equation is solved:

Y (income) = −$5,629 + 3774 − 5,100
Y (income) = −$5,629 + 3774 (× 10) − 5,100 (× 1 because women were coded 1)
Y (income) = −$5,629 + 37,740 − 5,100
Y (income) = $27,011

Which variable is the strongest? Looking at the beta weights (the standardized coefficients), which one has more impact on income? Highest year of education does; it has a higher beta coefficient than gender.

We still need to look at the strength of this model. How much change in income is predicted or explained by these two variables? The R-squared is 0.22. This means that 22 percent of the variation in income is explained by these two variables; 78 percent is explained by other factors. More research is needed to determine other variables associated with income.

reporter states that SATs account for 20 percent of the grades, he is referring to the *r*-squared.

Another example of embedded regression results appeared in a 2007 *New York Times* article, "Experts Question Study on Youth Suicide Rates" (Berenson and Carey 2007). A study had reported an increase in the suicide rate in 2004 for children and adolescents due to a warning by the Food and Drug Administration (FDA) about the potential harm of using antidepressants; the researchers believed that the warning resulted in parents refraining from having their depressed teenagers use antidepressants, thus increasing the number of suicides. Other studies challenged the need for the FDA warning. For example, one study analyzed data from 1990 to 2000 showed that "for every 20 percent increase in the use of antidepressants among adolescents, there were five fewer suicides per 100,000 people each year." These are regression coefficients that state the impact of the use of antidepressants on suicide rates.

Another example of multiple regression appeared in an article in the *Public Administration Review* on reinventing government (Kearney et al. 2000). The article discussed the attitudes of city managers and their self-reported actions in reinventing government. Researchers conducted a multivariate analysis using thirteen factors to explain why some managers have a more pro-reinvention attitude than others. While it might be tempting to glaze over all these numbers, the first thing to look at is the *R*-squared value. In this analysis, the *R*-squared is .05. This means that this complex model explains only 5 percent of the differences in attitudes or, alternatively, that 95 percent of the variation in attitudes is not explained by the variables in the model.

Not finding a relationship, however, is still important information. Future researchers can build on what was learned, either looking for other factors or changing the way the factors are measured. In either case, the initial research provides information that future researchers can use even though the findings are not immediately helpful in identifying factors that prompt innovation in government. Research, at its heart, is a process of discovery.

WHY DID THE VIOLENT CRIME RATE DROP AFTER 1991?

Research can shed light but it is also true that individual research studies dealing with complex public issues can read like blind men trying to describe an elephant. So it is with trying to explain why the violent crime rate in the United States declined after 1991. Violent crimes are defined as those offenses that involve force or threat of force: murder and nonnegligent manslaughter, forcible rape, robbery, and aggravated assault.

The violent crime rate peaked in 1991 at 758 violent crimes per 100,000 people and then began a steady decline. It dropped to 463 per 100,000 people in 2004 and rose slightly in 2006 to 473. Many researchers, interest groups and even politicians have offered explanations for the decline in violent crime, some using anecdotes and others using powerful regression techniques.

When running for the 2008 presidential nomination, former New York City mayor Rudy Giuliani touted his record, claiming "I reduced homicides by 67 percent" (Vedantam 2007). There is no question that the mayor implemented a number of actions intended to reduce crime during his tenure from 1994 to 2001. The political spin was "I reduced crime so vote for me." But did the crime rate drop solely because the mayor got tough? Stronger evidence is needed to draw that conclusion. For example, what was the crime rate trend in nearby areas? If the crime rate continued to increase while the crime rate went down in New York City, the mayor would have stronger evidence that his actions made a difference. If, however, the crime rate also declined in the nearby areas, then it would seem that other factors that Giuliani's efforts explain the drop.

The National Rifle Association also weighed in on this debate in 2007 with a paper titled "More Guns, Less Crime." It presented trend data showing the declining crime rate along with a decline in gun restrictions and an increase in gun ownership. This implies there is a relationship between the declining crime rate and the increase in gun ownership. Although the organization provided no correlations or measures of association, the political spin was to argue that increasing gun ownership decreases crime; therefore restricting gun ownership is bad.

However, trend data are just not strong enough evidence; there are too many other events occurring at the same time and none are being ruled out. The reader is left with insufficient information to assess whether this is a real relationship or just an attempt to make a political point by presenting things that appear to be associated but are not actually related.

Economists Donohue and Levitt (2001) claim that legalizing abortions explains the drop in crime rates, reasoning that legalization allowed women to avoid childbirth until they were in a position to care for their children. The underlying assumption is that unwanted babies growing up with mothers who are not ready to care for them are likely to become violent criminals. This assumption, however, is just an assumption; the authors do not provide evidence to support it. The political spin here is that if there is a relationship between abortions and crime reduction, those who support a woman's right to choose might argue that restricting access to abortions would have an unintended consequence of increasing future crime rates.

These social scientists provide evidence based on research to back up their theory, using multiple regressions in a display of statistical wizardry. The violent crime rate is the dependent variable. Looking at state data over time, they constructed a model that includes the effective abortion rate, along with prisoners per capita, police per capita, percent unemployed, income per capita, poverty rate, welfare generosity, the right to carry concealed weapons law, and gallons of beer consumption per capita as the independent variables. This regression model has more variables than the other examples presented in this chapter, but it gets interpreted the same way. The key information is an R-squared of .938 between the effective abortion rate and the violent crime rate, and an R-squared of .942 for the model with all the variables.

An R-squared of 0.9 seems to explain almost all the variation in crime rates. However, it is very rare to see such a high R-squared, so I am immediately suspicious. Certainly some of the independent variables in the model are likely to be highly correlated, such as income and poverty rate. That correlation will throw off regression models, which work best when the independent variables are not correlated with each other. It is also possible to get a high R-squared by eliminating extreme scores in the data, which by definition will reduce the variance.

For some reason that is not clear to me, there is a ridiculously high correlation between the effective abortion rate and the violent crime rate. In an explanation that is difficult for me to fully understand, the authors describe the effective abortion rate as a calculated figure that includes an estimate of the number of arrestees. Hmmm—there might be a problem here in including arrest data because arrest rates are likely to be highly correlated with crime rates. In order to determine the credibility of this study, I would have to dig a whole lot deeper. However, despite my skepticism, it does not mean that the researchers have not done a good job. They might indeed have found a relationship between legalization of abortions and crime rates.

The first takeaway lesson is that while I can raise some questions about this study and voice some skepticism, I need more than that to dismiss its results. I need solid evidence to refute this study. I also need to be mindful that some of my skepticism might be because the study challenges some personal beliefs. This awareness is a warning that I might not be able to make an objective assessment.

If I were an elected official being pressed to make a decision based on this study, I would hire my own experts to critique this complex and very statistically oriented study. So, the second takeaway lesson is that it is a good thing to recognize when some research study is beyond understanding and ask for help.

What else might explain the crime rate reduction? Could it be the reduction in lead poisoning? That is what social scientist Rick Nevin thinks (Vedantam 2007). Lead is toxic to the brain and lead poisoning is associated with aggression. Prior research revealed that geographic areas with high levels of lead had substantially higher murder rates than areas with lower levels, after controlling for socioeconomic and environmental factors.

Nevin tracked data looking at crime rates and lead poisoning in nine countries. Because other countries introduced policies to reduce lead exposure at different times, Nevin was able to do a comparative time series analysis using a regression technique. "Sixty-five to ninety percent or more of the substantial variation in violent crime in all these countries was explained by lead," he states. He is talking about R-squared here. He noted that lead poisoning is not the only factor but it is the strongest one according to his research. Again, there is much statistical wizardry here with a very high R-squared, which is a signal for closer inspection if a policy-maker is being pressed to make a decision.

Might there be some connection between reduced lead levels and the violent crime rate decline in New York City? Lead levels plummeted in New York City in the early 1970s; the number of children heavily poisoned by lead fell by more than 80 percent. Twenty years later, the drop in crime in the 1990s was dramatic. Is it possible that Mayor Giuliani's "get tough on crime" campaign benefited from the impact of actions to reduce lead taken in the 1970s that finally became measurable in the 1990s? Nevin's study is a good reminder about the complexity of the world and the unseen interconnections between events, including things that happened a decade or two earlier.

The difficulty in explaining the drop in violent crime is not unique. The policy arena is cluttered with competing theories about why something happened, some with strong analysis and some not. Some explanations may be designed to serve different political agendas, but truthfully, it is just plain hard to determine causality in complex social issues even with very advanced statistical techniques and the intention to be objective.

CONCLUSION

Regression is a very powerful analytical technique. When done well, it can identify causal factors as well enable prediction. One key element is the *r*-squared, which shows the strength of the model. Interpreted as how much variance is explained by the model, it varies from 0 to 1. The closer it is to 1, the stronger the model. The closer it is to 0, the weaker the model. It gets interpreted in terms of how much variation it explains. For example, an *r*-squared of 0.65 explains 65 percent of the variation; the other 35 percent is explained by other factors not in the model. The *r*-squared is the first thing I look at when assessing regression results.

In multiple regressions, the partial regression coefficients allow researchers to determine the independent effect of one variable on the dependent variable while other variables in the model are controlled. When the independent variables are measured using different scales, such as money, number of days, or a yes or no, beta coefficients are needed to determine which variable has the greatest impact.

Policy advocates often use statistics to persuade decision-makers to take a particular action. The fancy statistics are appropriate but can also bedazzle or intimidate. Darrell Huff, who wrote the classic *How to Lie with Statistics*, observed, "Many a statistic is false on its face. It gets by only because the magic of numbers brings out a suspension of common sense" (1954, 138). Maybe common sense is a better concept to use than skepticism when critiquing research results.

It is also true that even these powerful analytical techniques are sometimes too frail to give a clear answer. Warning bells should sound when someone tries to convince you that a single factor is causing a complex problem. It is rare to find simple answers to the complex policy issues faced in the public sector.

It is also important to remember that statistics can get so technical that only experts can make sense of complex and confusing research results. No one expects one research course—or a single book—to provide all the information managers will need. Perhaps the most important takeaway lesson is that it may be necessary to ask for help when the research results are based on unfamiliar, complex or confusing analytical methods.

EXERCISES

1. Solving the sunny days and tax revenue problem:
   a. The researchers calculated this bivariate regression analysis to predict the number of tourists per sunny day: $Y = 100 + 1,000X$. The analysts estimate that the city receives $50 per tourist. Using these figures, how much revenue will be generated if there are 75 sunny days as compared to 125 sunny days?
   b. Using the results from the multiple regression, how much revenue will be generated if there are 125 sunny days, $500,000 spent on advertising, and no hurricane as compared to a season with one hurricane?

2. You have been asked to determine what explains the GPA of MPA students. The analysts computed this multiple regression that included undergraduate GPA and gender as predictors. Interpret this table and decide whether either of these is a strong predictor.

GPA Multiple Regression Result

	Unstandardized coefficient B	Standardized coefficient beta
Gender	2.6	
Undergraduate GPA	.168	.371
R-squared = .275	.177	.323

3. Does country music cause suicides? Stack and Gundlach (1992) published results showing a relationship between country music and suicide. The results of their multiple regression analysis of forty-nine metropolitan areas show that the greater the airtime devoted to country music, the greater the suicide rate.

   They selected forty-nine large metropolitan areas for which data on music were available. They reported that the data on the proportion of airtime devoted to country music was calculated based on information from the Radio and Records Rating Report, spring 1985. Suicide data were extracted from the annual mortality tapes from University of Michigan national files. Gun availability was measured by the number of retail outlets per 100,000 people listed under "Guns" or "Firearms" in the yellow pages. A dummy variable was constructed, with southern states coded as 1 and the rest coded as 0; however, the researchers did not specify which states were counted as southern. Divorce rates were obtained from the U.S. Census data.

Explaining White Suicide Rates

Variable	Regression coefficient	Beta
Country music	.13	.27
Poverty	.28	.13
Southern region	2.17	.27
Divorce	.74	.30
Gun availability	.20	.08
R-squared = .51		

   a. How would you interpret the regression coefficients and R-squared in this study?
   b. Do you think the authors have provided sufficient evidence to support their conclusion? Why or why not?
   c. What other factors not included might explain suicides?

15 Data Analysis Using Inferential Statistics

OVERVIEW

The word *statistics* has two meanings. One is a general reference to numbers that are used to describe something. The other is a very narrow meaning that applies only to data from random samples. They are called inferential statistics and this chapter's subject.

Inferential statistics enable researchers to do two important things. First, they provide techniques to estimate how likely the research results are due to chance rather than being an accurate reflection of the population; these techniques are called tests for statistical significance. Second, inferential statistics enable researchers to make estimates about a population based on a random sample; these are called point estimates and confidence intervals.

These concepts were first presented in the sampling chapter. This chapter focuses on understanding how these techniques are used to interpret data. While formulas are provided in Appendix A (see page 230), this chapter assumes a belief that the statisticians have correctly figured out how to do the math. The mantra "I believe, I believe!" serves us well.

STATISTICAL SIGNIFICANCE: BASIC CONCEPTS

Results from random sample data have some probability of error because they are, after all, random. Are the results a function of some quirkiness of the sample rather than a fairly accurate picture of the population? Asked another way: If the researchers had selected a different random sample, would the results be fairly similar?

Statisticians have developed tests of statistical significance to estimate the likelihood of obtaining quantitative results by chance alone. Statistical tests come in 100+ varieties. You may have heard of some of the common statistical tests, such as chi-square and the *t*-test. But no matter which statistical significance test is used, they follow the same rules for interpretation. When these tests show that the results are not likely due to chance, researchers proclaim that the results are statistically significant.

The statistical significance level is called the alpha level or the p-value (probability value), and the social science standard is to set it at .05. This means that as long as the statistical test is .05 or less, the social scientists are 95 percent certain that the results reflect the population rather than being the consequence of a quirky sample. Put another way: the researchers are 95 percent sure that if they had surveyed everyone in the population of interest, the results would be similar.

The researchers set the benchmark. If they wanted to reduce the chances of being in error, they would set the alpha level at .01; if that test were met, the researchers would be 99 percent certain that the sample results are not due to chance alone. If they wanted to be really certain, they would set the alpha level at .001; at this test level, they would be 99.9 percent sure that the sample results accurately reflect the population.

All tests of statistical significance are partly based on sample size. If the sample is very large, small differences in the results are likely to be statistically significant. At the other end, it is hard to demonstrate statistical significance in very small samples (under thirty).

One thing to remember is that just because results are statistically significant does not mean they are important. The descriptors "significant" and "important" do not the mean the same thing. For example, the results may show that 75 percent of parents who send their children to public schools are satisfied with the education they receive, while 80 percent of parents who send their children to private schools are satisfied. If the sample is very large, this difference will be statistically significant. However, the bottom line is that most parents are satisfied with whatever school their children are attending. While statistical significance is determined by a mathematical formula, the importance of the results is always a judgment call.

The second key thing to remember is that the word *significant* is owned by statistics. It should only be used in the context of statistical significance tests. When talking about a study, researchers should not use *significant* when what they mean to say is that the results are important.

The third key thing to remember is that tests for statistical significance are not the same as measures of association. Statistically significant results do not mean relationships are strong; measures of association have to be used to make that determination.

The fourth key thing to remember is that statistical significance does not mean that design errors have been eliminated nor does it say anything about nonsampling errors. A test for statistical significance will not compensate for poorly worded survey questions or a low response rate.

The last key thing to remember is that, a result at the .01 level is not stronger than a result at the .05 level in any other sense than that the probability of getting these results based on chance is lower.

The main lesson about tests for statistical significance is that they have a very narrow purpose. They tell the sophisticated reader how likely it is that the results from a random sample are due to chance. That's all, folks! My favorite quote from a text I read in graduate school still holds true: "Unfortunately, researchers often place undue emphasis on significance tests," observed W. Phillip Shively. "Perhaps it is because they have spent so much time in courses learning to use significance tests, that many researchers give the tests an undue emphasis in their research" (1980, 172).

THE LOGIC OF STATISTICAL SIGNIFICANCE TESTING

While the interpretation of actual statistical significance tests is straightforward, many people find the logic of statistical significance testing bordering on mondo bizarro. I will walk through this step-by-step so it makes sense.

At the heart of tests for statistical significance is the concept of the null hypothesis. A null hypothesis is an assumption of no difference. It is framed this way: If there really is no difference between the salaries of men and women in the population from which the random sample was taken, then how likely is it that we would find this amount of difference in the sample results? For example, researchers gather data from a cross-sectional survey of randomly selected men and women in the United States. The results show that men earned $5,000 more than women. Are these results statistically significant; that is, is this difference an accurate reflection of the population?

Framed as the null hypothesis, the question is posed: How likely is it to get a $5,000 difference if there really is no difference between men's and women's salaries in the population? If the statistical significance test shows that the probability is small (.05 or less), then the researchers reject the null hypothesis and state: "There is a $5,000 difference in salaries, with men earning more than women. That difference is statistically significant."

If the statistical significance test shows that the probability is greater than the alpha level or p-value, then that means the $5,000 difference could be the result of chance alone. Therefore, the researchers would not reject the null hypothesis. In the jargon, the researchers would "fail to reject the null hypothesis." More simply, they would state: "There is no statistically significant difference between the salaries of men and women."

The steps in applying tests for statistical tests of significance are straightforward:

1. Set the test probability: the alpha level or p-value (default is .05).
2. State the null hypothesis.
3. Run the significance test.
4. Interpret the test results in terms of the null hypothesis; reject or fail to reject the null hypothesis.
5. Conclude whether the observed finding is statistically significant or not.

ERRORS IN TESTS FOR STATISTICAL SIGNIFICANCE

However much we long for certainty, the reality is that tests for statistical significance are about chance. Even when researchers are 99 percent certain that the results accurately reflect the population, there is still a 1 percent chance of being wrong. Conversely, when the test for statistical significance shows that the results in the sample are not statistically significant, it is possible that there really is a difference in the population. Social scientists label these as Type I and Type II errors.

A Type I error occurs when there really is no difference in the population even though the sample results show a difference. The null hypothesis is rejected but it is in error.

For example, suppose the test for statistical significance turns out to be .03. This is below the alpha level of .05, so the researchers reject the null hypothesis of no difference and state that the results are statistically significant. But what if there really is no difference between men and women's salaries in the population and their sample results are just a quirk? The researcher would have made a Type I error. When the p-value is .05, there is a 5 percent chance of making a Type I error. The researchers can make it harder to make a Type I error by setting the p-value to .01 or .001.

A Type II error occurs when there really is a difference in the population even though the sample results show no statistically significant difference. In this situation, the researchers fail to reject the null hypothesis, but are in error.

If the statistical test were .07, the researchers would "fail to reject the null hypothesis." The probability of getting that $5,000 difference between men's and women's salaries in the sample results if there really was no difference in the population is greater than 5 percent. The researchers would simply state, "There is no statistically significant salary difference." However, if there is a salary difference in the population that did not show up in this particular random sample, the researchers will make a Type II error. Failing to rejecting the null hypothesis in this scenario is an error.

Researchers are more likely to make a Type II error when working with small samples. Increasing the sample size or changing the benchmark from .05 to .10 will make it easier to reject the null hypothesis and reduce Type II errors.

So now we know the truth: there is no escape from the possibility of making an error when working with random sample data. If the researchers try to reduce the possibility of making a Type I error, they will make it harder to reject a null hypothesis. However, this action will increase the chances of making a Type II error. If they try to reduce the probability of making a Type II error by making it easier to reject the null hypothesis, they increase the chances of making a Type I error.

Which is worse: a Type I or a Type II error? It depends. Social scientists worry about making a Type I error; they fear concluding there is a difference in the larger population when there really is none. Program managers, however, might be more concerned about making a Type II error. If the sample results show no difference, it is possible for the conclusion to be simplified to a statement that the program did not work. Program managers would worry about a Type II error because if the researchers are wrong, a program that works might lose funding (see Application 15.1).

When working in the world of probabilities, researchers, program managers, and decision-makers should be very cautious in concluding that a program does not work because a single study fails to find statistically significant results. The study may have been too flawed or weak to detect the differences that actually exist. It is also possible that the sample mistakenly did not reflect reality and the researchers made a Type II error. Yes, more research is needed.

Application 15.1
The PTA and Computer Technology

The statewide PTA raises concerns about gender discrimination because of disparate opportunities for girls and boys to learn computer technology. The PTA believes that boys are more likely to be in computer classes than girls, which will unfairly limit the ability of girls to compete in the marketplace. The PTA requests that the state's Department of Education conduct a study to determine whether there is discrimination.

The Department of Education's director contracts a team of researchers. The researchers take a small sample of schools and compare the number of boys and girls in computer classes during the past year. The researchers analyze the data and find no statistically significant difference. What should the research team tell the Department of Education?

Technically, the researchers should say that the results of the study failed to reject the null hypothesis; however, few laypeople will understand what that means. More simply, they would say that their study did not find a statistically significant difference between the number of boys and girls in the computer classes.

However, there is a chance that the study's results are in error because it was based on a sample; there might be a difference even though the study did not find statistically significant results. The researchers should acknowledge that possibility even though that conclusion will not look nearly as definitive as the director might want. Still, I would sympathize with anyone trying to explain the possibility of a Type II error.

The director of the Department of Education has to report back to the statewide PTA. The director could say, "Based on the results of this particular study, there appears to be no statistically significant difference in the number of boys and girls in computer classes. No action needs to be taken." Note that she is careful to say "this particular study" and "appears." This wording softens the absolute statement.

On the other hand, the director could issue a statement something like this: "Our policy is that boys and girls have equal access to all computer technology classes. It appears that the policy is working; the researchers did not find any statistically significant differences between the number of boys and girls in the computer technology classes." This reaffirms the nondiscrimination policy just in case the study missed the discrimination that actually exists. The director could go further. Given that there is a possibility that the results were in error, she could state that she will continue to monitor the computer class enrollments. It is a way to signal that she is on the case.

COMMON TESTS FOR STATISTICAL SIGNIFICANCE

Many tests for statistical significance are available and are used in a variety of very specific situations. The most commonly used tests for statistical significance in public administration are chi-square, t-test, and ANOVA/f-test. Once again, the level of measurement of the variables—nominal, ordinal, or interval/ratio—is a factor in deciding which statistical test to use.

Exhibit 15.1 **Gun Permit Views by Gender** (in percent)

| | Favor or oppose gun permits | | |
	Favor	Oppose	Total
Men (n = 435)	77	23	100
Women (n = 528)	89	11	100

Source: National Opinion Research Center, General Social Survey, 1991.
Note: Statistical significance (chi-square) = .000.

CHI-SQUARE

Chi-square (χ^2) is used with nominal (categorical) data or nominal with ordinal data when using crosstab analysis. For example, does gender explain differences in attitudes about public policy issues, such are whether women are more or less likely than men to favor requiring gun permits? The null hypothesis is that gender makes no difference. The computer crunches the numbers and gives the results shown in Exhibit 15.1. Women (89 percent) are slightly more likely to favor gun permits than men (77 percent).

Chi-square is calculated in terms of the difference between the expected result count if there is no difference in the population and the actual sample results. That is, the computer determines the number of men and women who would favor and oppose gun permits if there was no difference in attitudes based on gender. This is the underlying logic for chi-square. The computer calculates how likely it is to get these differences based on chance alone. If the probability is .05 or less, then the null hypothesis is rejected and the results are interpreted to be statistically significant.

The computer reports a *p*-value of .000. This means the result is statistically significant at the .000 level, which is definitely less than .05. The researchers report, "While a majority of both sexes favor gun permit laws, a slightly higher proportion of women (89 percent) favor gun permits than men (77 percent). These results are statistically significant."

Once the differences in attitudes are found to be statistically significant, the next question is whether this is a strong relationship. A measure of association (phi or Cramer's *V*) is needed, but just looking at the results shows that they are not very strong. A key lesson is that it is possible to have statistically significant results even though there is a weak relationship. Tests of statistical significance say nothing about the strength of the relationship.

Do men and women have different attitudes about abortion? Using data from a national survey, the computer provides the information in Exhibit 15.2.

The chi-square is .788. This is greater than .05, so the researchers fail to reject the null hypothesis and conclude, "There is no statistically significant difference between men's and women's attitudes about abortion, with 52 percent of both men and women opposing abortion for any reason."

Exhibit 15.2 **Abortion Views by Gender** (in percent)

| | Abortion if woman wants for any reason | | |
	Favor	Oppose	Total
Men ($n = 424$)	48	52	100
Women ($n = 509$)	49	52	100
Total	449	484	933

Source: National Opinion Research Center, General Social Survey, 1991.
Note: Statistical significance (chi-square) = .788.

t-TESTS: ANALYZING DIFFERENCE IN MEANS

Three commonly used *t*-tests are single mean, paired means, and independent means. They are used in particular research situations.

A single mean *t*-test is used with interval or ratio data: it tests the mean of a single variable. The null hypothesis assumes the population has a known and specified average. For example, if a researcher assumes that people work a forty-hour workweek on average, then how likely is it to get survey results reporting forty-two hours? The computer calculates the *t*-test to give the probability of getting forty-two hours if the population average is forty. If the probability is low (less than or equal to .05), the researcher rejects the null hypothesis. The researcher will report that the average workweek is forty-two hours and that this result is statistically significant.

A paired means *t*-test is used with a before-and-after design. In this scenario, the sample received an exam before the treatment and another exam afterward; again, this *t*-test is used with interval or ratio data. A 15 percent difference is found between the before and after exams. How likely is it that this difference is the result of chance? In this scenario, the null hypothesis assumes that there is no difference between the before and after exam scores.

If the probability of getting a 15 percent difference is small—a *p*-value of .05 or less—then the null hypothesis is rejected. The researcher will report, "The 15 percent difference between the before and after exams is statistically significant."

An independent means *t*-test is used when working with two variables. One variable is interval or ratio data and the other is a nominal or ordinal variable with only two values. This *t*-test calculates the probability of getting differences in the mean scores between two groups.

In considering the connection between income (ratio data) and gender (nominal with two values), the computer will look at the average salary of the men and the average salary of the women and determine how likely it is that the differences are based on chance alone. The null hypothesis is that there is no difference between the mean income for men and women in the population. Exhibit 15.3 shows the comparison of means and the *t*-test = .00. The researchers would state, "Men earn an average of $38,965, while women earn an average of $33,096. This $5,000 difference is statistically significant."

Exhibit 15.3 **Average Salary by Gender**

Respondent's gender	n	Mean salary
Male	609	$38,965
Female	756	$33,096

Source: National Opinion Research Center, General Social Survey, 1991.
Note: Statistical significance *f*-test = .000.

Exhibit 15.4 **Average Income by Level of Education**

Educational Degree	n	Mean salary
High school or less	953	$29,225
College	303	$46,764
Graduate degree	108	$62,275
Total	1,364	$35,738

Source: National Opinion Research Center, General Social Survey, 1991.
Note: Statistical significance *f*-test = .000.

ANALYSIS OF VARIANCE

Analysis of variance (ANOVA) is similar to the independent *t*-test in that one variable is interval or ratio and the other is nominal or ordinal. However, the independent t-test can only be used with a nominal or ordinal variable that has only two values, like male and female. In contrast, ANOVA is the test to use when there are more than two values. For example, educational degree is ordinal data with four values (see Exhibit 15.4). If researchers wanted to know whether there is a difference in income based on whether a person has a high school diploma or less, has attended college or completed a bachelor's degree, or has a graduate degree, ANOVA would be used to test for statistical significance.

The table shows that average income increases as education increases. ANOVA uses the *f*-test to calculate statistical significance. In this analysis, the *f*-test is .000, which is less than .05. This is interpreted as: "There is a statistically significant difference in average income based on educational degree. Those with a high school diploma or less earn $29,225 on average, as compared to an average of $62,275 for those with graduate degrees."

A key point to remember is that the larger the sample size, the more likely it is to obtain statistically significant results even if the actually differences are small. Secondly, while *p*-values of .000 mean that it is very unlikely that this result is due to random chance alone, tests for statistical significance do not say anything about the strength of the relationship.

TESTS FOR STATISTICAL SIGNIFICANCE IN REGRESSION ANALYSIS

In the previous chapter, regression was presented as a way to understand both the strength of a relationship and the impact of the independent variable on the dependent variable.

Exhibit 15.5 **Regression Model Explaining Income**

	Partial regression coefficients	t-test Significance
(Constant)	7,174	.161
Highest year of school completed	3,880	.000
Age when first married	−142	.379
Homeowner or renter	−13,176	.000

Source: National Opinion Research Center, General Social Survey, 1991.
Note: R-squared = .33; f-test = .000.

Very often the data used are from a random sample, so tests for statistical significance are needed. Both an f-test (to measure the statistical significance of the entire model) and a t-test (for each of the independent variables in the model) are used.

For example, if researchers wanted to examine factors that might explain differences in income, they could construct a multiple regression model. In one model, the researchers included education, age when first married, and whether the respondents own or rent their home (see Exhibit 15.5).

Since these data are based on a random sample, statistical significance must be determined. The computer calculates the overall statistical significance of the model using an f-test; it is .000. This is less than .05, so the model is statistically significant.

The researchers would report the R-squared too. This model shows that highest year of school, age when first married, and home ownership explain 33 percent of the variation in income. This is pretty good for social science research.

The researchers would focus next on the statistical significance of the individual variables in the model. When the other variables are controlled, only two of the variables in the model are statistically significant in their relationship with income: education and home ownership.

Each independent variable is measured in relationship to income: how much change in income is caused by each unit change in the independent variable. This means interpretation of the partial regression coefficients. For every increase in year of education completed, income increases $3,880; this is a statistically significant relationship. Home ownership also is statistically significant. As ownership changes from owning to renting, income decreases $13,176. Age when the respondents first married, however, is not statistically significant and would not be added into the prediction.

REPORTING RESULTS OF STATISTICAL SIGNIFICANCE

The simplest and most direct way to report results of statistical significance in a narrative is to state that the results are or are not statistically significant at the .05 level. For example, "There is a statistically significant difference in men's and women's attitudes about requiring gun permits ($p < .05$). Eighty-nine percent of women favored gun permits compared to 72 percent of men." Both the descriptive percentage and statistical significance level should be presented.

Exhibit 15.6 **Selected Attitudes by Gender** (in percent)

	Gender	
	Men	Women
Favor gun permits*	77	89
Favor abortion for any reasons	48	49
Favor legalizing marijuana*	28	19

Source: National Opinion Research Center, General Social Survey, 1991.
*Statistically significant at $p < .05$.

When presenting data in a table, researchers often use an asterisk (*) to indicate statistically significant results and connect it to a note at the bottom of the table. For example, a summary table of gender and multiple social policy attitudes could be set up like Exhibit 15.6, which shows that two of the three are statistically significant.

Of course, not everyone follows this style of presentation, so sophisticated readers will have to read the notes to find out how the researchers handled statistical significance. Often a variety of unnecessary information is presented in research reports. In precomputer days, tests for statistical significance were calculated by hand (see Appendix A for the formulas). The results of these calculations were used to compare with a table that would tell the researcher whether the results were statistically significant; an example is also presented in Appendix A.

Some researchers continue to state the actual t-value or chi-square value, as if the readers are going to check the various tables in statistics books to determine for themselves whether the results are statistically significant. Clearly, I think this is silly, but it helps to know what these extra numbers are so you can ignore them.

Researchers writing for the general public or a practitioner audience are well advised to avoid unnecessary information and focus on what matters. When reporting results from a random sample, one key piece of information is whether the results are statistically significant. If more detailed social science information is needed, provide it in an appendix.

As you know by now, I like to use fake data to make my points dramatic. However, sometimes I cannot beat reality. "State workers more satisfied: scores improve from 2006 job survey" appeared as the top of the fold headline in the local newspaper (Wilson 2008). In a survey asking a number of questions on a five-point agree-disagree scale, with 5 being the strongest agreement, the overall average in 2006 was 3.78. In the 2007 study, the average score was 3.8. The state official stated: "You think, big deal. . . . [but] that is a statistically significant difference. It is an improvement. It's not just random." Assuming that the p-value was .05 or less, it is true that statistically significant results are not likely to be a quirk.

We are back to the issue of meaningful versus significant results. If I were the head of the state government, I would not be joyously jumping up and down because the average went from 3.78 to 3.8. While I can understand the desire to see improvement, in my view, this is spin. Statistically significant results are not inherently important or meaningful.

POPULATION ESTIMATES AND CONFIDENCE INTERVALS

Isn't amazing that researchers predict who will win a presidential election based on random samples of just 1,800 people? This is the magic of inferential statistics: they enable researchers to make estimates about what is true in the population based on a relatively small random sample.

Although I briefly presented this topic in the chapter on sampling, it makes sense to go through some of these concepts again. A point estimate is the specific estimate about what is true in the population. For example, when researchers report that the average salary in the population is $35,714, they are giving the point estimate. When they report that men earn $38,965 a year and women earn $33,096, they are also giving point estimates.

However, there is some degree of error. The researchers can then estimate the range of the true average salary if they had surveyed everyone. This is the confidence interval, where the true average can be found. The researchers would state: "We are 95 percent certain that the true average salary in the population is between $34,357 and $37,072."

Alternatively, the researchers could construct confidence intervals around the income of men and of women. The write-up might look like this: "We are 95 percent certain that the average salary for men in the population is between $36,938 and $40,992 and between $31,285 and $34,907 for women." The narrower the range, the more precise the estimates are.

Let us return to the estimate of the number of Iraqi deaths presented in the discussion of random cluster sampling in Chapter 10 (Burnham et al. 2006). In that study, the researchers state: "We estimate that as of July 2006, there have been 654,965 (392,979 – 942,636) excess Iraqi deaths as a consequence of the war." The 654,965 deaths is the point estimate. What is the true figure? The researchers are 95 percent certain that the true number of Iraqi deaths in the population is between 392,979 and 942,636. The researchers state that the wide confidence interval is the result of using relatively few clusters even though they surveyed over 1,800 households. They note that if they had used 470 clusters instead of just 47, the results would have been more precise. However, that was difficult given the situation.

It is also true that there is a 5 percent chance that the true number of deaths is outside of the confidence interval. It could be more or it could be less. The numbers based on random sample data give a sense of the situation but not an exact count. However, the fact that the numbers are not an exact count is no basis to completely discount the data as bogus. This is just the reality of working with sample data.

CONCLUSION

Statistical significance tests assume that a study was done properly: that the sample was randomly selected, that the measures were valid and reliable, and that the design ruled out other possible explanations. If these assumptions are violated, statistical significance tests are useless in telling us how much faith to put in the results. Statistical tests cannot fix serious design flaws. They indicate only how likely it is that the results are due to chance; they say nothing about importance or the strength of any relationships.

When working with random sample data, there is always some possibility of being wrong. Social scientists classify these potential errors as Type I and Type II. Certainty is an illusion when working with results from random sample data.

While the emphasis in research is to find statistically significant results, finding nonstatistically significant results can still be very important. For example, if the researchers are expecting to find differences in salary based on gender but the results are not statistically significant, it could be that discrimination does not exist. Researchers can also learn from these studies that did not find statistically significant results in order to design follow-up research.

Inferential statistics are a powerful analytical technique. They enable researchers to figure out the likelihood of getting the results by chance alone and to make estimates about the population based on the sample results. However, point estimates are not absolute; they only make sense within the estimated confidence intervals, which are also not absolute. Researchers need to acknowledge that even the most impressive statistical results might not be as solid as they appear.

If researchers want to avoid inferential statistics altogether, they should collect data from the entire population. If all the citizens, all the files, all the employees, or all the roads are included in the data collection, then inferential statistics are not needed.

EXERCISES

1. Interpreting tests of statistical significance:
   a. Are the GPAs of men and women significantly different?

Men	3.31
Women	3.50

   t-test = .001

   b. Are the GPAs of white and nonwhite students significantly different?

White	3.40
Nonwhite	3.47

   t-test = .056

   c. Are the GPAs of students from the large, small, and online MPA program significantly different?

Large MPA program	3.37
Small MPA program	3.58
Online MPA program	3.42

   ANOVA f-test = .001

2. Your boss wants to do an employee satisfaction study. Her plan is to survey everyone. She wants you to prepare an analysis plan, including tests for statistical significance. Are statistical tests necessary? Why or why not?

3. The mayor wants to survey citizens to find out their views. His plan is to have city employees interview citizens in the downtown areas from noon to 2 p.m.

during the first week of October. He remembers his statistics course from college but does not remember which statistical test would be appropriate. What is your response?

4. The United Way wants to survey citizens to find out their views. Questions will be ordinal scales rating whether the various issues are major, minor, or no problems. The plan is to do a telephone survey of 500 people using random digit dialing. What tests of statistical significance should be used? Explain.

5. The director of the child welfare agency is interested in the length of time that families receive protective services. She asks you to gather data and write a report about the average number of treatment hours received by clients per month and the average number of months the cases are open. The data are not in a computer, so you will have to look at closed files. She wants the results to be statistically significant and so it will be necessary to gather data from 300 files. Describe your sampling strategy. What test for statistical significance would be appropriate?

6. A program was implemented to improve reading scores. A group of fifth graders was randomly selected from across the school district to participate. The students were given a reading test before and after the program. What test of statistical significance should the researchers use?

7. The Portland City Survey states that caution should be used in comparing 2005 data with 2007 survey results. In 2007, the margin of error within any of the seventy-five neighborhood areas was between plus and minus 5 and 8 percent. What does this mean?

16 Communicating Research Results

OVERVIEW

What are the answers to the questions asked at the very beginning of the research process? What have the researchers learned? In the reporting phase, the researchers have often to decide which of the many possible stories to tell and how to tell them.

Reporting can take a number of forms; this chapter briefly covers formal reports, executive summaries, the use of charts, and oral briefings. Every audience is different and every organization has its own preferred communication style.

This chapter provides some guidelines for presenting research results. The first section focuses narrowly on how to write up data so that it makes sense to the reader. This is followed by general guidelines about writing reports, executive summaries, and oral presentations. These are general guidelines that should be adapted to the situation as needed.

EFFECTIVELY REPORTING RESULTS

The first step is to identify the major findings from the data analysis. Based on those findings, the researchers sometimes propose steps for action. It might be that more research is needed because the study ran into some unanticipated difficulties that reduced the quality of the research or because the study raised more questions that need to be answered before a policy or program action is clear. Other times, however, the research is strong enough to warrant recommendations. These should be very clearly stated: specifically who should do exactly what by when. The report should provide convincing evidence to support those recommendations.

The researchers begin by using the data analysis to answer their guiding research questions. It is likely, however, that other questions may have surfaced or some data have revealed surprising results. The story emerges as the researchers make sense of the data. There are multiple stories, so the researchers and those sponsoring the research must work carefully to distill the most essential story that best answers the research questions and convey it in an accurate and unbiased way.

When writing research for an organization, the researchers will adhere to the organization's preferred format for presenting research results. It is also likely that others besides the researchers will make the final decisions about the message of the report and any recommendations. Researchers working outside of an organizational structure will consider their primary audience as they craft the research report, and it is very likely that those contracting for the research will want to make edits. The style of research written for an academic publication will be different from that written for the general public. Professional journals have different styles and the researchers need to be ready to make changes suggested by the editors.

The major difference between writing for an academic audience and an organizational audience is in the overall format and flow. Academic writing builds up to the conclusions. Practitioners reverse that. Someone in one of my classes passed along this advice: BLUF. This does not mean fool people; it means putting the bottom line up front. When I worked at the U.S. Government Accountability Office (GAO), the writing style was similar but was framed in terms of a T-structure. The writer places the main message first and then supports it with the rest of the paragraph or the next several paragraphs. This is different from academic writing, where the style is to build to the conclusion. One needs to be mindful of what the audience expects.

The research results might be communicated through a written report. Typically, these reports lead with a very short, highly synthesized executive summary. It provides enough detail to explain the study along with the key findings and recommendations; it is as close to a bottom line as a report is going to get. The body of the report contains more detail but is still written simply and clearly; technical information or detailed analyses are typically placed in an appendix. Charts and tables are used to highlight the key points, not to dazzle or overwhelm the reader. Used sparingly, they will make the key messages clear and memorable.

It really does help to have others review the draft. Sometimes a small change— taking out a few words or changing a single word—will greatly improve the report. Writers can easily get too attached to what they have written. Detachment is very helpful here so that they can make the changes suggested by the reviewers. The goal is to write the best possible report, one that is clear, engaging, and on-point. The reviewers help. Their criticism is not personal.

Research results are also communicated through oral presentations. These presentations have to be very tightly focused and the main points communicated clearly. Less is typically better than more. A zillion PowerPoint presentations will only bore the audience: handouts and visual presentations can be very helpful but should be kept to the bare minimum needed to effectively tell the story. Everything else gets cut. Again, a friendly reviewer can help select the essential slides and cut the rest.

Presenting research results is a performance; rehearsal pays off. Unless you are a gifted speaker who is very familiar with the material, it really helps to have the presentation scripted. It will keep the presentation focused on the key points and avoid digressions that eat up precious time. It also helps to know how much time is available for the presentation and for discussion. Practice with a stopwatch so that the presentation does not exceed the time available.

If your presentation is likely to be given before a hostile audience, make sure you have some colleagues listen to the presentation first and ask the tough questions. Many of us need time to formulate a good response to a hostile or difficult question. These practice sessions give time for that reflective "I wish I had said" process.

REPORTING DATA

The goal is to present data so that it reads clearly in the English language. The intention is to make it simple and easy for the audience to understand. The challenge is to do that without sacrificing accuracy, depth, and insight. When presenting key findings, present the aggregate results first—that is, what percent of all the respondents said they would strongly or very strongly recommend the program? Then provide more detail. Were there some important differences based on key variables? If not, you just get to summarize, saying there were none. If there were some interesting differences, these become part of the story.

When reporting survey data, it helps to anchor English descriptors with the percents. For example, "Most men (60 percent) reported they would strongly or very strongly recommend the program while less than half of the women (43 percent) did." It also helps to round to the nearest whole number rather than use decimal places when working with survey data and any other data where the decimal places are not meaningful information.

Be careful not to use the word *significant* unless you are talking about statistical significance. Other words—such as *important*, *key*, *meaningful*, or *surprising*—can be used to describe findings. If the results are statistically significant, then try to write that up as simply as possible.

When means (averages) are used, the standard deviation should also be provided. It is necessary to provide enough explanation about standard deviations so the reader understands them. Do not assume your reader has taken a statistics course in the past six months.

If the data are from nonrandom samples, it is correct to point out that these results are not generalizable to the larger population. It helps to use some reminders from time to time, such as "participants in the focus group said" or "four of the five senior executives that were interviewed told us."

While many people panic over statistics, the real problems are often in how the data are interpreted. It is all too easy to accidentally distort the statistical results in the write-up. Exhibit 16.1 presents common mistakes in writing up data results.

GENERAL GUIDE FOR COMMUNICATING RESEARCH RESULTS

- Keep the text simple and free from jargon. Avoid acronyms, or spell out when first used and place the acronym in parentheses; if the acronym has not been used recently in the text, provide the full name and acronym in parentheses again. Present variables in English, not the variable names used by the computer. V8 sounds like juice, not the Recommend the Program.
- Use active voice ("The respondents report that . . . "), which is less wordy and more direct than passive voice ("It was reported by the respondents that . . . ").

Exhibit 16.1 **Common Mistakes in Writing Up Results**

- Reporting perceptions as fact. For example, students are asked to rate the effectiveness of a program. The reporting mistake occurs if the analysts state, "The program is effective" rather than "A majority of the participants rate the program effective."
- Changing words midstream. For example, the respondents are asked to identify the barriers and supports to the program but the results are reported as "pros" and "cons."
- Overgeneralizing the results. For example, students are asked to rate various components of a course but the report states, "Most (70 percent) students rate the course as a success"—even though they were never asked that question. Assuming a majority rate all components as effective, it would be more accurate to say, "A majority of the students rate all components of the course as effective."
- Confusing proportion with majority. For example, analysts report that a majority of women favor curriculum changes, when in fact only 40 percent favor curriculum changes. It would be correct to say a greater proportion of women (40 percent) favor curriculum changes as compared to men (30 percent).
- Failing to provide context. For example, analysts say "All of the instructors report . . ." when they should say "All five instructors out of a total of twenty instructors that we interviewed report . . ."
- Using percents when the numbers are small. For example, the report reads "Eighty percent of the participants state . . ." when a more accurate wording would be "Four out of five participants interviewed state . . ."
- Using misleading percentage changes: For example, the analysts report a 100 percent increase in the number of political appointees in an agency when the actual number of political appointees increased from one to two.
- Attributing causality when it is not demonstrated. For example, the report says that a program "caused" a $980 increase in income when what is really known is that those in the program earned $980 more than those not in the program. The analysts need to demonstrate that there was a strong enough design before concluding a causal relationship.

- Provide enough information about your research methods so others can judge its credibility. Full disclosure is essential. It may be helpful to give a brief description in the body of the report and then include a fuller presentation of methods in an appendix.
- Use white space and graphics to break up the narrative. A few charts and tables will highlight your major points, but too many can be distracting.
- Place technical information and additional tables of results in an appendix.
- Always state the limitations of the study, including any cautions about interpretations.
- Provide only the necessary background about the issue needed to set up your report. The exception here is academic papers, which often include more background and a fully cited literature review.
- Organize around major themes or the primary research questions.
- Place major points in the beginning. Lead each paragraph with your point.
- Leave time to revise, revise, revise!
- Find a detail-oriented person not involved with the research project to serve as a "cold reader"—someone who is detached enough to quickly spot when you have left things out or where things are not clear.

GUIDE FOR WRITING AN EXECUTIVE SUMMARY

Provide an executive summary for your report if this will go to public officials and/ or citizens or is required in your organization. The audience may not have the time to read the whole report, so a quick overview highlighting the major points is essential. If it is well written, the readers will get the message. If they are intrigued and want to know more, they can turn to the other sections of the report.

An executive summary should be short: one page is ideal and more than four is too much, even for a lengthy report and complex study. However, some reports have very lengthy executive summaries of more than ten pages; there are no firm rules and each organization will decide what works best. Remember that writing short is harder than writing long; the process of reducing the length usually makes the message much clearer. The first version is likely to be too long, so continue to cut it down until you are communicating just the essence. Look at other public reports that use executive summaries to get an idea of how tightly it should be written.

Use consistent formatting for the executive summary. I prefer to place headings at the left margin and indent the narrative under them (hanging indents). This style makes the headings easily visible so the reader can quickly scan the report. Boldface type might also work to highlight the key parts of the report, but keep bolding to a minimum.

The basic components of an executive summary are as follows:

1. Brief overview or introduction to the report, defining the purpose of the study, the situation, or the issue of concern. This opening is your chance to grab the reader's attention.
2. Description of the study, identifying the major research questions and explaining briefly how the study was conducted.
3. Background information to place the study in context.
4. Major findings. These should relate to the purpose or research questions. This section reflects the researcher's judgment: what findings are most important or interesting? What should the audience take away from this research? Explain the findings in simple, clear, jargon-free language, perhaps in bullet format. Refer readers to the text or appendix for more detail.
5. Conclusions and recommendations. These should flow from the findings and be supported by the key evidence.

GUIDE FOR WRITING A FORMAL REPORT

The format of a report should be specific to the customs of the organization and the desires of the audience. Typically, a report that goes to public officials and citizens will be an expanded version of the executive summary and generally follow this type of format:

1. Introduction. What is the purpose of the study, situation or issue of concern? What is the big research question? What is already known about this issue? Why is this issue important and worth the reader's attention?
2. Background. Provide enough information to place the study in context. While not a cited literature review (as would be needed if this was an academic report), a fuller description of what is known already and/or the major issues

or perspectives may be useful. Information about what the organization (city, state, federal government) has done in the past might be helpful.

3. Methodology. State the major and minor research questions. Present essential information about how the study was conducted: key measures, data collection strategy, how participants were selected, number of participants, and response rate (if appropriate). More detail can be placed in an appendix. The survey instrument itself should be presented in a separate appendix. This section should also explain the boundaries and limitations of the study.

4. Major findings. What are the major points that the reader should understand? What are the answers to the research questions? Which findings were expected? Which were not? What is interesting or surprising? Major points can be highlighted with judicious use of charts and tables.

5. Conclusions and recommendations. Provide the answers to the big issues and questions. Present the key evidence to support any conclusions or recommendation. Recommendations should be placed in context and be specific: who should do what when and how. State any major limitations about the study's conclusions.

GUIDE FOR USING CHARTS AND TABLES

Charts and tables can be very persuasive because they draw attention to key points, making it easier for the reader to remember the information. Tables are useful for presenting data; charts are more effective in communicating the message. Use them for the following purposes:

- Communicate complex ideas clearly, precisely, and efficiently
- Present data in a way that makes it easy to understand
- Show the big picture, patterns, and trends
- Give your message impact
- Increase audience acceptance
- Increase memory retention
- Provide visual relief from narrative

A table or chart should:

- Show the data simply and accurately
- Entice the audience to think about the information
- Avoid distortion
- Make large data sets coherent
- Encourage the eye to compare different pieces of the data
- Enhance the statistical and verbal descriptions of the data
- Serve a clear purpose: to describe, explore, tabulate, elaborate, or compare

Choose the type of chart that is most appropriate for the type of material you are presenting. A line chart depicts trends over time; a pie chart shows the parts of a whole, always adding up to 100 percent; a single bar chart shows the percent distribution of a single variable; a cluster bar chart compares several items. No matter what type of chart you use, the graphic should present sufficient data to tell the story and make sense to a reasonable person. Keep scales honest. Make the chart easy for the audience to read by using clear typefaces with upper- and lowercase lettering; avoiding many different sizes and types of lettering; avoiding busy and unnecessary patterns; and using white space to provide visual relief. Include data tables to support your charts in an appendix.

GUIDE FOR ORAL PRESENTATIONS

- Follow the classic structure: tell them what you will tell them, tell them, and tell them what you told them.
- What is your point? What are the three things you want the audience to remember?
- Who is your audience? What do they expect? How much detail do they want?
- How much time do you have? As a general rule, short is always better than long.
- What are the resources of the room for delivery: slides, overheads, poster boards? Always bring a backup plan. If you are going to do a PowerPoint presentation, bring overheads too. If possible, get there early enough to set up and do a trial run of any equipment.
- Make handouts if you have a lot of information on your slides or overheads; the handouts can have far more detail than is on the slide.
- When developing overheads and handouts, use minimum text, clear visuals, and lots of white space.
- Talk to the audience, not to your notes or overheads. It is important to make eye contact with many people in the audience.
- Rehearse, rehearse, rehearse! Get feedback on your rehearsal, and time your presentation and cut as needed to stay within the allotted time.

PRESENTING UNWELCOME INFORMATION

Researchers sometimes uncover unwelcome information, such as programs that do not work as intended, questionable expenditures, policy failures, disparate treatment of some employees, inadequate services delivered to a particular segment of the community, poor organizational communication, disgruntled volunteers or inept supervisors. Negative results can make people very defensive and the research might be discredited out of hand. Alternatively, researchers may be afraid to tell the bad news to their employer or requester even though they have an ethical responsibility to report their results truthfully. This is a difficult situation.

When research results are critical of the policy, program or officials, it is important to go back and recheck all the data analyses to make sure they are absolutely accurate. Yes, it is important to double check the analyses with positive research results too but they are less likely to be subjected to the same level of scrutiny as negative results.

It is also important to consider how strong the research is before drawing damaging conclusions. The point to remember is that there is rarely any forgiveness for mistakes in a highly critical research report.

If the analyses are correct and the research design is solid, the researchers might want to meet with the requesters to discuss preliminary results that might be surprisingly different from what they were expecting. The requesters might provide some context for interpreting the results, information that might not have been available to the researchers, or specific information that disagrees with the researchers' findings. The organization's disagreement with the research findings might be included in the final report. The U.S. GAO, for example, will include the agency's response to the draft evaluation report. This disclosure reflects the reality that in complex situations reasonable people may disagree about what constitutes the best measures or criteria for determining success.

While researchers should not be afraid to provide unwelcome information, there are some choices about how it can be conveyed. In many cases, they have the choice of portraying the glass half full or half empty; even when there is a criterion for what constitutes good performance, it will be rare to find that nothing works at all. As with any evaluation of performance, the message is easier to hear if it starts with the positives: what works well and the assets that contributes to success.

The researchers should also consider the tone of the report as well as how they frame the issues most likely to be unwelcome. For example, saying the program "failed miserably" is far more critical in tone than saying the program "encountered challengers that limited success." It also helps to assume that most people want to do the right thing, so instead of focusing on the mistakes made and implying ineptness, it is more helpful to identify areas that work well at least to some extant and can be improved.

The researchers might choose to focus only on a few important factors where action is likely to bring about positive change. Realistically, most people cannot focus on more than a few things to change at one time and that is also true of organizations: identifying the three most important lessons learned from the research might be more effective than a list of ten.

It is also possible to raise some issues in a briefing rather than in the report. This might be especially useful for researchers within an organization who have an ongoing relationship with the senior officials. For example, responses to an employee satisfaction survey and focus groups results might reveal a serious problem in one division. The researchers might not want to identify that division head in a written report, but might share that information with the director of human resources in an informal briefing. However, care must be taken to ensure that there is no breach of confidentiality and that no one is made vulnerable by the information. Sometimes it will be necessary to withhold information in order to protect the participants from reprisals. For example, if a focus group was held with six people from the problem division, it may be necessary to withhold that information in the formal report so those six people are not made vulnerable to a possibly vengeful division director.

Researchers have a responsibility to report the information in a way that is honest and accurate. While they need to be sensitive to the likely reactions the research results will generate, they must find a way to convey the results in a way that is most likely to be heard and used. At the same time, they need to be mindful of watering down the results so much in order not offend anyone that the research no longer honestly reflects what was learned. At each step of the research process, the researchers have choices as they search for ways to balance the conflicting ethical demands. This is a time where researchers may want to consult professional colleagues about how to handle these kinds of difficult situations.

CONCLUSION

The report connects the research back to the initial questions. After a journey into detail, the reporting phase pulls back to look at the whole picture. This is where the researchers tell their story. They face several challenges. One is to make the story simple and clear. A second challenge is to find the balance between presenting too much and not enough information. A third challenge is to make sure bias does not sneak in when drawing conclusions and making recommendations. The fourth challenge is to convey unwelcome results in a way that can be heard and used.

There are many possible stories. Managers overseeing a research project should make sure that everyone remains focused on answering the research questions while remaining open to unexpected findings. Recommendations should be offered only if there is sufficient evidence to support them, and they should be very specific: who should do what when.

The report should clearly describe the actual research as well as the findings and conclusions. All the dots should be connected so that the reader, presumably a sophisticated user of research results, has enough information to make an independent assessment about the credibility of the results.

EXERCISES

1. Gather three public administration reports or articles. Which one is the best in terms of how the data is presented? What factors make it the best?
2. Go to Portland's Citizen Survey posted on the city auditor's website, www. portlandonline.com/auditor/auditservices/residentsurvey2007/. Assess how the data are presented on this website. What types of charts are used? Do you think these are an effective way to display data? Why or why not?
3. Go to Portland's Service and Accomplishment Report at www.portlandonline. com/auditor/index.cfm?c=25948.
   a. Critique how the website presents goal achievement in the various areas of city service (pages 1–8). Think about the clarity of the writing and the usefulness of the charts. What works and what does not?
   b. Critique the explanation about how the report was produced (pages 9–12). What works and what does not? Is this too much information or not enough? What, if anything, has been left out?

4. Go back to Exhibit 3.5 on oil profits.
   a. Construct a chart that shows the changes (use rate of change) in total profits of all the oil companies from year to year. What story do the data tell?
   b. Construct a chart that shows the changes (use rate of change) each year of Exxon's and Conoco-Phillips's profits. What story do the data tell? How do these rates of change compare to what you found with the total profits?

17 Conclusion
Research at the Intersection of Politics and Administration

OVERVIEW

Did the war on poverty work? Did legalizing abortion cause the crime rate to decline? Is there a relationship between race and the death penalty? How many Iraqis were killed after the United States invaded? These controversial questions take us to the intersection of research, politics, and public administration.

Research on controversial issues challenges us to adopt a research perspective. This requires two things. One is a basic knowledge of research methods. The second is a critical thinking ability that enables us to detach from our beliefs in order to see things clearly and ask the tough questions. Both are essential if public administrators are to make judgments and decisions that best serve the public's interest based on research results.

This chapter sums up the key points about research methods in the context of public administration. The research process and ethics are revisited. Suggestions are made for managers who oversee research projects as well as the key questions to ask in order to assess the credibility of research results. Lastly, the limitations of research and the particular challenges within the political environment are discussed. The key takeaway lesson is that while research results can be helpful, public administrators often make decisions in the midst of uncertainty and political conflict.

THE RESEARCH PROCESS REVISITED

As public administrators grapple with the tough issues of policy and governance, good research can be an ally. It not only provides information to guide decisions and actions, but also engages people in a dialogue about the differences between what they believe and what they know. It provides a basis for learning about what works and what does not. All these learning opportunities serve the public's interest.

Once the scientific veneer is peeled away, research is revealed to be a very logical process. No matter the purpose of the research, the research process is always the same: planning, doing, reporting. Researchers must plan the research, collect and analyze data, and report the results in ways that are accurate, useful to the intended audience, and without spin. All the pieces of the research process must fit together, with ethical considerations guiding every step.

PLANNING

Planning is essential in producing high-quality research because no statistical magic can save a flawed design. Research begins with a question about an issue, policy, program or problem. Sometimes the researchers choose but often funders, stakeholders, or bosses decide the questions. Prior research can provide valuable information about what is already known as well as ideas about how to approach this new project. Enlisting the advice of other researchers and stakeholders can help in refining the questions so they are researchable.

The journey into concrete detail begins with developing conceptual and operational definitions of every key term in the research question. What specific data do the researchers need to answer the questions? How can that data be measured?

The design also begins to take shape. In the narrowest sense of design, researchers find the Xs and Os framework helpful. The X might be the program, treatment, causal factor, or independent variable. The O is the observed measure or measure of the effect, which could be a test score or the percentage of clients that get a job; more generically, it is the measure of the dependent variable.

The design elements—when measures are taken and whether to use comparison groups—can be combined in a variety of ways, creating different types of designs. These include classical experiments that use random assignment; quasi-experimental designs such as non-equivalent designs, correlational designs using statistical controls and longitudinal studies; and nonexperimental designs such as the one-shot design.

Cause-and-effect or impact questions are the hardest to answer because four conditions must be met: a logical theory, the right time order, covariation between the variables, and the elimination of rival explanations. The classical experimental design is technically the best for controlling for all kinds of possible rival explanations because of random assignment to the treatment and comparison groups; random assignment makes the groups equivalent. However, researchers are more likely to use a quasi-experimental design because random assignment is often not an option. When working with quasi-experimental designs, researchers will need to account for threats to internal validity, such as an event, a volunteer sample, or changes in measures that might alter the observed outcomes. Nonexperimental designs are the weakest for answering impact or cause-and-effect questions because they lack the power to control for rival explanations.

Other research approaches, such as analysis of secondary data, meta-analysis, content analysis, case studies and cost-benefit analysis, are often used in public administration research but do not fit comfortably into the Xs and Os framework. But regardless of which design or approach is used, it must be appropriate given the question and situation.

The data collection methods flow from the desired measures and the location of the data. If the desired data are located in files, researchers will probably use a data collection instrument. If people's behavior constitutes the data, the researchers might use an observational approach. If they want to know people's opinions, they might conduct a survey, interviews or focus groups.

Samples are often necessary if researchers cannot gather data from every unit in the population of interest. They might choose a random or nonrandom sampling technique. The power of random samples, if of sufficient size, is that they enable researchers to make generalizations or inferences about the larger population.

The planning process is not as linear as presented here. Researchers move back and forth between these steps until finally the plan clicks into focus. The key point here is that researchers make choices that affect the quality of the research and nothing should be assumed or taken for granted by the sophisticated reader of research results.

DOING

Getting ready to collect data begins with pretesting all data collection instruments and procedures. The researchers need to build in quality control procedures to limit bias and ensure the accuracy of data entry. The data collection itself should be systematic. This is true for both qualitative and quantitative data. Any limitations of the data collection need to be identified and reported.

The analysis should be appropriate to the data, using the simplest techniques that are technically correct. Researchers have the greatest choice of analytical techniques when working with interval or ratio level data and fewer choices with nominal and ordinal data. These choices should be considered in the planning phase.

Cross-tabs, comparison of means, and correlations are commonly used analytic techniques. Measures of association or regression analysis should be calculated if the researchers are exploring the strength of relationships. Lastly, tests for statistical significance should be used with random sample data. Depending on the questions at hand, the researchers might also need to run sampling errors, point estimates, or confidence intervals.

As the researchers make sense of the data, they need to be open to results that turn out differently than expected. Research is a process of discovery and all findings can guide future research.

REPORTING

The presentation of research results can be a formal report, an article, a briefing paper, or an oral presentation. Typically, the requester chooses the format and the researchers write to their primary audience.

The results should tell the story that emerges from the data analysis in a way that is simple, clear, accurate, sufficient, and honest. One challenge is to find the balance between providing enough information and overwhelming the reader with detail; further detailed information can be placed in an appendix if using a report format.

Another challenge arises when the results are critical of a program, policy or organization. Researchers must find a way to present unwelcome findings in a way that can be heard. It helps to identify what works and focus on a few key areas that can be improved. Sometimes softening the tone can help by using more neutral words. Another strategy is to present the results in a briefing. Lastly, it is important that the researchers tell the story in a way that protects the confidentiality of the participants; no one should be identifiable from the research results if confidentiality was promised.

Limitations should be stated along with any cautions about conclusions that can be drawn. If recommendations are made, they should be very specific and supported by evidence. It is not unusual to recommend that more research is needed.

ETHICS AND SOCIAL JUSTICE

Adherence to ethical principles ensures that research does not harm participants or the larger population. Participants must give informed consent to any experiment after being notified about any potential risk. No one should be forced to participate in research nor should anyone have benefits denied to which they are entitled (such as health care or food stamps) if they refuse. Nor should harm be done because of decisions based on flawed designs, limited results, or predictions based on weak models.

The ethical stance of analysts in the public sector is to provide the most accurate and honest data possible. Shading the truth to get a result that supports an ideological, political, or personal position is never acceptable. The intention of analysis in public administration is to illuminate problems and inform discussions, not to win an argument. Managers and advocates have to resist the temptation to pressure analysts to spin the data.

Social justice in public administration research is a variation of the ethical principle to do no harm. Research, when misused, may unfairly disadvantage some people. Small studies or deeply flawed studies can result in unnecessary programs being funded and needed programs being cut.

The injustice begins with the choices about who is asked to prove positive impacts. Why are social programs that benefit the poor typically required to prove their efficacy but income transfer programs to the middle class are not? A program to feed poor pregnant women and their children has to demonstrate positive results, but the "business lunch" income tax deduction is not required to prove that it has positive results for the taxpayers.

Given how difficult it is to prove program impact, it seems the cards are stacked against the programs that serve the least powerful. Think about the logic of Type II errors. When the researchers fail to find a statistically significant difference, all they should say is that they failed to reject the null hypothesis. However, it is very possible that the program made a difference even though the researchers did not find a statistically significant result. This is a social justice issue, and public administrators should be cautious in drawing conclusions that result in programs being cut based on weak research designs and small samples.

MANAGING RESEARCH PROJECTS

While most public administrators do not conduct research, many are likely to oversee research contracts and projects. Knowledge of basic research concepts provides man-

Exhibit 17.1   **Building Quality Into the Research**

- Obtain expert review of research questions, measures, the design, the program logic model, the assumptions and hypotheses, the data and data collection strategy, and the proposed data analysis strategy.
- Engage stakeholders early and often to ensure that the questions make sense and are the right ones given the situation.
- Identify and explicitly state biases, beliefs, and assumptions at all stages of the research process.
- Have others review the plan, the analysis, and the final report to make sure the work is unbiased: engage reviewers with different perspectives who are not afraid to ask tough questions.
- Pretest all data collection instruments before full implementation of the research project.
- Establish procedures that allow team members to collect data consistently.
- Strive for at least a 60 percent response rate when gathering data from people.
- Verify a sample of the data entered into a computer back to its source. If the error rate is high (more than 1 percent), reenter the data.
- Use more than two raters when coding qualitative data for analysis and test for inter-rater reliability on a sample before coding all the data.
- Do a reliability assessment to determine the accuracy of the data if using a database prepared by someone else; if the error rates are high, go to Plan B.
- Hire expertise if highly technical analysis is needed.
- Have statistical analyses reviewed independently.
- Have someone verify all the data in the report to make sure they are correct.
- Have both an expert and a cold reader review the draft report to make sure that the evidence presented actually supports the conclusion and any recommendations.

agers with the confidence to ask the researchers tough questions. Understanding that there is no one best way enables managers to engage researchers in a dialogue about the process and to set realistic expectations. The shared goal is to build in quality; Exhibit 17.1 lists a number of important steps to achieve that goal.

When contracting for research, the steps in the research process are typically specified in a contract's scope of work. The scope of work will describe the research questions, provide context and background of the issue, and state the purpose of this research. The contract might specify the design and methods to be used or those may be left open as something to be determined as more information becomes available. The contract typically states the desired qualifications of the research team and the schedule for deliverables, such as interim status reports, final products, and briefings.

A Gantt chart is one way to visually specify the tasks and the due dates (see Exhibit 17.2). The tasks are listed in the down the left-hand column the dates in the top row, and markers indicate expected start and completion dates. The tasks can be as general or specific as needed, although specific is usually better. Some tasks are likely to slip, and the Gantt chart makes it easy to see the likely impact on the other tasks and the completion date because the chart shows the interconnectedness of the various tasks.

Ongoing dialogue is part of this process. Problems will arise and unanticipated events will occur. Even the best researchers cannot avoid surprises. Flexibility will help everybody involved get through these challenges. In addition, managing a research project often requires some negotiation about what gets included in the final report. It is possible that what the researchers think is important may not align with the contract's expectations or requirements. On the other hand, the unexpected information might be useful even though it was not specified in the contract.

Exhibit 17.2   **Gantt Chart**

TASK	MONTH									
	1	2	3	4	5	6	7	8	9	10
Initial meeting	▲									
Planning	—	—	▲							
Data collection			—	—	▲					
Data analysis				—	—	▲				
Interim report						—	—	▲		

It is also important for managers to be mindful that the research might surface problems they would prefer to deny or ignore. When asking for feedback from employees or customers, it raises expectations that identified problems will be fixed. Unmet expectations might increase cynicism and distrust, making things worse. Managers need to be prepared to take action if they decide to initiate a research project.

ASSESSING CREDIBILITY

When reading the research results produced by others, it is essential to be able to distinguish fact from fiction, even if the fiction has the appearance of science. The sophisticated user of research results must ask the tough questions about the methods used. Managers should be suspicious of overly complex and convoluted research reports. Whether due to a weak ego or an attempt to hide the weaknesses of the research, obfuscation is a misuse of statistics.

Wendell Potter, a former head of communication for the health insurance giant CIGNA, stated in an interview:

> One of my favorite textbooks when I was in college was *How to Lie with Statistics*, and I think that we in PR [public relations] often will throw statistics out that are true to a certain extent but are also misleading and don't disclose the full story. That is what, more often than not, was what I was doing. I don't recall intentionally or knowingly lying to a reporter; I wouldn't have done that. But I think there are times when by withholding all the information or providing selective information or data, you definitely are misleading. And that's what I did more often than not. (2009)

Skepticism is the appropriate lens through which to view research results. However, skepticism does not mean cynicism and it definitely does not mean rejecting research because it is imperfect. All research is flawed, so perfection is not a helpful standard. Some flaws are relatively unimportant while others are fatal. The challenge is deciding when the flaws cross the fatal line.

Several studies discussed in this book had serious flaws: the immigration reform study, the teenage mothers on welfare study, and the Iraqi mortality estimates. The question is whether the research could have been done better, not just differently. If each study was the best that could be done in the situation, flawed though it might be, and if the limitations were honestly stated, then the results should be taken seriously.

I know of no rulebook to cover every situation and no simple formula that says three strikes and throw the research results out. Yes, at the extremes, it is easy to bounce out clearly bogus results like *American Idol* polls; and yes, there are some standards, like not generalizing to all people based on interviews with your two best friends. However, for all the appearance of concreteness, the decision about whether to believe the social science results falls into the sea of subjectivity. The best I can do is to suggest questions to ask in order to make an informed judgment about the credibility of the research (see Exhibit 17.3).

That said, it is important to remember that is easy to dismiss a study when you disagree with the results; at such times, many people can become overly and un-fairly critical. It is also remarkably hard to assess a study with a critical eye when you agree with the results. The researcher perspective is important when assessing research results, with no attachment to the outcomes. The key is to read research articles or research reports nonlinearly so you are not tricked into suspending critical thinking by elegant writing or the power of the story. My strategy is to first read the introduction and then the conclusion, a method I obviously do not follow when reading a mystery novel. This gives me the big picture of what the researchers are trying to do and sets the frame for the next step: reading the methodology section. It should make sense given the question and purpose of the research. Then I turn to any data presented in tables to make sense out of them, although sometimes I will only look at the R-squared if they used a multiple regression. I make an independent interpretation before reading what the researcher writes. For example, I might conclude that an R-squared of .06 is extremely weak although the author might have characterized it in the narrative as "not a really strong relationship." I prefer to make my own judgment.

You may find that another approach to breaking apart a research study works for you. The key point is that it is easier to assess research results when the specific elements are identified and considered. The design matrix in Appendix E (see page 263) might prove helpful as a way to identify the components of the research design.

Another point to remember is that arguments about controversial policy issues will often be about whose judgment is correct, as was the case with the Iraqi mortality study. It helps to know the basis for the judgments.

The last takeaway is to remember that a lot of research goes far beyond the basics provided in this book. If I had to make a decision based on research that I did not understand, I would not hesitate to call in some research experts to provide me with their assessment. I advise you to do the same.

Exhibit 17.3 **Assessing Research Credibility: Questions to Ask**

1. Does the report reveal any bias? Consider whether the authors, sponsors, or funders of the report have a particular point of view or an axe to grind. Keep in mind, however, that they may still have done an objective job. Considering the possibility of bias just means paying attention, not dismissing the research entirely.
2. Can the data really be known? If not, how do the researchers come up with it?
3. Is the research methodology fully reported? Are the limitations stated?
4. What types of research questions are asked?
   a. If normative, do the researchers report their criteria for making a judgment and how it was obtained? Do the criteria make sense?
   b. If cause-and-effect, do the researchers use a strong enough design to draw conclusions? Do they meet all the conditions necessary to answer cause-and-effect questions?
5. How are key terms defined and measured? Do they make sense? If the researchers use estimates, do they explain how the estimates were calculated? Is it in their interest to estimate high or low?
6. Who is included in the study and who is left out? Do those choices affect the results?
   a. Do the researchers use a census or a sample? If a sample, what kind? What is the sampling frame? How many people, files, roads, whatever, are included?
   b. Do the researchers report the response rate? If the rate is low, do they report results only in terms of those who participated?
7. Were the data collected in a consistent and nonbiased way?
8. Do the data analysis techniques make sense given the type of data?
   a. Are measures of association used when analyzing relationships in order to answer cause-and-effect questions?
   b. Are statistical significance, sampling, and nonsampling errors reported with results based on random sample data?
9. Do the researchers answer the research questions that they started with?
   a. Do the conclusions match the data collected?
   b. Do the conclusions stay within the limitations of the research?
10. Are recommendations supported by evidence from their study?

THE LIMITATIONS OF SCIENCE

Even when statistics are used correctly and research is done as objectively as possible, there are some limitations that researchers have to contend with. Sometimes the data required to answer public research questions are not available or may not be reducible to measurable terms. This poses a challenge for researchers asked to e measure results, an approach that is being adopted in many federal, state and local governments as well as in non-profit organizations. The logic model (discussed in Chapter 2) is often used in planning research to measure program results; it helps researchers in identifying inputs, activities, outputs and outcomes. While it is relatively easy to measure inputs and activities, it is difficult to measure outcomes and impacts. Even if outcomes can be measured, it is hard to say that the program alone caused them. However, as a manager, I am willing to take credit for positive outcomes even though I know they do not necessarily fulfill the social science requirements for causality.

While the scientific method is intended to reduce bias, sometimes bias is already built into how questions are framed. Carol Tarvis, in *The Mismeasure of Woman* (1992), lists a familiar inventory of what is wrong with women, as measured against men: they have low self-esteem, they undervalue their own work, they are too emotional, and they are not competitive enough. She suggests that the bias is embedded into the research questions themselves: a typical research question asks why women undervalue their work as compared to men but not why men overvalue their work as compared to women, or why women are not competitive enough to be leaders rather than why men are not cooperative enough to be leaders. Tarvis is not suggesting, nor am I, that research should be used as a forum for replacing one target of stereotyping with another. Replacing "women as the problem" with "men as the problem" will not move us forward. However, her questions do illustrate the subtleness of bias.

Another limitation is that science is not immune from clinging to theories that do not work. Thomas Kuhn (1962) observes that science changes incrementally only to the point where anomalies arise that cannot be explained by a current theory. Then, after much struggle—he calls it a revolution—there is a paradigm shift to a better theory. How long did it take before scientists accepted that the world is not flat and that the sun does not revolve around the earth? Shifts happen eventually, but a good question to ask when listening to policy debates is whether the theory is true. Social scientists, like the rest of us, often have a hard time accepting new theories. "Faced with having to change our views or prove that there is no need to do so," economist John Kenneth Galbraith observes, "most of us get busy on the proof" (1971, 50).

The financial meltdown in 2008 and the worsening economy raise questions about the dominant economic theories (Buchanan 2008). Does the "invisible hand" of market equilibrium theory still work if the government has to step in to keep specific businesses afloat, thus making the hand visible? Does deficit spending at the national level based on Keynesian economic theory make sense in a government with an $11 trillion debt? Perhaps these are the anomalies that Kuhn says signal that a revolution in theory is needed. From a public administration perspective, however, can science be of use if governmental actions are based on the earth-is-flat theories?

Social science is limited in its ability to fully explain complex social behavior. Yes, it is possible to use regression analysis to consider multiple explanations, but they rarely explain much. There are also difficulties in doing national studies or controlled experiments, obtaining clear goals from enabling legislation, and implementing one-size-fits-all programs across the United States. It is very unlikely that social scientists will be able to prove programmatic success; in fact, social science is not set up to prove anything. Social science tools are far too weak and error-prone, and the methods are actually stacked against finding program success. As a result, public programs often get translated as not working, which then becomes a platform for cynicism about the efficacy of government to solve complex social problems.

The uncomfortable reality is that all too often research just reveals that we really do not know as much as we think we do.

At this point you may be asking, "If science is so limited a tool to use in public administration, why have you written this book?" Great critical question!

I wrote this book because I believe that the search to determine what works and what does not, even if the results are only a partial truth, provides a useful framework for looking at a problem or program more deeply. Logical thinking is what matters. Building a model to capture the various factors that are connected to the problem, program, or outcome can be illuminating. The process may generate new ideas and approaches. The logic model presented in Chapter 2 can be a very useful way to think through a public program in order to improve program design and delivery. The lessons learned in the process of doing research may help others as they work on solving problems in their organizations or communities.

The main reason, however, is that I prefer that decisions be based on evidence and facts rather than emotion or raw political power. Critical thinking requires more than understanding the intricacies of research methods, although that is important. It also means recognizing our beliefs and being able to set them aside in order to see things clearly, to not be blinded by our preconceived judgments. This clarity is part of what I call a research perspective, which asks for evidence and uses data to back up statements about how the world works.

Now this desire for rationality coupled with an awareness of the limitations of social science brings us to a place of compassion. Research is hard to do! The world is not organized in a way to meet the requirements of social scientists, so it is necessary to pursue rationality with an acceptance of uncertainty. This awareness of uncertainty also brings recognition of the necessity for changing one's mind. The "facts" that today seem solid and true and based on the best research may prove false tomorrow. As General Dwight D. Eisenhower observed: "Neither a wise man nor a brave man lies down on the tracks of history to wait for the train of the future to run over him" (1952). The willingness to adapt to new information goes hand-in-hand with accepting the inherent limitations of science when decisions have to be made.

Public administrators are placed in a tough spot. They are pressed to act but the data might not be as good as they need. They must find a balance between jumping to quick fixes that rarely work and waiting for "perfect" information before taking action. In these places of uncertainty, small incremental steps make sense, especially if feedback mechanisms are put in place to monitor what happens. This continuous feedback is just another way to say that more research is needed.

This recognition of how little we know for sure might also turn down the volume in public discourse. When we accept that what we know is very limited compared to what we believe is true, we can listen to people with different views and open up a deeper conversation. Ideally, these deeper conversations will lead to solutions that actually have a good chance of working.

THE INTERSECTION OF RESEARCH, POLITICS, AND ADMINISTRATION

Public problems and their solutions are usually interwoven with values, so the "truth" often is subjective. At this intersection of research, politics, and administration, beliefs are entwined with policy and ideology clashes with science. The research perspective is an attempt to resist ideological blinders.

It is not easy. One of my favorite stories about life at this intersection is about C. Everett Koop when he was surgeon general under the Reagan administration. He was asked to prepare a report to document the long-term negative effects of abortion on women. The research available, however, was weak—mostly small studies using anecdotal evidence gathered from women who had sought therapy. Clearly, these studies did not represent all women who had abortions. Although Koop opposed abortion on religious grounds, he sent a letter to the president stating that there was insufficient evidence of a long-term harmful effect. He thus maintained his research perspective and professional standards even though his conclusions were in opposition to his personal values as well as what the president wanted.

"Facts" in the political arena are often ephemeral, and policy issues that are controversial will often turn on values and verbal arguments rather than data. While there is a desire for the "facts," the "facts" alone will not eliminate the need for public administrators to exercise reasonable judgment in making decisions. Decisions made in a political context have to take into account citizens' preferences and reactions as well as the many competing interest groups. Experts weigh in, but not all who speak are really experts, and experts often wear their own ideological blinders

The number of expert voices weighing in on big policy issues can be so overwhelming that it makes it difficult to discern the truth. For example, in a report by the Center for Public Integrity, "more than 770 companies and interest groups hired an estimated 2,340 lobbyists to influence federal policy on climate change in the past year. . . . That's an increase of more than 300 percent in the number of lobbyists on climate change in just five years. . . ." (Lavelle 2009). It can become very difficult to assess the credibility of all the statistics tossed around as the lobbyists try to persuade Congress to adopt a particular policy.

We live in a pluralistic society that welcomes and protects the expression of conflicting views. The challenge of governance is to find a middle way that respects those differences and seeks a consensus in order to move forward and solve problems. Public administrators wind up in the middle of these debates. The more controversial the issues, the more likely public administrators will find themselves bombarded with all kinds of data, facts, and emotional arguments supporting conflicting policy positions. It may make life difficult for the public administrators, but this messy process serves democracy.

CLOSING OBSERVATIONS

The intention of this book was to provide public administrators with the basic concepts, tools, and techniques used in conducting research, so that people who conduct research can enhance their skills, people who contract for research can more effectively ask for what they want, and people who use research results will have the information needed to decide whether to believe them.

One of my goals in writing this book is to help readers become savvy users of research results who seek out opportunities to use research to guide their decisions. Feedback is necessary in an uncertain environment so that midcourse corrections can prevent us from going over the falls.

My second goal is that "What's the evidence?" will become the critical question every public administrator asks before making a decision. While beliefs and values have their place, they need to be moderated by a serious conversation about what is actually known. Simple solutions to complex social problems are almost always false, no matter how scientific the research appears or how compelling the story. The caution and common sense embedded in a research perspective can help public administrators judge the credibility of research results, especially when they want to assume the research is good because the results match what they already believe.

EXERCISES

1. Think about any organizational or government programs with which you are familiar that were implemented before there was sufficient research to guide the action. Describe the situation. Why was quick action necessary? Do you agree or disagree with the action? Explain.

2. What public issue that you care about is being currently debated? What are the arguments for and against proposed actions by government? To what extent are data being used as evidence or support for the arguments? How good are the data and do you think they are credible enough to sway the policy decision? If not, what data, if any, might be persuasive? Explain your reasoning.

3. Of the studies referenced in this book, which ones were the most helpful in understanding the concepts? Which were the least helpful? Explain.

4. What are the challenges in relying on research results? Are you more or less likely to look at research in guiding choices you make as an administrator and as a citizen? Explain.

5. What does critical thinking mean to you? How is it the same as, or different from, skepticism? Why is either or both important in deciding whether to apply research results to policy or program decisions?

6. The legislature's judiciary committee is concerned about the deterrent effect of citizen action groups to combat drugs. Over the past few years, groups like Neighborhood Guardians have started to patrol streets that serve as open-air drug-markets in an attempt to prevent drugs from being bought and sold. These groups claim that they not only reduce drug transactions but also serve as positive role models in the community. The judiciary committee would like to know if these groups are effective in reducing the number of drug transactions, what types of risks are associated with this type of citizen action, and what benefits does their presence provide. The committee would like to hold hearings in one year.

   You have been called in as a consultant to advise the researchers who will conduct the study. They would like you to help them identify the strengths and weaknesses in their possible research strategies and the challenges they are likely to face. They also want your opinion about which of these approaches you recommend and why.

   Option A: Do a multiple time series analysis of all communities with Neighborhood Guardians compared to communities with similar demographic characteristics but who do not have Neighborhood Guardians (or an equivalent group) present. The study will determine if drug arrests, drug sales, and drug usage have changed over time in cities that have Neighborhood Guardians as compared to cities without them.

   Option B: Select four communities for in-depth case studies. The research team proposes to survey a random sample of community residents and ask their opinions about the Neighborhood Guardians' positive and negative effects in their community. In addition, the team will interview church and community leaders about the Neighborhood Guardians' effect.

Option C: Interview the Neighborhood Guardians' leaders to determine what kind of training they provide, what types of situations they have encountered that put them at risk, and how many of their members (or their families) have been physically injured as a result of their activities.

Option D: Interview police officials in those communities. In addition to collecting data about drug transactions, the team will obtain the police officials' views about the Neighborhood Guardians' effectiveness in reducing drug transactions and their risk in being involved.

Appendix A
Mathematical Formulas for Selected Statistics

This book is intended to provide an overall understanding of research and statistics, with an emphasis on designing research and interpreting statistical results. However, some people find it helpful to see the formulas in order to understand what these statistics mean. The formulas for the most commonly used statistics are presented here. In-depth information is beyond the scope of this book, so you may wish to consult a statistics book.

The formulas for many statistics are complicated because there are variations depending upon the exact circumstances. For example, formulas vary slightly depending on whether you are working with sample or population data. The formulas also can be confusing because they use Greek and other symbols that may be unfamiliar and because different statistics books use different symbols. The formulas presented here are intended to provide an overall sense of the mathematics but will not cover every possible situation.

COMMON COMPARISON TECHNIQUES

Several statistical techniques can be used to make comparisons, such as the crime rates of various cities, student-teacher ratios, and changes in budget expenditures over time.

CALCULATING RATES

Comparisons of rates are useful when you want to compare the incidence of an event (such as crime) to a standardized point of reference, such as the population. If just the numbers of crimes in different cities were compared, large cities would be likely to have a high number of crimes, but that would not necessarily mean they have a greater crime problem than a small city with a smaller number of crimes. The more accurate comparison is in terms of which cities have the most crime relative to their population. Typically, population is standardized in terms of 1,000 people or 100,000 people. Which city has the highest crime rate: city A with a population of 1,500,000 and 6,000 reported crimes or city B with a population of 200,000 and 3,000 reported crimes?

This is a two-step process. The first step is to standardize the population; that is, divide the population by 1,000 since that is the base rate we will be using (number of crimes per 1,000 people). The second step is to divide the number of crimes by the standardized population.

Step 1: Standardize the population:
    City A: 1,500,000 / 1,000 = 1,500.
    City B: 200,000 / 1,000 = 200.

Step 2: Divide the number crimes by the standardized population:
    City A: 6,000 / 1,500 = 4.
    City B: 3,000 / 200 = 15.

Although city A has more reported crimes, its crime rate of 4 crimes per 1,000 people is less than city B's reported crime rate of 15 per 1,000 people.

CALCULATING A RATIO

Another way to compare two items is in terms of one item relative to the other. For example, if we want to know if one school district has enough teachers, just counting the number of teachers does not provide accurate information. A more useful method is to compare the number of students to the number of teachers: the student-teacher ratio. While this figure still does not answer the question whether there are enough teachers, it does provide a way to compare this school district to a professional standard or to another school district.

A ratio is calculated by dividing the number of items (in this case, the number of students) by the reference item (the number of teachers). How does district A compare to district B in terms of how many students there are per teacher? District A has 1,500 students and 45 teachers and district B has 2,000 students and 50 teachers.

To calculate the ratios, divide the number of students by the number of teachers:

District A: 1,500 / 45 = 33. The student-teacher ratio is 33:1.
District B: 2,000 / 50 = 40. The student-teacher ratio is 40:1.

Even though district B has more teachers than district A, it also has more students per teacher. District B may want to make a case for hiring more teachers so its student-teacher ratio is comparable to that of district A.

CALCULATING THE RATE OF CHANGE

A third frequently used comparison is the rate of change. This shows how much change there is between two points in time, such as changes in budget expenditures. The number from the older point in time is always the reference point. The number from the most recent point is expressed as a percentage relative to the number from the older point in time and is calculated this way:

[(New time / Older time) – 1] × 100.

Step 1:   Divide the number for the most recent year by the number for the older time.
Step 2:   Subtract 1 from that number.
Step 3:   Multiply by 100 to get the percentage.

For example, the budget expenditure for salaries was $12 million in FY 2000 and $14 million in FY 2001. What was the percent change in salaries from FY 2000 to FY 2001?

Step 1:   14,000,000 / 12,000,000 = 1.16.
Step 2:   1.16 – 1 = .16.
Step 3:   .16 × 100 = 16%.

In this scenario, salary expenditures increased 16 percent from FY 2000 to FY 2001. But what happens if the salary expenditures declined to $10 million? What is the percent change?

Step 1:   10,000,000 / 12,000,000 = .83.
Step 2:   .83 – 1 = –.17.
Step 3:   –.17 × 100 = –17%.

In this scenario, the salary expenditure declined 17 percent (notice the minus sign).

COMMON DESCRIPTIVE TECHNIQUES

There are many ways to describe data. The most common ones are presented here. The mean and median are used to describe central tendency while variance and the standard deviation are used to describe the dispersion or variability of distribution.

MEAN

The mean is the average and is used with interval and ratio data. All the values are summed up and divided by the number of cases. The formula is typically presented as follows:

$$Mean\ (\bar{X}) = \frac{\sum_{i}^{N} X_i}{N}.$$

The mean is often portrayed as X with a bar over it, although sometimes it is presented as M. The Greek letter sigma $\sum$ is the symbol for "sum"; in this case, it tells the researcher to add up all the values of variable X. The small i indicates however many values there are. The number of cases is noted as N. Sometimes researchers use slightly different symbols depending on whether they are working with population or sample data, but the calculation is done in exactly the same way. For example, if we wanted to calculate the mean for the salaries of five people in distribution A, we would add up all five salaries and divide by 5. The total of all five salaries is $190,000. When divided by five, the average salary is $38,000.

> Salary distribution A
> $20,000
> $25,000
> $35,000
> $40,000
> $70,000

MEDIAN

The median is the midpoint of a distribution. It is the point in the distribution where 50 percent of the measures are above and 50 percent are below. When the distribution contains an uneven number of cases, the median is the middle score. For instance, if there are five cases, then the third case is the midpoint. In salary distribution A, the midpoint is $35,000.

> Salary distribution A
> $20,000
> $25,000
> $35,000
> $40,000
> $70,000

When there is an even number of cases, as in salary distribution B, then the midpoint is the value between the two middle cases. In this distribution, there are six cases so the midpoint is between the third and fourth case. The salaries for the third and fourth cases are added together and then divided by 2 to find the midpoint. Since the third salary is $35,000 and the fourth is $40,000, the median is $37,500.

> Salary distribution B
> $20,000
> $25,000
> **$35,000**
> **$40,000**
> $70,000
> $100,000

VARIANCE

While variance is a way to measure how much variability there is in a distribution, the standard deviation (described below) is more typically used. However, variance is used in calculating other statistics, so it is useful to know this formula:

$$\text{Variance } (S^2) = \frac{\Sigma(X_i - \overline{X})^2}{N-1}.$$

Variance is the sum of all the squared differences for each value and the distribution mean divided by one less than the number of cases. It can be calculated in three steps:

Step 1: For each value, subtract it from the mean and square it.
Step 2: Sum all the squared differences.
Step 3: Divide by one less than the number of cases.

Using salary distribution A, the variance can be calculated:

Step 1: Obtain the squared differences:

Difference	Difference squared
$20,000 – $38,000 = –18,000	324,000,000
$25,000 – $38,000 = –13,000	169,000,000
$35,000 – $38,000 = –3,000	9,000,000
$40,000 – $38,000 = 2,000	4,000,000
$70,000 – $38,000 = 32,000	1,024,000,000

Step 2: Sum the squared differences = 1,530,000,000.
Step 3: Divide the sum of the squared differences by one less than the number of cases: 5 – 1 = 4; 1,530,000,000 / 4 = 382,500,000.

The variance is = 382,500,000. As mentioned earlier, the variance is rarely used by itself since it is hard to interpret.

STANDARD DEVIATION

The standard deviation (S or SD) is the more commonly used measure to describe the variation or dispersion in a distribution. Basically, the standard deviation is a measure of how far each value is from the mean. If the values are far from the mean, there is a lot of variation in the distribution; if the values are not far from the mean, then there is not a lot of variation. In a normal distribution, which resembles a bell-shaped curve, 65 percent of the scores are within plus and minus one standard deviation and 95 percent are within plus and minus two standard deviations. The formula for the standard deviation looks like the formula for variance, except that it is under a radical sign. The standard deviation is the square root of the variance:

$$\text{Standard deviation } (S) = \sqrt{\frac{\Sigma(X_i - \overline{X})}{N-1}}.$$

To obtain the standard deviation:

Step 1: The difference for each value is subtracted from the mean and then squared.
Step 2: Sum the squared differences.
Step 3: Divide the sum of the squared differences by one less than the number of cases.
Step 4: Take the square root of the result of Step 3.

For example, what is the standard deviation of salary distribution A, which has a mean of $38,000?

Step 1: Obtain the squared differences of each value from the mean:

Difference	Difference squared
$20,000 − $38,000 = −18,000	324,000,000
$25,000 − $38,000 = −13,000	169,000,000
$35,000 − $38,000 = −3,000	9,000,000
$40,000 − $38,000 = 2,000	4,000,000
$70,000 − $38,000 = 32,000	1,024,000,000

Step 2: Sum the squared differences = 1,530,000,000.
Step 3: Divide the sum of the squared differences by one less than the number of cases: 1,530,000,000 / 4 = 382,500,000.
Step 4: Take the square root of 382,500,000 = $19,558.

The standard deviation of this distribution is $19,558. This means that 65 percent of the values are between $18,442 and $57,558 (the mean plus and minus one standard deviation). There is a lot of variation in this distribution.

Steps 1–3 are the same as the steps used in calculating the variance. The standard deviation is the square root of the variance; alternatively, the variance is the standard deviation squared.

Z-SCORE

The z-score is used to show how a particular score compares to all the rest of the scores in terms of a distribution. The z-score expresses this comparison in terms of the standard deviation; specifically, it shows the score in terms of its standard deviations from the mean. The z-score is calculated in a two-step process expressed in this formula:

$$z\text{-score} = \frac{X_i - \overline{X}}{S}.$$

Step 1: Subtract the average score from the actual score.
Step 2: Divide that difference by the standard deviation.

A common use of z-scores is to construct a "curve" for exams. For instance, a professor gives an exam and the average score is 60. She decides she wants to grade on a curve so few students fail; only those whose grade is two standard deviations below the mean will fail. She determines that the standard deviation is 10. If a student gets a 70, the professor can calculate where the student stands in terms of the standard deviation.

Step 1: Subtract the mean from the actual score: $70 - 60 = 10$.
Step 2: Divide by the standard deviation: $10 / 10 = 1$.

This student's score is one standard deviation from the mean. If the average score is 60, then one standard deviation (70) above becomes a B and two standard deviations above the mean (80) becomes an A. A student who gets a 40 will still pass with a D since the professor decided that only those people with test scores more than two standard deviations below the mean will fail.

MAKING ESTIMATES USING SAMPLE DATA

When working with sample data, there is always some degree of error; the data from samples will not be exactly the same as data gathered from the entire population. Researchers may present the estimate of the error or the estimate of what the population mean is likely to be. Typically, researchers give estimates in which their confidence level is 95 percent (they are 95 percent certain their estimate is correct). When working with interval or ratio data (such as salary or test scores), they will present their estimate as a range or interval within which they believe the population mean is captured. When working with proportions (such as in polling data), researchers will provide an estimate of the sampling error (expressed as plus or minus X percent). To calculate estimates based on sample data, several formulas are needed; the standard deviation and the z-scores are used to calculate these estimates.

THE CONFIDENCE INTERVAL

When working with sample data, it is sometimes necessary to determine the accuracy of the estimate of the mean. Typically, the confidence interval is calculated at the 95 percent confidence level: the researchers want to be 95 percent certain that the true population mean would be within a specific interval. The first step is to calculate the standard error of the mean. Basically, this is the standard deviation divided by the square root of the sample size (n). The formula is as follows:

$$\textit{Standard error (se)} = \textit{standard deviation} \; (S) \Big/ \sqrt{n} \; .$$

Using the data from the professor's exam, where the average score is 60 and the standard deviation is 10, the standard error can be calculated. Suppose seventy-five people who were randomly selected from 1,000 students took this exam. When the standard deviation is known, the standard error is calculated in two steps:

Step 1: Find the square root of the sample size.
  In this case, the square root of 75 is 8.66.
Step 2: Divide the standard deviation by the square root of the sample size:
  10 / 8.66 = 1.15.

The standard error is 1.15. The standard error, combined with the z-score, is then used to calculate the confidence interval, according to this formula:

Upper confidence interval (CI) = mean + (z-score × standard error).
Lower confidence interval (CI) = mean – (z-score × standard error).

The z-score for 95 percent confidence level is always 1.96, so that is used in the basic formula. Determining the confidence interval is done in two steps:

Step 1: Multiply the z-score by the standard error:
  1.96 × 1.15 = 2.25.

Step 2: To obtain the upper confidence interval, add the result of step 1 to the mean.
  The mean was 60, so the upper confidence interval is 60 + 2.25 = 62.25.
  To obtain the lower confidence interval, subtract 2.25 from the mean: 60 – 2.25 = 57.75.

If everyone had taken the exam, the professor is 95 percent certain that the average would have been between 57.75 and 62.25.

The precision of the confidence interval is affected by the sample size. The larger the sample size, the smaller the confidence interval; the smaller the sample, the larger the confidence interval. For example, if the sample were 300, the confidence interval would be 58.86 to 61.14. In contrast, if the sample were 30, the confidence interval would be 56.44 to 63.56.

SAMPLING ERROR

A related concept is sampling error, which is the estimated amount of error between the sample results and the population as a whole. Sampling error is typically reported in polling data. For example, survey results might be reported as 48 percent in favor and 52 percent opposed, with a 5 percent margin of error (plus or minus 5 percent).

Sampling error is based on the standard error of the proportion; that is, the proportion that answer "yes" and "no" to a question. The standard error is essentially based on the proportions (p) and the sample size (n). The formula for the standard error of the proportion is as follows:

$$Standard\ error\ of\ the\ proportion\ (se_p) = \sqrt{p \times (1-p)/n}.$$

Step 1: Multiply the proportion (p) by 1 – proportion ($1-p$).
Step 2: Divide the result of Step 1 by the sample size.
Step 3: The square root of this result gives the sample error.

If the results of a poll of 1,500 randomly selected people show that 55 percent support capping gasoline prices and 45 percent oppose, what is the sampling error?

Step 1: Multiply the proportion by 1 – the proportion: $p = 55$ and $1-p = 45$: .55 × .45 = .2475.
Step 2: Divide by the sample size: .2475 / 1,500 = .000165.
Step 3: Take the square root.
$\sqrt{.000165} = .012$.

The researcher would report that the results were 55 percent for and 45 percent against, plus or minus 1 percent. This means that if everyone were surveyed, the researcher is confident that between 54 and 56 percent would favor capping gasoline prices and between 44 and 46 percent would oppose.

Sample size plays an important role here: the larger the sample, the smaller the sample error; the smaller the sample, the larger the sample error. If the sample were 200, the sample error would be 3.5 percent. In this scenario, if the researcher had surveyed everyone in the population, the true proportion favoring capping gasoline prices would be between 51.5 percent and 58.5 percent, and the true proportion opposing capping gasoline prices would be between 41.5 percent and 48.5 percent. While the actual percentages can vary over a wider range, in this example it is still clear that a majority favor capping gasoline prices.

CALCULATING TESTS FOR STATISTICAL SIGNIFICANCE

All tests of statistical significance provide an estimate of how likely it is that the obtained results were due to chance. Because the data are based on random samples, it is possible that the results are due to the particular sample rather than an accurate reflection of the population as a whole. Tests for statistical significance are always set up in terms of a null hypothesis. For example, the null hypothesis is that there is no difference in the salaries of men and women. The question then is how likely is it to find the amount of difference in their salaries obtained in the data, if there is no difference in the population? If the probability of getting these results by chance is small, then the researcher will conclude that the differences obtained in the sample data are statistically significant.

There are many tests for statistical significance, using slightly different formulas to account for different situations. However, they are conceptually doing the same thing and are interpreted in the same way. Typically, the standard for tests of statistical significance (called alpha or the *p*-value) is .05. If the probability of getting the obtained results is .05 or less, then the results are interpreted as being statistically significant.

CHI-SQUARE

In surveying a sample of public administration students to measure their public service motivation, a researcher will want to determine if these results are statistically significant. Since tests of statistical significance are based on the concept of the null hypothesis—that there really is no difference in the population—then the researcher would expect to see the same number of people reporting high, medium, or low motivation. Chi-square is essentially a way to calculate the difference between what was expected and what was observed for each value.

Calculating chi-square is a two-stage process. First, a chi-square value is obtained. The second stage involves using a chi-square distribution table to determine whether the value is higher than what is predicted; this table is typically included in statistics textbooks.

The formula for obtaining the chi-square value is as follows:

$$Chi\text{-}square = \sum [\,(f_0 - f_e)^2 / f_e].$$

Obtaining the chi-square value is done in four steps:

Step 1: Subtract the observed value (f_o) from the expected value (f_e) for each cell.
Step 2: Square the difference.
Step 3: Divide the squared difference by the expected value for that cell.
Step 4: Sum up all the results from Steps 1–3.

For example, a researcher surveys 300 randomly selected students and finds that 130 report high public service motivation, 95 report medium public service motivation, and 75 report low public service motivation. Because this is random sample data, the researcher wants to determine whether these results are statistically significant. If there were no difference (the null hypothesis), the researcher would expect to see 100 at each level of motivation (300 people divided by 3 possible choices = 100). To calculate the chi-square value:

Steps 1–3: For each level of motivation, determine the difference between what was observed and what was expected, square it, and then divide by what was expected.
High motivation: 130 – 100 = 30. Squared = 900.
Divide by expected value: 900 / 100 = 9.
Medium motivation: 95 – 100 = –5. Squared = 25.

Exhibit A.1 **A Modified Chi-Square Distribution Table**

	Probability (p-value)		
Degrees of freedom	.10	.05	.01
1	2.7	3.8	6.35
2	4.6	5.9	9.2
3	6.2	7.8	11.3
4	7.8	9.5	13.3

Exhibit A.2 **Gender and Public Service Motivation**

		Gender	
Public service motivation		Women (n = 100)	Men (n = 200)
High	(expected)	50	100
	(observed)	55	110
Low	(expected)	50	100
	(observed)	45	90

Divide by expected value: 25 / 100 = .25.
Low motivation: 75 – 100 = –25. Squared = 625.
Divide by expected value: 625 / 100 = 6.25.

Step 4:   Sum the results of each level:
9 + .25 + 6.25 = 15.5.

The chi-square value is 15.5.

The second phase of the process is to look up the value in the chi-square distribution table. To do this, the researcher must first determine the degree of freedom. The degree of freedom in this example is one less than the number of choices. There are three possible choices: high, medium, and low. The degree of freedom is calculated: 3 – 1 = 2. There are two degrees of freedom. Next, the researcher selects the probability value (alpha level or p-value), which is typically .05. To determine whether the results are statistically significant, the chi-square value should be greater than the value in the chi-square distribution table for two degrees of freedom and the .05 level.

An abbreviated version of the chi-square distribution is presented in Exhibit A.1. According to the table, the results would have to be greater than 5.9 for the results to be statistically significant. The chi-square value obtained from this analysis is 15, which is greater than 5.9. The researcher would conclude that these results are statistically significant.

Another common application of chi-square is in cross-tabulations using nominal and ordinal data. For example, a researcher decides to examine whether men and women differ in terms of their reported public service motivation (see Exhibit A.2). There are differences but are they statistically significant? In this example, there are only two choices, so the researcher would expect to find the men and women equally distributed across the two options if the null hypothesis is correct: half the women should report high motivation, and half should report low, just as half the men should report high motivation and half report low.

To determine whether these results in Exhibit A.2 are statistically significant, the chi-square value has to be computed. Again, this is a two-stage process. First, the researcher calculates the difference between what was expected and what was observed, then squares it, and then divides it by the expected frequency for each cell. Then these results are summed up to obtain the chi-square value. In the second stage, the researcher looks up the value in the chi-square distribution table. If the value obtained is greater than the one in the table, then the results are statistically significant; if it is not, the results are not statistically significant.

Steps 1–3: For women and high motivation, the difference between what was expected and the actual result is calculated by first taking the difference: $55 - 50 = 5$. Next, that difference is squared: $5^2 = 25$. Next, this is divided by the expected frequency. $25 / 50 = .5$

Moving to the next cell, men with high motivation scores, the score would be computed by taking the difference between the actual result and what was expected: $110 - 100 = 10$. Then, that difference is squared: $10^2 = 100$. This figure is then divided by the expected frequency: $100 / 100 = 1$.

Each cell would be calculated in the same way.

Step 4: Sum the results from Steps 1–3: $.5 + 1 + .5 + 1 = 3$.

The sum is the chi-square value that gets compared to the chi-square distribution table. If the chi-square value is higher than what is expected, then the researcher would conclude that the results are statistically significant. The table is arranged by the p-values along the top and the degrees of freedom down the side (see Exhibit A.1). Degrees of freedom are a measure of the number of choices (or values for each variable). In this example, there are two choices for gender (male and female) and two choices for motivation (high or low). In a crosstab, the degrees of freedom depend on the number of rows and columns. The formula for calculating the degrees of freedom in a crosstab is as follows:

Degrees of freedom (df) = (number of rows – 1) × (number of columns – 1).

For Exhibit A.2, the degree of freedom is calculated: $df = (2 - 1) \times (2 - 1) = 1$. If the researcher set the p-value at .05, and the degree of freedom is 1, then the chi-square value would have to exceed 3.8 in order to be statistically significant. The chi-square value is 3, so these results are not statistically significant. If, however, the results were more dramatic, the chi-square value would be higher (see Exhibit A.3).

Computing the value for the women and high motivation begins with taking the difference between the expected and actual results: $85 - 50 = 35$. Next, that difference is squared: $35^2 = 1225$. This figure is divided by the expected frequency: $1225 / 50 = 24.5$. Computing the value for men with high motivation begins with taking the difference between the expected and actual results: $130 - 100 = 30$. Next, that difference is squared: $30^2 = 900$. Then this figure is divided by the expected frequency: $900 / 100 = 9$. The other cells would be calculated in the same way—for a total value of 67. The total sum would be compared to the chi-square distribution to determine

Exhibit A.3 **Gender and Public Service Motivation**

Public service motivation		Gender	
		Women (*n* = 100)	Men (*n* = 200)
High	*(expected)*	*50*	*100*
	(observed)	85	130
Low	*(expected)*	*50*	*100*
	(observed)	15	70

whether it is statistically significant; since the value is greater than 3.8 (see Exhibit A.1), these results are statistically significant.

t-TESTS

t-tests are used with interval and ratio level data. In a single distribution, a *t*-test can be done to see if the mean is statistically significant. While tests for statistical significance are in terms of the null hypothesis, this test has a slight variation to it. In this analysis, the mean from the sample data is compared to a hypothesized or assumed mean. The question then is how likely is it to get this mean if we think (hypothesize) the population mean is something different? If a survey were done to determine how many hours people work per week, the researcher might hypothesize that the population average would be 40 hours per week, but the sample average is 43. If the hypothesized population average is true, how likely is to get an average of 43 from sample data? A *t*-test would be done using this formula:

$$t = (\text{mean of the sample } (\overrightarrow{X}) - \text{assumed mean }) / (\text{standard error of the mean}).$$

To calculate this *t*-test, the difference between the sample mean and the assumed mean is divided by the standard error. The standard error is the square root of the standard deviation divided by the number of cases. If the researcher surveyed 200 people and found that the mean was 43 hours and the standard deviation was 1.2, the equation would be solved in these steps:

Step 1: Subtract the assumed mean from the sample mean: $43 - 40 = 3$.
Step 2: Obtain the standard error of the mean: $\sqrt{}$(standard deviation / number of cases): $1.2 / 200 = .006$.
Step 3: Take the square root of the results from Step 2: $\sqrt{.006} = .077$.
Step 4: Divide the results from Step 1 by Step 3: $3 / .077 = 38$.

There is another step. The results of these calculations are compared to a table of *t*-value distributions (see Exhibit A.4 for a modified version). If the *t*-value is greater than what is expected, the results are statistically significant. The *t*-test value comparison is based on the degree of freedom, which is one less than the number of cases ($200 - 1 = 199$). It is also based on the probability criteria (the *p* or alpha value), which is typically .05. If the *t*-value obtained in Steps 1–4 is greater than the value listed

Exhibit A.4   **A Modified *T*-Value Distribution Table**

| | Probability (*p*-value) | | | |
| | One-tailed test | | Two-tailed test | |
Degree of freedom	.05	.01	.05	.01
1	6.3	31.8	12.7	63.7
2	2.9	7.0	4.3	9.9
3	2.4	4.5	3.2	5.8
10	1.8	2.8	2.2	3.2
30	1.7	2.5	2.0	2.8
60	1.7	2.4	2.0	2.7
Infinity	1.6	2.3	2.0	2.6

on the table, then the results are statistically significant. In this case, it is; it would be very unlikely to get an average of 43 hours in a sample of 200 if the real population average is only 40. The researcher would conclude that the average hours worked per week is actually closer to 43 and that this result is statistically significant.

A *t*-test could be done on the salary distribution A used earlier where the mean was calculated to be $38,000 and the standard deviation $19,558. If the researcher assumes that the population mean is $35,000, how likely would it be to get a sample mean of $38,000?

Step 1:   Subtract the assumed mean from the sample mean: 38,000 – 35,000 = 3,000.

Step 2:   Obtain the standard error of the mean: $\sqrt{}$ (standard deviation / number of cases):
19,558 / 5 = 3,911.6.

Step 3:   Take the square root of the results from Step 2: $\sqrt{3,911.6}$ = 62.5.

Step 4:   Divide the results from Step 1 by Step 3: 3,000 / 62.5 = 12.5.

The *t*-value derived would be compared to the t-distribution table. This value is greater than what is expected at the .05 level with four degrees of freedom, so the difference is statistically significant.

Another typical analysis for the *t*-test is to determine whether differences are statistically significant. For example, is there a difference in salary between men and women and if so, is that difference statistically significant? Data from a random sample are collected and the data shows that men have a higher average salary than women. To determine whether this difference is statistically significant, an independent means *t*-test is computed using the following formula:

$$t = \frac{\overline{X}_1 - \overline{X}_2}{\sqrt{\dfrac{S_1^2}{n_1 - 1} + \dfrac{S_2^2}{n_2 - 1}}}.$$

Step 1: Calculate the difference in means between the men and the women:
Mean salary for women = $31,000.
Mean salary for men = $38,000.
Difference = $7,000.

Step 2: Divide the variance for women by one less than the number of women in the sample. The variance is the square of the standard deviation. The standard deviation is $3,000, so the variance is 9,000,000. There are 1,000 women in the sample: 9,000,000 / 999 = 9009.

Divide the variance for men by one less than the number of men in the sample. The standard deviation is $5,000, so the variance is 25,000,000. There are 1,500 men in the sample:
25,000,000 / 1,499 = 16,677.

Step 3: Add these two results together and then obtain its square root.
9,009 + 16,677 = 25,686. Square root =160.

Step 4: Divide the differences in the means (obtained in Step 1) by the results of Step 3:
7,000 / 160 = 43.

Again, the results of these calculations are compared to a table of t-value distributions (see Exhibit A.4). If the t-value is greater than what is expected, the results are statistically significant.

The probability values in the t-distribution are divided between one-tailed and two-tailed tests (in one-tailed tests, the hypothesis states a direction, such as that men will earn more than women; two-tailed tests do not have a direction, stating just that there is a difference between men and women). The degrees of freedom are calculated as the sample size minus 2. The sample consisted of 1,000 women and 1,500 men, so the degrees of freedom (df) = 2,498. The researcher would then consult the t-distribution table and look for the value based on the degrees of freedom and probability for the one- or two-tailed test (see Exhibit A.4).

Sample size will affect the t-values. If the mean salaries and standard deviations remain the same, but the sample size is much reduced, the t-value would be different. For example, if there are only 50 women and 75 men in the sample, the t-value will be smaller.

Step 1: The difference in means between the men and the women is calculated.
Mean salary for women = $31,000.
Mean salary for men = $38,000.
Difference = $7,000.

Step 2: Divide the variance for women by one less than the number of women in the sample. The standard deviation is $3,000, so the variance is the square = 9,000,000. There are 50 women in the sample:
9,000,000 / 49 = 183,673.

Divide the variance for men by one less than the number of men in the sample. The standard deviation is $5,000, so the variance is 25,000,000. There are 75 men in the sample: 25,000,000 / 74 = 337,837.

Step 3: Add the results together and then take its square root.
$183,673 + 337,837 = 521,510$. Square root = 722.

Step 4: Divide the differences in the means by the results of Step 3:
$7,000 / 722 = 9.7$.

While the t-value is lower with the smaller sample size, checking the t-distribution will show that this result will still be statistically significant at the .05 level (two-tailed column) with 123 degrees of freedom (N–2).

MEASURES OF RELATIONSHIP

Many different kinds of formulas are used to calculate the strength of the relationships depending upon the type of data being used and the particular circumstances. But while the formulas differ, all measures of relationships can vary only between 0 (meaning no relationship) and 1 (meaning a perfect relationship). Some measures of relationship also show the direction of the relationship: a plus sign indicates that the changes are in the same direction (as X decreases, Y decreases) and a negative sign indicates that the changes are in the opposite or inverse direction (as X decreases, Y increases). Some measures of relationship are relatively easy to calculate while others involve many small calculations. With large data sets, these become far too time-consuming to calculate by hand and the probability of making errors greatly increases.

The formula for Pearson's r (product moment correlation) is shown here:

$$\textit{Pearson's product moment (r)} = \frac{N\sum XY - \left(\sum X\right)\left(\sum Y\right)}{\sqrt{\left[N\sum X^2 - \left(\sum X\right)^2\right]\left[N\sum Y^2 - \left(\sum Y\right)^2\right]}}.$$

Pearson's r measures the strength of relationship between two variables (X and Y). The calculations include taking the sum of all the values of X, all the values of Y, the sum of the product of X and Y for each case, the sum of the squares of X and the sum of the squares of Y. The number of cases (N) is also a factor included in the calculations. Then they are multiplied, subtracted, divided, and square-rooted. The easiest way to do these calculations is to first set up a table (Exhibit A.5) that does the basic calculations and then plug them into the formula. In this example, we have a sample of five people who have been given two tests. The question is whether the scores on test A are related to the scores on test B.

To calculate the Pearson's r, first calculate the top half (numerator) of the equation:

$N\sum XY - \left(\sum X\right)\left(\sum Y\right)$.

Step 1: Multiply each person's score on test A by that person's score on test B and then sum.
$\sum XY = 197$.

Step 2: Multiply the sum obtained in Step 1 ($\sum XY$) by the number of cases (N):
$5 \times 197 = 985$.

Exhibit A.5 **Calculation Table**

Person	Test A	Test B	XY	X^2	Y^2
1	8	7	56	64	49
2	8	6	48	64	36
3	5	6	30	25	36
4	4	7	28	16	49
5	5	7	35	25	49
Σ Sum	30	33	197	194	219

Step 3: Multiply the sum of the values of X by the sum of the values of Y:
$(\Sigma X)(\Sigma Y) = (30)(33) = 990$.

Step 4: Subtract the result of Step 3 from the result of Step 2:
$985 - 990 = -5$.
The numerator is -5.

Next, calculate the denominator: $\sqrt{\left[N\sum X^2 - \left(\sum X\right)^2\right]\left[N\sum Y^2 - \left(\sum Y\right)^2\right]}$.

Step 5: Sum of the square of each value of X:
$\sum X^2 = 194$.

Step 6: Multiply $\sum X^2$ by the number of cases (N):
$5 \times 194 = 970$.

Step 7: Square the sum of all values of X $(\sum X)^2$:
$(30)^2 = 900$.

Step 8: Subtract the results of Step 7 from the results of Step 6:
$970 - 900 = 70$.

Step 9: Sum of the square of each value of Y:
$\sum Y^2 = 219$.

Step 10: Multiply $\sum Y^2$ by the number of cases (N):
$5 \times 219 = 1095$.

Step 11: Square the sum of all values of X $(\sum Y)^2$:
$(33)^2 = 1089$.

Step 12: Subtract the results of Step 11 from the results of Step 10:
$1095 - 1089 = 6$.

Step 13: Multiply the results of Step 8 by the results of Step 12:
$70 \times 6 = 420$.

Step 14: Take the square root of 420:
$\sqrt{420} = 20.5$

Step 15: Divide the result of Step 4 (the numerator) by the result of Step 14 (the denominator):
$-5 / 20.5 = -.24$.

The Pearson's r is $-.24$. This suggests that there is a weak, inverse (note the minus sign) relationship. People with the lower scores on test A got higher scores on test B (maybe they tried harder on the second test!).

FORMULA FOR DETERMINING SAMPLE SIZE FOR POPULATION CHARACTERISTIC EXPRESSED AS A PROPORTION

Sometimes the sample size is calculated based on the proportion of the characteristic in the population. For example, researchers might have already determined that the proportion of women in the population is 50 percent. They could then determine the sample size based on their desired confidence level (the science standard is 95 percent) and level of precision (the social science standard is plus or minus 5 percent).

$$\sqrt{n} = \sqrt{p(1-p)} \times \textit{z-score / accuracy}$$

where:

n = sample size
p = proportion of the population. Conservative measure is 50 percent.
z-score = desired confidence level, related to standard deviation
95 percent confidence level = z-score = 1.96

Accuracy is the level of precision. Standard is .05.

Solving the equation:

$$N = \sqrt{(.50)(1 - .5)} \times 1.96 / .05$$

$$(.5) \times (39.2) = 19.6$$
$$n = 384$$

The desired sample size is 384.

Appendix B
Statistics as a Second Language

alpha level	The standard for determining statistical significance: if there really is no difference in the population, what is the probability of getting these sample data results by chance alone? The social science standard is .05; if the probability is .05 or less, the researcher will conclude that the results are statistically significant. It is also known as the *p*-value.
ANOVA	It provides a measure of statistical significance when working with an interval or ratio-level dependent variable and a nominal or ordinal-level independent variable that has more than two categories.
association	Two variables that appear to be related; that is, as one variable changes, so does the other. This relationship might also be referred to as a correlation. However, association or correlation does not mean causality.
beta weight	Used in multiple regression, this is the standardized regression coefficient that makes variables using different measurement scales comparable; it enables the researcher to determine which independent variable has the greatest effect on the dependent variable.
case study	A type of study in which the researcher will select one or more subjects or sites in order to make an in-depth analysis of a process, organization, or other event. It can include both quantitative and qualitative data collection and analysis.
causality	A relationship in which a change in one variable (the independent variable) causes change in another variable (the dependent variable). *X* causes *Y* to happen. The necessary elements needed to determine causality are a logical theory, time order, covariation, and elimination of rival explanations.
census	Data collected from all members or units of the population of interest.

chi-square test A statistical test to estimate the probability of getting the results solely because of random chance. Chi-square is used with categorical variables (nominal and ordinal, and interval data that have been collapsed into categories).

Chronback's alpha A test to determine the internal consistency of survey answers. The results vary from 0 (little consistency) to 1 (great consistency). The test should be at least .7. It is also called a reliability coefficient.

coefficient of determination In linear regression analysis, this tells the extent to which the independent variable explains the variance in the dependent variable. It is more typically called r-squared. A small r is used with bivariate regression and a capital R is used with multiple regression.

confidence interval The range that is very likely to contain the true population mean or proportion based on results from a sample drawn from that population. For example, polling results typically give a margin of error of plus or minus 3 percent when reporting the percent of people supporting different presidential candidates; this is one way to present the confidence interval.

confidence level It is the estimated probability that a population parameter lies within a specific range. The standard is 95 percent, meaning the researchers are 95 percent confident that the true population value resides within a specified range of values. Confidence levels and confidence intervals go together. One way to present the confidence level is as follows: In nineteen out of twenty cases (95 percent of the time), the results based on this sample will differ by no more than 5 percentage points in either direction from what would be obtained by seeking out all the people in the population of interest.

controls and control variables Accounting for an observed relationship between two variables by controlling for a third variable, sometimes called a control variable. It is also sometimes called a suppressor or confounding variable. Researchers call this process "holding constant" or "controlling for" that third variable. If the initial relationship persists, then the third variable has no effect. If the initial relationship disappears, then the relationship is said to be spurious. If specific relationships emerge, then the third variable helps to specify the nature of the relationship.

Cramer's V A measure of association typically used with cross-tabulations with nominal data. Phi is another measure of association used with nominal data.

cross-tabulations (contingency tables) Method for analyzing nominal, ordinal, or interval data that have been converted into categories variables. When used to explore a relationship, the table is interpreted by looking at the each category of the independent variable (such as gender) and comparing the percentage distribution of the dependent variable (such as for or against a particular public policy).

degrees of freedom	A measure of how many choices there are; used to calculate tests of statistical significance.
dependent variable	The variable that the researcher is trying to understand or explain. In terms of the particular theory used, the dependent variable is thought to be the result of (or related to) some other factor (the independent variable). It therefore "depends" upon another factor.
descriptive statistics	In its narrowest definition, mathematical techniques to describe and summarize quantitative data for an entire population. The most common being frequencies, percentages, rates, rates of change, ratios, means, medians, ranges, and standard deviations.
dummy variable	A variable with only two categories, such as gender: male or female; it is coded 0 and 1 and is often used in multiple regression.
frequency distribution	A description of the number of times the various attributes or values are observed; for example, the ages of people in an MPA program.
experimental design	A research design that uses random assignment to treatment and control groups. It is the strongest design for answering cause-and-effect or impact questions.
generalization	The ability to make a statement about a larger population based on the results of a sample from the same population.
hypothesis	A statement of something that ought to be observed if a theory is correct; stated expectations about the relationship of two or more variables.
hypothesis test	The empirical determination of statistical significance. Hypothetical tests are framed in terms of rejecting or failing to reject the null hypothesis when working with random sample data: if there is no difference in the population, how likely is it that these findings are the result of random chance?
independent variable	The variable believed to explain changes in the dependent variable or believed to be the causal factor.
inferential statistics	A body of statistical computations that enable the researcher to make inferences from random sample results to the larger population as well as determine how likely it is that the results are due to chance.
inter-rater reliability	The extent of agreement between researchers when coding qualitative data such as presidential speeches or focus group transcripts.
interval data	Measures that are numeric but do not contain zero, such as IQ or GRE scores.

least squares   In regression analysis, the researcher wants to fit a line to the data in a way that minimizes the distance between the line (which represents the predicted values if there is a relationship between the two variables) and the actual data. The calculation is based on squaring the distance between the actual data and the predicted values, hence the name. It is also known as ordinary least squares.

level of measurement   The type of data: whether it is ratio, interval ordinal, or nominal.

Likert scale   Ordinal responses for survey questions; these typically contain 5 possible responses with a neutral category in the middle. For example: strongly agree, somewhat agree, neither agree or disagree, somewhat disagree, strongly disagree.

measures of association   Statistics that measure the strength of a relationship. The closer to 0, the weaker the relationship; the closer to 1, the stronger the relationship. Some measures go from plus 1 to minus 1 to reflect the direction of the relationship; a plus sign signals a direct relationship while a minus sign indicates an inverse relationship. Common measures of association are Cramer's V, Phi, gamma, Tau b, Tau c, Spearman's rho, Pearson's r, and correlations.

measures of central tendency   A single number that summarizes and describes the center of a set of data. There are three measures: the mean is the arithmetical average of a set of data; the median is the middle point in a set of data; and the mode is the most common value in a set of data.

measures of dispersion   A way to summarize the amount of variation in the distribution of data by describing how much the data cluster around the mean. The variance is the differences from the mean. The standard deviation is the most common measure, which shows how the data vary from the mean; the higher the standard deviation, the greater the spread of the data from the mean. The range presents the highest and lowest values in the distribution.

nominal data   Measures whose values are names or categories, with no order to them. For example, names of cities or religions.

nonexperimental design   A type of design that might have a comparison group but no before-and-after measure, or might have a before-and-after measure but not a comparison group, or lack both a comparison group and before-and-after measures. This design is typically used to answer descriptive questions.

nonlinear relationships   Unlike linear relationships in which both variables change in a single direction (a direct relationship where both change in the same direction or an inverse relationship where one variable increases while the other decreases), variables in nonlinear relationships can both increase and decrease. For example, youth from low-income and high-income families are more likely to use illegal drugs than youth from middle-income families.

nonrandom samples	Sampling methods that are used when it cannot be ensured that each item has an equal chance of being selected or when it makes sense to make selections based on specific criteria. Selection is based on expert knowledge of the population. Common nonrandom samples methods are judgmental, quota, accidental, convenience and snowball.
non-sampling error	Non-sampling errors are problems that arise because of a volunteer sample, low response rates or poorly worded survey questions that limit the ability of researchers to make estimates about the population. Unlike sampling errors that can be mathematically estimated, the impact of non-sampling errors on the results is unknown.
normal curve	A theoretical concept suggesting that data are arrayed in a bell-shaped curve and that the mean, median, and mode have the same value.
null hypothesis	The null hypothesis is stated as an assumption that there is no relationship between the variables.
operational definition	Defining a concept in measurable terms so it can be studied.
ordinal measure	A ranking order of a variable's categories going from most to least; it assumes an underlying continuum. For example, extent scales are ordinal measures.
parameter	A measure used to summarize the characteristics of the population from which a sample was drawn.
percentage distribution	A description of the proportional distribution of all observations for each category of the variable. For example, of 300 respondents, 55 percent are women and 45 percent are men.
population	The total set of items or people that a researcher is interested in studying.
probability	An estimate of how likely it is that certain events will occur, or an estimate of how likely it is that the results are due to chance.
product moment correlation coefficient (r)	A measure of association used with interval and ratio data.
qualitative research	Research focusing on a nonnumerical understanding of the world, based on observations or verbal statements; useful for understanding context, perspective, and complex phenomena.
quantitative research	Research focusing on numerical measures of things using mathematical analysis.

quasi-experimental design	A research design that lacks random assignment. It typically has a comparison group, either existing or created using statistical controls (correlational design). Longitudinal and interrupted time series designs are often categorized as quasi-experimental. These are not as strong as experimental designs in demonstrating causality but they are often as good as it gets in public administration research.
***R*-squared**	Used in regression analysis, this tells how much of the variation in the dependent variable is explained by the independent variable(s). If 0, nothing is explained by the independent variable; if 1, everything is explained. A .3 is considered respectable in social science research.
random sample	A sample in which every member or unit of the population has an equal chance of being selected. Also called a probability sample. This is the fundamental requirement for using inferential statistics. Simple random, stratified random, and cluster samples are common.
range	Presents the highest and lowest values in a set of data.
ratio-level data	Numerical data that contains a zero. It is therefore possible to add and subtract, multiply and divide ratio measures and to state a given score is twice as great as another score. This is not possible with interval-level data.
regression coefficient	Used in predicting the value of the dependent variable for every one unit change in the independent variable: for a one unit change in the independent variable there is a specific amount of change in the dependent variable.
reliability	A measure is reliable to the extent that it gives the same result again and again if the measurement is repeated. Analogy of measuring with a wooden yardstick vs. an elastic tape measure: the wooden yardstick will tend to give reliable measures every time, while the elastic tape measure will give different results.
rounding rule for decimals	To round to the nearest whole number, round down if the decimal is less than .5 or less; round up if it is .5 or higher. In a percentage distribution, the total might not add to 100 percent but it should never add to less than 99 or more than 101 percent.
sample	A subset of the population; can be a random or nonrandom selection.
sampling distribution	A sampling distribution shows what proportion of the time each particular result could be expected to occur if the sampling technique used was repeated a very large number of times and the set of assumptions (including the null hypothesis) was true. That is, it gives the probability of getting any particular result with repeated samples. It enables the researcher to estimate the probability of getting the observed result or estimate the risk of rejecting a null hypothesis when it is really true and should not be rejected.

sampling error	The estimate of the expected differences between the results from a random sample and the results if data had been gathered from the entire population.
sampling frame	The rules and procedures that specify how a sample is to be selected, including a statement about the characteristics used for selection; it is the specifics about the population of interest from which the sample will be drawn.
scatterplot	A graphic that plots all the observations for how each case scored on both the independent and dependent variable; also called a scattergram.
significance test	Statistical significance refers to whether the results of data from a random sample are due to chance; significance tests give an estimate of how likely it is that these results are due to chance alone. The social science standard for the test (often called the p-value or alpha level) is .05. These tests include chi-square and t-tests.
skewness	A measure of how well a set of data conforms to a normal distribution. If the measure is close to 0, the data are close to a normal distribution. If the measure is positive, it is positively skewed: the mean will be higher than the median. If the measure is negative, the distribution is negatively skewed: the mean will be lower than the median.
social desirability bias	When participants tell the researchers what they think is politically correct, socially acceptable, or what they feel the researchers want them to say.
spurious correlation	When an association between X and Y disappears when a control is applied, the original association between X and Y is said to be spurious. For example, when temperature is controlled for, the seeming relationship between ice cream sales and drownings disappears.
standard deviation	Obtained by squaring the variance, it is a single number that shows how much dispersion (or spread) there is in a frequency distribution. The smaller the standard deviation, the less variation or dispersion from the mean in the set of numbers.
standard error of the mean	This is an estimate of the amount of error in a sample estimate of a population mean. This allows the researcher to state the level of confidence that the estimated population mean lies within a specified range (i.e., the confidence interval).
statistics	The word *statistics* derives from Latin, meaning "of state affairs" and grew out of the need to keep records for the state. It generally refers to collecting, analyzing and presenting numerical data.
suppressor variable	When a third variable hides a relationship but when it is controlled for, the relationship between X and Y becomes apparent.

Tau *b* and Tau *c*	Measures the strength of association between ordinal variables as part of a cross-tab analysis; Tau *b* is used with square tables and Tau *c* is used with rectangular tables.
triangulation	A research approach that uses multiple methods of collecting data to answer a research question in a single study; it is intended increase the validity of its results.
***t*-test**	A test of statistical significance used with interval or ratio data; when used with two variables, a dependent variable must be interval or ratio data and the independent variable must be nominal or ordinal data with only two categories.
Type I error	An error that occurs when the researcher rejects a null hypothesis that is actually true, concluding there is difference when, if everyone had been surveyed, there would be no difference.
Type II error	An error that occurs when the researcher fails to reject a null hypothesis, concluding there is no difference, when there really is.
unit of analysis	The object whose characteristics are being measured; for example, if the researcher is measuring individual characteristics in explaining student drop-outs, then the unit of analysis is "student's propensity to drop out." If the researcher is measuring school characteristics in explaining dropout rates, then the unit of analysis is "school characteristics" in predicting dropout rates of schools.
validity	A measure is valid if it measures the concept it is meant to measure: Are you measuring what you think you are measuring? Face validity refers to a measure that appears to measure the concept; it looks like an appropriate operational measure even though it has not been tested.
values	These are the concrete categories or measures of the variables. For example, the values for gender are male and female.
variables	Attributes or characteristics whose variations are of interest to the researcher. The same variable may be an independent variable in one theory and a dependent variable in another. The designation of "dependent" or "independent" depends upon the researcher's theory or assumptions, not on some inherent quality of the attribute itself.
variance	A measure of how widely the observed values of a variable may vary among themselves. Calculated as the average squared deviation of values from their means. If they do not vary at all, the variance will be zero. The more the values vary among themselves, the further each will be from the mean of them all, and the greater the sum of the squared deviations from the mean will be. Thus, the more they vary among themselves, the higher their variance will be.
weight	A way to accurately estimate a population mean or proportion based on data from a disproportinate stratified sample. It is computed by dividing the number of items in each strata by the sample size for each strata.

Appendix C
References and Resources

REFERENCES

Adler, Matthew D., and Eric A. Posner. 2006. *New Foundations of Cost-Benefit Analysis.* Boston: Harvard University Press.

Agnew, Neil McK., and Sandra W. Pyke. 2007. *The Science Game: An Introduction to Research in the Social Sciences.* 7th ed. New York: Oxford University Press.

Associated Press. 2008. Did Tuskegee damage trust on clinical trials? CNN.com, April 2. www.finalcall.com/artman/publish/article_4522.shtml.

Bardach, Eugene. 2005. *A Practical Guide for Policy Analysis.* 2nd ed. Washington, DC: CQ Press.

Barker, Joel. 2001. Paradigms: The business of discovering the future. www.thenewbusinessofparadigms.com/media/preview/TranscriptClassicPreview_NBOP.pdf.

Berenson, Alex, and Benedict Carey. 2007. Experts question study on youth suicide rates. *New York Times*, September 14.

Bracey, Gerald W. 1999. The numbers game in higher education. *Washington Post Weekly Edition*, November 1, 34.

Brown, David. 2006. Study claims Iraq's "excess" death toll has reached 655,000. *Washington Post*, October 11.

Buchanan, Mark. 2008. This economy does not compute. *New York Times*, October 1.

Burnham, Gilbert. 2006. Response to the *Wall Street Journal*'s "655,000 war dead?" Johns Hopkins Bloomberg School of Public Health. www.jhsph.edu/refugee/publications_tools/iraq/wsj_response.html.

Burnham, Gilbert, Riyadh Lafta, Shannon Doocy, and Les Roberts. 2006. Mortality after the 2003 invasion of Iraq: A cross-sectional cluster sample survey. *Lancet*, October 11. www.thelancet.com/journals/lancet/article/PIIS0140673606694919/abstract.

California Newsreel. 2003. *Race: The Power of Illusion. Public Broadcasting Service (PBS).* www.pbs.org/race/000_General/000_00-Home.htm.

CBS News.com. 2007. Video games may divert kids from homework. July 2. www.cbsnews.com/stories/2007/07/02/health/webmd/main3009349.shtml.

Children's Defense Fund. 2008a. Every day in America. www.childrensdefense.org/site/PageServer?pagename=research_national_data_each_day.

———. 2008b. Protect children, not guns. www.childrensdefense.org/site/PageServer?pagename=Safe_Start_Gun_Report.

Clark, Kim. 2008. How much is that college degree really worth? *U.S. News and World Report*, October 30. www.usnews.come/article/education/10/30/how-much-is-that-college-degree-really-worth?

CNNMoney.com. 2005. Surprise! Pretty people earn more. April 11.

Creswell, John W. 2008. *Research Design: Qualitative, Quantitative, and Mixed Methods Approaches.* 3rd ed. Thousand Oaks, CA: Sage.

Curtis, Karen A., and Stephanie McClellan. 1995. Falling through the safety net: Poverty, food assistance and shopping constraints in an American city. *Urban Anthropology* 24: 93–135.

DeYoung, Karen. 2007. Experts doubt drop-in violence in Iraq: Military statistics called into question. *Washington Post*, September 6.

Dillman, Don, Jolene D. Smyth, and Leah Melani Christian. 2008. *Internet, Mail, and Mixed-mode Surveys: The Tailored Design Method.* 3rd ed. New York: Wiley.

Donohue, John D., III, and Steven D. Levitt. 2001. The impact of legalized abortion on crime. *Quarterly Journal of Economics* 116 (2): 379–417.

Dougherty, Connor. 2008. High-degree professionals show power. *Wall Street Journal*, September 10.

Duggan, Mark. 2001. More guns, more crime. *Journal of Political Economy* 109 (5): 1086–1114.

Dunham, Will. 2008. France best, U.S. worst in preventable death ranking. *Reuters*, January 8. www. reuters.com/article/newsOne/idUSN0765165020080108.

Eggen, Dan, and Kimberly Kindy. 2009. Familiar players in health bill lobbying: Firms are enlisting ex-legislators, aides, *Washington Post*, July 6. www.washingtonpost.com/wp-dyn/content/article/2009/07/05/AR2009070502770.html.

Ehrenreich, Barbara. 2001. *Nickel and Dimed: On (Not) Getting By in America.* New York: Henry Holt.

Einstein, Albert, and Leopold Infeld. 1938. *The Evolution of Physics: The Growth of Ideas from Early Concepts to Relativity and Quanta.* New York: Simon & Schuster.

Eisenhower, Dwight David 1952. quoted in "Republicans: Man of Experience," *Time*, November 3. www.time.com/time/magazine/article/0,9171,806506,00.html.

Fisher, Deborah, Pamela Imm, Matthew Chinman, and Abe Wandersman. 2006. *Getting to Outcomes with Developmental Assets: Ten Steps to Measuring Success in Youth Programs and Communities.* Minneapolis, MN: Search Institute Press.

Fowler, James H., and Nicholas A. Christakis. 2008. Dynamic spread of happiness in a large social network: Longitudinal analysis over 20 years in the Framingham Heart Study. *British Medical Journal* 337 (December): a2338.

Frechtling, Joy A. 2007. *Logic Modeling Methods in Program Evaluation.* San Francisco: Wiley.

Galbraith, John Kenneth. 1971. *A Contemporary Guide to Economics, Peace, and Laughter.* Boston, MA: Houghton Mifflin.

Gellene, Denise. 2007. Study finds left-wing brain, right-wing brain. *Los Angeles Times*, September 10.

Goodman, Amy. 2009. They dump the sick to satisfy investors: Insurance exec turned whistleblower Wendell Potter speaks out against healthcare industry, *Democracy Now!* July 15. www.democracynow.org/2009/7/16/former_insurance_exec_wendell_porter.

Gosche, Mary. 2007. Homework: Too much or not enough. Missouri Families newsletter. http://missourifamilies.org/features/parentingarticles/parenting20.htm.

Grier, Peter, and Patrik Jonsson. 2004. LBJ launched a major national battle 40 years ago this week. *Christian Science Monitor*, January 9.

Gueron, Judith M. 1988. Work-welfare programs. *New Directions for Program Evaluation* 37: 7–28.

Harris, Gardiner. 2007. Teenage birth rate rises for first time since '91. *New York Times*, December 6.

Harrison, Michael. 2004. *Diagnosing Organizations: Methods, Models, and Processes.* 3rd ed. Thousand Oaks, CA: Sage.

Hatry, Harry P. 2007. *Performance Measurement: Getting Results.* 2nd ed. Washington, DC: Urban Institute Press.

Huff, Darrell. 1954. *How to Lie with Statistics.* New York: Norton.

Jacobe, Dennis. 2008. U.S. Congress, gouging blamed equally for gas prices, *Gallup,com.* August 6. www.gallup.com/poll/109303/us-congress-gouging-blamed-equally-gas-prices.aspx.

James, Delores C.S., W. William Chen, and Jiunn-Jye Sheu. 2005. Comparison of three tobacco survey methods with college students: A case study. *International Electronic Journal of Health Education* 8: 119–124.

Johnson, Gail. 2001. Teenaged mothers on welfare: Views on reform and necessary supports. *Journal of Poverty* 5 (2): 67–86.

Kearney, Richard C., Barry M. Feldman, and Carmine P.F. Scavo. 2000. Reinventing government: City managers' attitudes and actions. *Public Administration Review* 60 (6): 535–548.

Keeter, Scott, Juliana Horowitz, and Alec Tyson. 2008. Young voters in the 2008 election. Pew Research Center for the People and the Press. http://pewresearch.org/pubs/1031/young-voters-in-the-2008-election.

King, Cheryl, and Gail Johnson. 2002. Where the rubber meets the road: Analysis of citizens' reaction to a bridge closure. Unpublished report.

Klass, Gary. 2008. *Just Plain Data Analysis: Finding, Presenting, and Interpreting Social Science Data.* New York: Rowman and Littlefield.

Klein, Stephen P., Richard A. Berk, and Laura J. Hickman. 2006. *Race: The Decision to Seek the Death Penalty in Federal Cases.* Prepared for the National Institute of Justice by the Rand Corporation, CA.

Krejcie, R.V., and D.W. Morgan. 1970. Determining sample size for research activities. *Educational and Psychological Measurement* 30: 607–610.

Krueger, Richard, and Mary Anne Casey. 2008. *Focus Groups: A Practical Guide for Applied Research.* 4th ed. Thousand Oaks, CA: Sage.

Kuhn, Thomas S. 1962. *The Structure of Scientific Revolutions.* Chicago: University of Chicago Press.

Kume, Hitoshi. 1985. *Statistical Methods for Quality Improvement.* New York: Productivity Press.

Lahart, Justin. 2008. Daylight savings wastes energy, study says. *Wall Street Journal Online*, February 27. http://online.wsj.com/article/SB120406767043794825.html.

Lavelle, Marianne. 2009. "The Climate Change Lobby Explosion: Will Thousands of Lobbyists Imperil Action on Global Warming?" The Center for Public Integrity, February 24. www.publicintegrity.org/investigations/climate_change/articles/entry/1171/.

Lenhart, Amanda, Sydney Jones, and Alexandra Rankin McGill. 2008. Video games: Adults are players too. Pew Internet & American Life Project, December 7. http://pewresearch.org/pubs/1048/adults-are-players-too.

Liptak, Adam. 2008. New look at death sentences and race. *New York Times*, April 29. www.nytimes.com/2008/04/29/us/29bar.html?partner=rssyahoo&emc=rss.

Livio, Susan K. 2008. Anti-poverty programs aren't working in NJ, report says. *New Jersey Star-Ledger*, February 19. www.nj.com/news/index.ssf/2008/02/government_programs_fail_to_ma.html.

MacQuarrie, Brian. 2006. Disputed study says 600,000 Iraqis killed during war. *Boston Globe*, October 12. www.boston.com/news/world/middleeast/articles/2006/10/12/disputed_study_says_600000_iraqis_killed_during_war/.

Mallick, Ross. 2002. Implementing and evaluating microcredit in Bangladesh. *Development in Practice* 2 (2): 153–163.

Maslow, Abraham. 1987. *Motivation and Personality.* New York: HarperCollins.

McLennan, Louisa. 2005. Two children die of malaria each minute, warns UN. *Times Online*, May 3. www.timesonline.co.uk/tol/news/world/article1079394.ece.

McNabb, David E. 2002. *Research Methods in Public Administration and Nonprofit Management: Quantitative and Qualitative Approaches.* Armonk, NY: M.E. Sharpe.

Meier, Kenneth J., Jeffrey L. Brudney, and John Bohte. 2008. *Applied Statistics for Public and Nonprofit Administration.* 7th ed. New York: Wadsworth.

Milgram, Stanley. 1974. *Obedience to Authority: An Experimental View.* New York: Harper and Row.

Money.cnn.com. 2008. Fortune global 500. *Money.* http://money.cnn.com/magazines/fortune/global500/2007/industries/20/1.html.

Moore, Michael. 2007. *Sicko.* Dog Eat Dog Films.

Moore, Steven E. 2006. 655,000 war dead? A bogus study on Iraq casualties. *Wall Street Journal*, October 18. www.opinionjournal.com/editorial/feature.html?id=110009108.

Naff, Katherine C., and John Crum. 1999. Working for America: Does public service motivation make a difference? *Review of Public Personnel Administration* 19 (Fall): 5–12.

National Academy of Sciences. 1995. *Measuring Poverty: A New Approach*. Washington, DC: National Academy of Sciences Press.

National Institutes of Health, Office of Human Subjects Research. 1949. Nuremberg Code. Reprinted from *Trials of War Criminals before the Nuremberg Military Tribunals Under Control Council Law* 10 (2): 181–182. Washington, DC: U.S. Government Printing Office. www.ohsr.od.nih.gov/guidelines/Nuremberg.html.

National Rifle Association. 2007. More guns, less crime. NRA Institute for Legislative Action. www.nraila.org/Issues/FactSheets/Read.aspx?id=206.

New York Times. 2008a. Poverty's real measure. July 22.

———. 2008b. The corporate free ride. August 18.

Nolte, Ellen, and C. Martine McKee. 2008. Measuring the health of nations: Updating an earlier analysis. *Health Affairs* 27 (1): 58–71.

Olympian. 2002. Our views: Help out United Way. November 7.

Parrott, Sharon, Isaac Shapiro, and John Springer. 2005. Selected research findings on accomplishment of the safety net. Washington, DC: Center on Budget and Policy Priorities. www.sbpp.org/pubs/accomlishments.htm.

Perry, James L. 2000. Bringing society in: Toward a theory of public-service motivation. *Journal of Public Administration Research and Theory* 10 (April): 471–488.

Pew Forum on Religion and Public Life. 2008a. The faith factor in the media's primary campaign coverage. July 10. http://pewresearch.org/pubs/894/running-on-faith.

———. 2008b. Public support falls for religion's role in politics. August 21. http://pewresearch.org/pubs/930/religion-politics.

Pew Research Center for the People and the Press. 2008. Bush and public opinion: Reviewing the Bush years and the public's final verdict. December 18. http://people-press.org/report/478/bush-legacy-public-opinion.

———. 2007. Today's journalists less prominent; fewer widely admired than 20 years ago. March 8. http://people-press.org/report/309/todays-journalists-less-prominent.

Phillips, Scott. 2008. Racial disparities in the capital of capital punishment, *Houston Law Review* 45 (3): 808–840.

Portland Auditor's Office. 2008. *Services, Efforts and Accomplishments: 2007–08: Eighteenth Annual Report on City Government Performance*. Portland, OR. www.portlandonline.com/auditor/.

Potter, Wendell. 2009. They dump the sick to satisfy investors: Insurance exec turned whistleblower Wendell Potter speaks out against healthcare industry. *Democracy Now!* July 15. www.democracynow.org/2009/7/16/former_insurance_exec_wendell_porter.

Rabin, Roni Caryn. 2008. What happy people don't do. *New York Times*, November 19. www.nytimes.com/2008/11/20/health/research/20happy.html.

Radostiz, Rita. 2008. Harris County death penalty: Race matters. *Austin Chronicle*, June 6.

Rector, Robert, and Kirk Johnson. 2004. Understanding poverty in America. Washington, DC: Heritage Foundation. www.heritage.org/Research/Welfare/bg1713.cfm.

Rimer, Sara. 2008. College panel calls for less focus on SATs. *New York Times*, September 22.

Scientist. 2007. Comparison of the top 15 U.S. academic institutions. November 11, 65. www.the-scientist.com/2007/11/1/65/2.

Shively, W. Phillip. 1980. *Craft of Political Research*. 2nd ed. New Jersey: Prentice Hall.

Smith, Mary Lee. 1994. Qualitative plus/versus quantitative: The last word. *New Directions for Program Evaluation* 61: 37–44.

Stack, Steven, and Jim Gundlach. 1992. The effect of country music on suicide. *Social Forces* 71 (1): 211–218.

Tanner, Michel. 2006. More welfare, more poverty. Washington, DC: Cato Institute. www.cato.org/ pub_display.php?pub_id=6698.

Tarvis, Carol. 1992. *The Mismeasure of Woman.* New York: Simon & Schuster.

Thee, Megan. 2007. Cellphones challenge poll sampling. *New York Times,* December 7.

Tague, Nancy R. 2004. *The Quality Toolbox,* 2nd ed. Milwaukee, WI: ASQ Press.

U.S. Census Bureau. Table 2. Poverty status of people by family relationship, race, and hispanic origin: 1959 to 2007. www.census.gov/hhes/www/poverty/histpov/hstpov2.xls.

———. Table H-9. Race of head of household—all races by median and mean income: 1980 to 2006. www.census.gov/hhes/www/income/histinc/h09ar.html.

———. Table P-36. Full-time, year-round all workers by median income and sex: 1955 to 2006. www. census.gov/hhes/www/income/histinc/p36ar.html.

———. Table P-40. Woman's earnings as a percentage of men's earnings by race and Hispanic origin: 1960 to 2007. www.census.gov/hhes/www/income/histinc/p40.html.

U.S. Congressional Budget Office. 2009. The budget and economic outlook: Fiscal years 2009 to 2019. www.cbo.gov/ftpdocs/99xx/doc9957/01–07-Outlook.pdf.

———. 2008. CBO's estimates of the president's budget for fiscal year 2009. In *An Analysis of the President's Budgetary Proposals for Fiscal Year 2009.* March. www.cbo.gov/ftpdocs/89xx/doc8990/ Chapter1.4.1.shtml#1045449.

U.S. Congressional Research Service. 2008. *Oil Industry Profit Review 2007.* Report number: RL34437.

———. 2006. *Oil Industry Profit Review 2005.* Report number: RL 33373.

———. 2005. *Oil Industry Profits: Analysis of Recent Performance.* Report number: RL33021.

U.S. Department of Housing and Urban Development. 2000. Random digit dialing surveys: A guide to assist larger housing agencies in preparing fair market rent comments. www.huduser.org/Publications/pdf/rddlarge98.pdf.

U.S. Federal Register. 2008. *Poverty Guidelines.* 73(15): 3971–3972. January 23. http://aspe.hhs.gov/ POVERTY/08poverty.shtml.

U.S. Government Accountability Office (GAO). 2007a. Securing, stabilizing, and rebuilding Iraq: Iraq has not met most of legislative, security and economic benchmarks. September 4. GAO-07–1230T.

———. 2007b. DOD should provide Congress and the American public with monthly data on enemy-initiated attacks in Iraq in a timely manner. September 28. GAO-07–1048R.

———. 1993. Drug use among youth: No simple answers to guide prevention. HRD-94–24.

———. 1992. Early intervention: Federal investments like WIC can produce savings. GAO/HRD-92–18.

———. 1990a. Immigration reform: Employer sanction and the question of discrimination. GGD-90–62.

———. 1990b. Death penalty sentencing: Research indicates patterns of racial disparities. GGD-90–57.

U.S. Government Printing Office. Table 10.1. Gross domestic product and deflators used in the historical tables: 1940–2009. www.gpoaccess.gov/usbudget/fy05/sheets/hist10z1.xls.

———. Table 3.2. Outlays by function and subfunction: 1962–2013. www.gpoaccess.gov/usbudget/ fy09/sheets/hist03z2.xls.

U.S. Office of Management and Budget. 2009. Budget of the United States government fiscal year 2009: Historical tables. www.whitehouse.gov/omb/budget/fy2009/.

U.S. Treasury. The national debt. www.ustreas.gov/education/faq/markets/national-debt.shtml.U.S. Treasury, Internal Revenue Service. Statistics of income. www.irs.gov/taxstats/.

Vedantam, Shankar. 2007. Research links lead exposure, criminal activity. *Washington Post,* July 8.

Wholey, Joseph S., Harry P. Hatry, and Kathryn E. Newcomer, eds. 2004. *Handbook of Practical Program Evaluation.* San Francisco: Jossey-Bass.

Wilson, Adam. 2008. State workers more satisfied: Scores improve from 2006 job survey. *Olympian,* June 16.

W.K. Kellogg Foundation. 2004. *Logic Model Development Guide.* www.wkkf.org/Pubs/Tools/ Evaluation/Pub3669.pdf.

Yin, Robert K. 2002. *Case Study Research: Design and Methods.* 3rd ed. Thousand Oaks, CA: Sage.

USEFUL WEBSITES

Federal Government: www.usa.gov/.

FedStats: www.fedstats.gov/.

National Aeronautics and Space Agency. Online deflator calculator: http://cost.jsc.nasa.gov/inflateGDP .html.

National Institute of Standards and Technology. Random number table: http://ts.nist.gov/ts/ htdocs/230/235/h133/appenb.doc.

National Institute on Drug Abuse (NIDA): www.nida.nih.gov/NIDAHome.html.

National Longitudinal Survey of Youth (NLSY): www.bls.gov/nls/.

U.S. Agency for International Development (AID): Evaluations. http://evalweb.usaid.gov/.

U.S. Census. Census Data: www.census.gov/.

U.S. Congressional Budget Office: www.cbo.gov/.

U.S. Congressional Research Service: http://digital.library.unt.edu/govdocs/crs/index.tkl.

U.S. Department of Commerce, Bureau of Economic Analysis: www.bea.gov/.

U.S. Department of Education: www.ed.gov.

U.S. Government Accountability Office: www.gao.gov.

OTHER ORGANIZATIONS, THINK TANKS, AND PROFESSIONAL ASSOCIATIONS

American Evaluation Association: www.eval.org.

American Society for Public Administration: www.aspanet.org.

American Society for Quality: www.asq.org.

Association for Policy and Public Management: www.appam.org/home.asp.

Cato Institute (libertarian think tank): www.cato.org/.

Center on Budget and Policy Priorities (liberal think tank): www.cbpp.org/.

Center for Responsive Politics (nonpartisan): www.opensecrets.org/index.php.

Gail Johnson's Blog: www.researchdemystified.org.

Heritage Foundation (conservative think tank): www.heritage.org/.

Institute for Research on Poverty: www.irp.wisc.edu/.

Just Plain Data Analysis, by Gary Klass: http://lilt.ilstu.edu/jpda/.

National Opinion Research Center (NORC), General Social Survey: www.norc.org/GSS+Website.

Pew Research Center for the People and the Press. Survey results: http://pewresearch.org.

Portland, Oregon, Service Efforts and Accomplishment Reports: www.portlandonline.com/auditor/ index.cfm?c=48978.

United Way of Thurston County, Washington: www.unitedway-thurston.org.

World Bank. Data and research: www.worldbank.org.

Appendix D
Logic Model Template

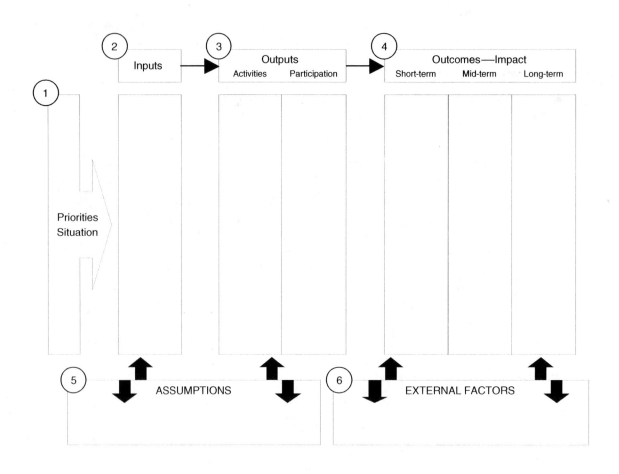

Appendix E
The Generic Design Matrix

DESIGN MATRIX: Planning the Research								
Questions	Subquestions	Design	Measures	Source of information	Data collection approach	Sample	Analysis	Comments
What is the program doing? Is the program doing meeting its targets? What are the costs and benefits? What are the supports and barriers? What is the impact of the program?	Who? What? Where? When? Why? How? How much? How many? Meeting target or criteria? Results? Impact? Type of question: descriptive, normative, or cause-effect	Non-experimental Quasi-experimental Time-series Cross-sectional Correlational with statistical controls Experimental Case study Cost-benefit Evaluation synthesis Content Analysis	Policies regulations Amount (counts) of: Money People Products Services Current or constant dollars Rates Percents Ratios Means Test scores Behaviors Perceptions Opinions Changes over time Comparison Years/time to be included	Documents Budgets Records Files Computers Reports Physical environment Other studies People Key players Implementers Beneficiaries Citizens Customers Experts	Literature review Review studies Gather available data Data collection instrument Observe Participant observation Tests Interviews Surveys Focus groups Expert panel Verify data protocols Pre-tests	Census Sample: Random Simple Stratified Multi-stage Non-random Convenience Judgmental Snowball Select cases Best Worst Typical Mixed Convenient	Quantitative: Frequencies Percentages Percent change Means Cost/Benefit Time-series Before/after comparisons Comparisons Crosstabs Correlation Regression Measures of association Tests for statistical significance Graphical information (GIS) Qualitative: Description Narrative summary Themes Patterns	Criteria: Available, Asserted, or Not available Problems with the data Site selection criteria Time constraint Potential problem Things yet to be determined Limits

Index

The letter e following a page number denotes an exhibit.

About the Author

Gail Johnson (PhD, University of Connecticut) has worked in several public agencies, including the U.S. Government Accountability Office, the U.S. Environmental Protection Agency and the U.S. Department of Health and Human Services. She has taught in MPA programs for more than fifteen years. She is the author of two books in addition to contributing to GAO reports about management of federal agencies, transforming the civil service, and drug use among youth. She is currently doing research about the first generation of women governors.

Her consulting and volunteer work includes designing a measuring-for-results workshop, conducting Appreciative Inquiry workshops, designing program evaluation training programs for the World Bank, and conducting a community assessment.